What They Say About Us

*"One organization with a long record of success
in helping people find jobs is The Five O'Clock Club."*

FORTUNE

"Many managers left to fend for themselves are turning to the camaraderie offered by [The Five O'Clock Club]. Members share tips and advice, and hear experts."

The Wall Street Journal

"If you have been out of work for some time . . . consider The Five O'Clock Club."

The New York Times

"Wendleton has reinvented the historic gentlemen's fraternal oasis and built it into a chain of strategy clubs for job seekers."

The Philadelphia Inquirer

"Organizations such as The Five O'Clock Club are building . . . an extended professional family."

Jessica Lipnack, author, *Professional Teams*

"[The Five O'Clock Club] will ask not what you do, but 'What do you want to do?' . . . [And] don't expect to get any great happy hour drink specials at this joint. The seminars are all business."

The Washington Times

"The Five O'Clock Club's proven philosophy is that job hunting is a learned skill like any other. The Five O'Clock Club becomes the engine that drives [your] search."

Black Enterprise

"Job hunting is a science at The Five O'Clock Club. [Members] find the discipline, direction and much-needed support that keeps a job search on track."

Modern Maturity

"Wendleton tells you how to beat the odds—even in an economy where pink slips are more common than perks. Her savvy and practical guide[s] are chockablock with sample résumés, cover letters, worksheets, negotiating tips, networking suggestions and inspirational quotes from such far-flung achievers as Abraham Lincoln, Malcolm Forbes and Lily Tomlin."

Working Woman

"On behalf of eight million New Yorkers, I commend and thank The Five O'Clock Club. Keep the faith and keep America working!"

David N. Dinkins, former mayor,
The City of New York

What Job Hunters Say

"During the time I was looking for a job I kept Kate's books by my bed. I read a little every night, a little every morning. Her commonsense advice, methodical approach, and hints for keeping the spirits up were extremely useful."

Harold Levine, coordinator, Yale Alumni Career Resource Network

"I've just been going over the books with my daughter who is 23 and finally starting to think she ought to have a career. She won't listen to anything I say, but you she believes."

Newspaper columnist

"Thank you, Kate, for all your help. I ended up with four offers and at least fifteen compliments in two months. Thanks!"

President and CEO, large banking organization

"I have doubled my salary during the past five years by using The Five O'Clock Club techniques. Now I earn what I deserve. I think everyone needs The Five O'Clock Club."

M. S., attorney, entertainment industry

"I dragged myself to my first meeting, totally demoralized. Ten weeks later, I chose from among job offers and started a new life. Bless You!"

Senior editor, not-for-profit

"I'm an artistic person, and I don't think about business. Kate provided the disciplined business approach so I could practice my art. After adopting her system, I landed a role on Broadway in Hamlet."

Bruce Faulk, actor

"I've referred at least a dozen people to the Five O'Clock Club since I was there. The Club was a major factor in getting my dream job, which I am now in."

B. R., research head

"My Five O'Clock Club coach was a godsend!!! She is truly one of the most dynamic and qualified people I've ever met. Without her understanding and guidance, I wouldn't have made the steps I've made toward my goals."

Operating room nurse

"The Five O'Clock Club has been a fantastic experience for my job search. I couldn't have done it without you. Keep up the good work."

Former restaurant owner who found his dream job with an organization that advises small businesses

What Human Resources Executives Say about
Five O'Clock Club Outplacement

*"**This thing works.** I saw a structured, yet nurturing, environment where individuals searching for jobs positioned themselves for success. I saw 'accountability' in a nonintimidating environment. I was struck by the support and willingness to encourage those who had just started the process by the group members who had been there for a while."*

—Employee Relations Officer, financial services organization

*"**Wow! I was immediately struck by the electric atmosphere** and people's commitment to following the program. Job hunters reported on where they were in their searches and what they had accomplished the previous week. The overall environment fosters sharing and mutual learning."*

—Head of Human Resources, major law firm

*"The Five O'Clock Club program is **far more effective** than conventional outplacement.Excellent materials, effective coaching, and nanosecond responsiveness combine to get people focused on the central tasks of the job search. Selecting the Five O'Clock Outplacement Program was one of my best decisions this year."*

Senior Vice President, Human Resources, manufacturing company

*"**You have made me look like a real genius** in recommending the Five O'Clock Club [to our divisions around the country]!"*

Senior Vice President, Human Resources, major publishing firm

*"Selecting Five O'Clock outplacement was **one of my best decisions this year.**"*

Senior Vice President, Human Resources, consumer products firm

The Five O'Clock Club®

Advising Professionals, Managers, and Executives for Over 25 years

REPORT FROM THE FRONT LINES
JOB HUNTERS AND CAREER COACHES TELL YOU HOW TO HAVE A SUCCESSFUL SEARCH

DAVID MADISON, PH.D.

www.FiveOClockClub.com

THOMSON

™

DELMAR LEARNING   Australia Brazil Canada Mexico Singapore Spain United Kingdom United States

THOMSON

DELMAR LEARNING

Report from the Front Lines: Job Hunters and Career Coaches Tell You How to Have a Successful Search
David Madison, Ph.D.

Vice President, Career Education SBU:
Dawn Gerrain

Managing Editor:
Robert L. Serenka, Jr.

Acquisitions Editor:
Martine Edwards

Product Manager:
Jennifer Anderson

Editorial Assistant:
Falon Ferraro

Director of Production:
Wendy A. Troeger

Production Manager:
J.P. Henkel

Associate Content Project Manager:
Angela Iula

Production Assistant:
Jeffrey Varecka

Director of Marketing:
Wendy E. Mapstone

Channel Manager:
Gerard McAvey

Marketing Coordinator:
Jonathan Sheehan

Cover Design:
TDB Publishing Services

Library of Congress Cataloging-in-Publication Data

Madison, David, Ph.D.
   Report From the Front Lines : Job Hunters and Career Coaches Tell You How to Have a Successful Search/David Madison.
      p. cm.
   Includes index.
   ISBN-13: 978-1-4180-3784-0
   ISBN-10: 1-4180-3784-2
   1. Job hunting. 2. Jub hunting--Psychological aspects. 3. Vocational guidance. I. Title.

HF5382.7.M33 2006
650.14--dc22

To David Pandozzi

"We'll always have Paris."

Acknowledgments

When I reflect on the process that brought this book together, I must extend my deepest thanks to two groups of people especially: the job hunters who come to the Five O'Clock Club for help and the coaches who have mastered the Club's methodology and apply it conscientiously with our clients.

There would have been no book if our successful job hunters had not been willing to return to the Club to tell their stories. They do it because they know that telling their stories helps those who are still in the job search process. There's a reason, after all, that we're a *club;* people come to the Club during their searches to get help and offer help to others. That's what the weekly small groups are all about. Coming back to report is a reflection of this collaborative approach to job search. We are grateful to our job hunters past, present, and future for their willingness to be generous and supportive.

There would also have been no book without the coaches. It took many years of research to create and perfect the Five O'Clock Club methodology, but all would have been for naught if we didn't have our Guild of Career Coaches to bring the methodology to life. In most cases, these folks had many years of coaching experience before they came to the Five O'Clock Club; and they underwent the rigors of *our* training program. Without exception I have found our coaches to be extraordinarily caring individuals. They love what they do, and they really do what is in the best interest of our job hunters. They help to assure the quality and integrity of our efforts.

The team at the Five O'Clock Club home office is the powerful engine that keeps everything going and that certainly keeps *me* going on a daily basis. We all have our Forty-Year Vision of the Club and its mission, and we pull together to assure delivery of the quality career coaching that the Club is famous for. So my gratitude must be voiced to our president, Kate Wendleton, Richard Bayer, COO, and Kim Hall, vice president of client services. Among the others who keep things running smoothly, I am indebted especially to Nydia Reid, Shakhnoza Shamirzaeva, and Julie Di Stasio, who see the things on my desk that need attention and keep me from falling too far behind.

And, finally, a special thank-you to my companion of 28 years, David Pandozzi, who puts up with the weekends when I have to write, gets me out of the house to Broadway, and who is "the wind beneath my wings."

David Madison

Foreword

The Five O'Clock Club is the only small-group job search program in the country that is based on research—25 years of research. Every week, job hunters report to their groups and to their career coaches. Many of our coaches have been with us for a decade or more. They see the trends over time and notice what is working in this market. In addition, we continually conduct surveys of our members to keep up with what is happening.

For example, we recently conducted a survey to determine how a job hunter *should* spend his or her time trying to get meetings. Most people who are not Five O'Clock Clubbers contact search firms or answer ads. Job hunters can spend endless hours on the Internet and make very little progress in their searches. Some people think networking is the only way to go. But we wanted to find out what really works.

Our survey clearly showed that job hunters get more meetings for the time spent through "direct contact" than through any other single technique. Networking (using someone else's name to get a meeting) is important, but very time-consuming. You have to find people who are willing to let you use their names. "Direct contact" means aggressively pursuing people whom you may have known in the past or people you may have never met. These might include association members or people identified on the Internet, through newspaper or magazine articles, or from library research. For entry-level people, direct contact even includes going from one human resources office to another in an office center.

Our survey showed that search firms accounted for only 11 percent of the meetings job searchers got. Newspaper ads and company websites each accounted for 6 percent; online job boards accounted for 13 percent. And what about networking? Surveyed job hunters spent 61 percent of their time on networking, but networking accounted for only 28 percent of their meetings! On the other hand, surveyed job hunters spent 11 percent of their time on direct contact, which resulted in 35 percent of their meetings. Direct contact is a more efficient way to get meetings because there is no middleman. Job hunters get more meetings for the time spent through direct contact than through any other single technique. But you never know what will work for your search, so we tell our job hunters to try *every* technique and see which ones result in meetings. Then they should do more of the same.

That's what it means to be a "research-based" organization. Finding out what works and letting our members know. Without the research and the methodology, there would be no Club. The job hunters could get together every week, but they would not have great things to report. Yes, David Madison recruits the best coaches, but still the coaches use the methodology as the foundation of their coaching.

David, as head of the Five O'Clock's National Club Guild of Career Coaches, is a hard taskmaster. The coaches are already highly skilled when we meet them, but they don't know the Five O'Clock Club techniques. By the time they have completed the Five O'Clock Club training with David, they have mastered the methodology.

The same is true with our job hunters. By the time they have attended the Club meetings for a few weeks and have studied the books and CDs, they too become very knowledgeable about the methodology. In fact, we've been in business so long that we have seen the same job hunters come back five or ten years later—when they need to search again. They tend to have shorter searches the second time around because now they have mastered the techniques and use them in their everyday work lives. At the Club, we say we are not teaching just job search skills, but life skills.

David has been a senior vice president and a member of the senior management team at the Five O'Clock Club for eight years. He is in the best position to tell you what's happening on the front lines because he works closely with all of the coaches and interviews our job hunters when they have had a successful search.

I like hearing from people who have had difficult searches. What good is it to hear that someone landed a job in three weeks because a cousin had a job opening? I'd rather hear about the person with no contacts trying to make a difficult career change who had other hardships to overcome. Those stories are the most inspirational to me.

For the 19 years I coached at the Club, the successful job hunter reports were always the highlight of the meeting. When you read this *Report from the Front Lines,* I hope you'll feel the same way.

I wish you the best in your career. If you need help, you know where to find us.

Kate Wendleton
President

Contents

Introduction

In this book, you will find the success stories of well over a hundred job hunters from many different walks of life. For over a decade we have published in our magazine, *The Five O'Clock News*, the reports from successful job hunters. With this wealth of information in our archives and with positive feedback from our readers that these reports are greatly appreciated, it seemed to be the logical next step to bring most of the articles together in one book, which is how *Report from the Front Lines* was born.

As the director of the Guild of Career Coaches of the Five O'Clock Club, one of my responsibilities is to train coaches to give speeches on career topics. I do this because our coaches are in high demand to give talks about career topics to professional and alumni associations, churches, libraries, and education institutions. I don't handle the training from the standpoint of public speaking *techniques,* that is, maintaining eye contact and breathing properly (we have other trainers who do that).

My focus is exclusively on content: what should you *tell* your audiences. What's your message? Of course there's our methodology, which provides the framework for any speech, whether it's about doing proper assessment or gearing up for interviews. But my constant refrain to the coaches is this: *talk about your clients.* Tell the real stories about how real people have put the Five O'Clock Club methodology into practice in the real world—and have come out winners. Of course, in most cases, when our coaches do this, they use made-up names to protect the confidentiality of their clients, but it is very important for audiences to hear how our job hunters have adopted the methodology and achieved success. So I say to our coaches, "When you give a 45-minute talk, make sure you tell one client story after another. That will make your presentation *come alive.*"

For many years, Kate Wendleton, the Club's founder and now its president, managed the Club's Grand Central branch in Manhattan on Monday evenings. When the time came to introduce the job hunters who had come back to report on their successful searches, Kate would say: "This is always the highlight of the night for me—getting to hear how the job hunters have made it happen." Getting job hunters to come back for their reports remains a top priority, and we usually hear a pretty upbeat and inspiring account of how the person landed interviews and turned them into offers.

We are careful to capture these moments on audiotape. In my role as associate editor of *The Five O'Clock News,* I listen to the tapes and write brief summaries to publish in the magazine. After our Insider Program (the weekly groups held by teleconference) was introduced in 1999, I also adopted the practice of interviewing successful job hunters by telephone, since most of them are scattered around the country; I write summaries of their reports as well. On occasion, it can be noted, I also write articles profiling selected job hunters, in which case we identify the person by name and include his or her photo.

This book is designed to be *another tool* to keep you moving ahead in your job search; here you can benefit directly from the experience of others. If you are already a member of the Club, you are familiar with *the other tools.* There are the four main Five O'Clock Club titles to help you master the methodology, and we really do mean it when we say that you should study them as if you were in graduate school; there are 8 CDs containing 16 lectures on the methodology (these are used primarily by those who participate in their small groups by telephone); there are the weekly lectures at the in-person branches, delivered by the coaches on the staff at the branch; there are the small groups for hammering out weekly strategy; there is the alumni database available on our website to job hunters who have attended at least four group sessions; there are your job search buddies, that is, two or three of the folks in your small group of peers who also are mastering the methodology and who are familiar with *your* search.

So *Report from the Front Lines* is another tool, one that can help you get *unstuck,* if that's how you're feeling about your job search today. You may be saying:

- "How in the world am I going to get more interviews?"
- "How in the world can I influence those people who interviewed me for that wonderful job?"
- "How in the world am I going to get out of my dead-end career?"
- "Why in the world should I go to all that trouble of doing the Seven Stories Exercise?"

In this book you will read the real-life accounts of how job hunters—who were as stuck, scared, or insecure as you may be—turned things around and came out on top. None of these accounts have been made up, by the way. Truth is stranger than fiction, as the old saying goes, and we've had no shortage of job hunters who have been eager to tell us their true stories.

In Chapter one you will read about "The Perfect Job Search," which is designed to help you get a grasp of the whole scope and sweep of an effective job search. This is a primer to get you braced for the hard work that lies ahead! At every point along the way, you need to refer to the four main Five O'Clock Club books for in-depth study.

In Chapters 2 through 10 you will find job hunter reports arranged by aspects of the job search. Chapter 2, for example, is on assessment; Chapter 7 is on acing the interview. When you read so many of these job hunters' reports, you may wonder why they are in a particular chapter and not another. Many of these reports could have been placed in *several* of the other chapters. Job hunters usually mentioned a few elements of the Five O'Clock Club methodology that paid off; sometimes it was a hard call knowing which chapter was most appropriate.

Chapters 11 through 14 are not job hunters' reports at all, but are reports from the front lines of another kind. Chapter 11, "Powering Through the Emotional Roller Coaster," is based on a panel presentation to one of our Guild training workshops by three of our seasoned coaches, Bill Belknap, Renée Lee Rosenberg, and Mary Anne Walsh. Bill, Renée, and Mary Anne have truly been on the front lines for many years helping job hunters and had a lot to say about helping people deal with the emotional ups and downs of job search.

Chapter 12, "Forging Career Security," is designed to help you maintain the front lines mentality—even when you're not job hunting. *Especially* when you're not job hunting you need to be minding your career. We say that the Five O'Clock Club is for *career-minded* professionals, managers, and executives, and we don't just give lip service to *career-minded.* If you take the Fifteen-Year Vision or Forty-Year Vision seriously, you know that your career won't unfold the way you want it to without careful plotting. Chapter 12 gives practical suggestions to help you with the plotting.

Chapter 13, "The Holiday Job Search: Full Steam Ahead" is designed to keep you in the trenches during November and December. So many job hunters retire from the front lines at the end of the year, but the subtitle of Chapter 13 makes the point that you'll discover in this chapter: ". . . burying the myth that the holidays are a time to slack off."

Chapter 14, "How to Get Fired" is about smart exit strategies—no, it's not about how to provoke your boss. But if you're about to get the ax, there are ways to handle the departure so that if you're about to be back on the front lines, you'll be in the best shape possible, both financially and emotionally. This chapter is based on a presentation by coaches Bill Belknap and Chip Conlin to a coach training workshop.

It is my sincere hope that *Report from the Front Lines* will prove a useful tool and that one day I'll be writing about *your* success story in *The Five O'Clock Club News.*

David Madison, PhD
Director of the National Guild of Career Coaches
The Five O'Clock Club

CHAPTER ONE

The
Five
O'Clock
Club

The Perfect Job Search

"When you land your new job,
be sure to come back to report."

For years we have been saying this every week at Five O'Clock Club meetings, and the job hunter report has become an established tradition. People look forward to the night when it will be their turn to stand in front of the group to announce the good news about a new job or consulting assignment. We also encourage those who have attended the telephone groups to call in one last time to share their success stories.

It has been our custom for years to capture the job hunter reports on audiotape and then summarize them in our monthly magazine, *The Five O'Clock News.* One Five O'Clock Club coach, Ruth Robbins, once characterized these testimonials about *putting the methodology into action* as the "lore of the Five O'Clock Club." It is part of the impressive body of evidence that the Five O'Clock Club methodology is *effective.* It propels people forward in their endeavor to get back to work or move on to better jobs.

Of course, it is most important that Club attendees hear the reports in person; these exciting extemporaneous stories about *how the methodology paid off* provide inspiration for people to keep going. On some evenings people come to the Club to discuss big forward steps in

their job searches; just as often, however, they're stuck, or they're trying to recover from setbacks. It's encouraging to hear from graduating job hunters who *got unstuck,* beat the competition, and ended up with offers. The reporters have suggestions about how to overcome the rough patches and dark days.

Perhaps the next best thing to being there at the Club to hear job hunters reporting in person, or on the phone, is to read about their successful searches—hence we publish their reports several times a year in our magazine. This book is, in fact, a collection of job hunter reports that have been published since the late 1990s. You will read about many people who were turned on by the Club's methodology and worked hard to apply it to their searches. For many, the methodology came as a revelation: *there is a method I can follow,* rather than haphazardly answering ads, posting résumés on the Internet, and simply telling anyone who will listen, "I'm looking for work" (otherwise known—incorrectly—as networking).

Maybe you're reading this book because you feel stalled in your job search, and you're looking for clues about how other people managed to get their act together and pull off a successful search. In fact, you will see how people from very different walks of life landed new jobs. Some had long, hard searches, others seemed to stumble onto the right opportunity. Of course, being prepared for opportunity has a lot to do with it and our main goal at the Five O'Clock Club is to *prepare you for opportunity.*

Aiming for the "Perfect Job Search"

In baseball there's the *perfect game.* Pitchers fantasize about achieving a perfect game— although it's been done fewer than twenty times in the history of baseball!—and any fan who witnesses the event has something to talk about for years. Likewise, bowlers dream about getting a perfect 300 score. Figure skaters strive to have the row of perfect 10s across the board. Years ago, actress Bo Derek, in the film *10,* gave currency to the concept of a Perfect 10 in the realm of human beauty.

Is it realistic to talk about a *perfect* job search? What would that mean, anyway? Hunting for a job—especially if you're unemployed—is usually considered such a distasteful task that doing it perfectly doesn't have much appeal. Pitching, bowling, skating, or looking beautiful—these are things that people *like* to do, *want* to do, can't *wait* to do. But job hunting? Most of us just want to get it over with—never mind doing it so well that you'd get a prize.

But job offers are the prize. Getting an offer for a dream job—that's the supreme prize. In other words, if you're forced to job hunt—no matter what the circumstances—*why not do it right?* Why not *come as close to perfect* as possible?

"I'm Pretty Rusty at This." What to Do?

Since we're forced into a job search (usually) only every few years, for most of us it is an *unpracticed* skill, and it's not uncommon to feel uncertain and adrift when the day comes to look for work. We commonly think of adding a few lines to the résumé, turning to the newspaper ads, and flipping through the Rolodex to look for people to call, and, oh yes, clicking résumés into cyberspace on the Internet. Not uncommonly, in these early stages of taking the tentative first steps, people make costly mistakes.

But there is a *methodology,* there is a *template* for the perfect job search. If you work hard to learn and master the template, you will assuredly spend far less time on the search (in terms of weeks or months lapsed) and get closer to your dream job.

The blueprint for the perfect job search is the eight-page spread found on pages 10–18. This is a quick-glance summary of the entire Five O'Clock Club methodology, based on more than 20 years of research. This is such an important guide that we print it two or three times every year as the centerfold of our monthly magazine. As a fold-out laminate (similar to college study guides) it is available at a modest cost from the Five O'Clock Club home office. Of course it's important to read the four main Five O'Clock Club books to get the full sweep—and all of the details—of the methodology. If you learn better by listening, we recommend that you make full use of the sixteen lectures available on CDs. Many job hunters have reported that they listen to the CDs repeatedly—while driving, at the gym, or jogging. (Visit our website www.fiveoclockclub.com for information on how to buy the books and CDs.)

So there *is* a methodology you can follow, but mastering it takes focus and commitment. But the payoff will be substantial, as you can see when you read the reports of job hunters in the chapters that follow.

Some of the Components of a Perfect Job Search

Let's take a brief look at some of the major building blocks of a *good* search. The more you can incorporate these elements, the closer you will come, in fact, to the *perfect* search—and the prize you're looking for.

A Full-Time Effort: 35 Hours a Week

Many times over the years, job hunters have arrived at the Club after several months of frustrating job search: "I've been hard at this since last April, and I'm banging my head against the wall. I can't get any traction. Nothing is happening."

We have learned the right questions to ask to find out why there's "no traction." And most commonly we discover that people aren't entirely honest with themselves about *the amount of time* they spend on their searches: "hard at this since April" turns out to be an exaggeration, because the hours actually spent per day or per week on job search fall far short of what is realistically required.

We say that a full-time job search is 35 hours a week; a part-time search is 15 hours a week. So, if you're unemployed, you should be devoting *7 hours a day*—no fudging and no fooling!—to your job search. Complaining about a six-month job search really isn't appropriate (and you're not being honest with yourself) if, in fact, you're working hard at job search only a couple of hours a day.

Without the discipline of getting up early to get to the office, it's easy to miss the mark of a *full day* spent on job search. But it can be done. For example, one unemployed Five O'Clock Clubber made a point of rising at 6:00 as usual, being settled with his coffee and *Wall Street Journal* by 7:00, and by 8:00 was working on his job search, whether that meant doing fresh Internet research, writing targeted letters, or making phone calls. One of our employed members—in a very demanding role at her company—wanted to find a job in another state. For several weeks she relentlessly devoted her evenings and weekends to crafting targeted letters to companies in the city she was aiming for and she managed to log *at least* 15 hours a week in the effort. She *really* wanted to make the move, so, although she would have preferred to have a normal life during evenings and weekends, she knew that the job search came first.

It's very easy to make excuses and come up with rationales for not searching *all day:*

- I deserve a rest after getting on that commuter train for six years.
- I didn't sleep so well last night.
- My cat is sick.
- I have to get to the dry cleaners before they close.
- I'll feel better when that closet is all cleaned up.

But, chances are, *none of these* would have held up as reasons to *skip work* when you had a job. You shouldn't skip work *now*—when the work is the job hunt. If you want to build toward a perfect job search, don't be swayed by *excuses* from your 35-hour obligation.

We do stress the importance of downtime during your job search, hence we say, "be sure to have two hours of fun per week." For example, that might mean going to a museum one morning—which you couldn't do when you were working. The problem, of course, is that many of us can easily slide into the fun/goofing off/procrastination mode for *far more* than two hours, especially if we're depressed or "just can't face" the job search today.

So it's best to try to structure your days and hours just as you would if you were organizing your schedule at the office. Build your to-do list for the day, either the night before or early in the day. Fill up your calendar with genuine job hunt activities, for example:

- Tuesday 9:00 to 11:00: do Internet research on ten more companies in my primary target.
- Tuesday 11:00 to 12:00: make follow-up phone calls to the targeted letters sent last week.
- Tuesday 12:00 to 1:00: write a letter for direct mailing to 50 companies, and prepare the mailing.
- Tuesday 2:00 to 3:30: write e-mails to all the people met with or contacted last month.
- Tuesday 3:30 to 5:00: do in-depth research for Friday interview, call two job search buddies to practice Two-Minute Pitch and review strategies.

How do you fill up *five days* with such a schedule? Look ahead a few paragraphs in this chapter to the section *The Missing Ingredient: Your Personal Marketing Plan,* and you'll see that a 35-hour week can fill up fast. But be careful—and honest—with yourself: a two-hour session at a job support group might make you feel better, but *it doesn't really count as job search* because it isn't part of your marketing strategy. The Five O'Clock Clubbers who are most successful are those who follow the methodology and *work hard.* It's an old cliché to say that searching for a job is a full-time job—but *we* really mean it!

And, by the way, if the support group you attend is filled with depressed unemployed people who want to vent and complain, stop going. You don't want to be around people who can drag you down. Those hours can best be spent talking with your Five O'Clock Club job search buddies and figuring out ways to get your résumé into the right hands.

The Best Foundation for a Successful Search

"I don't have time for that. I just need to get a job fast." We sometimes hear this from job hunters who balk at doing the assessment. They come to the Club in a rush to get a new job, and don't want anything to "slow them down." But *skipping* assessment will slow them down in ways they don't understand and can often result in complete derailment.

Our primary assessment tools are the Seven Stories and the Forty-Year Vision, and our experience has shown that people who *put a lot of effort into these exercises* do better on their job searches. Of course, people who don't know what they want to do next *must* do the exercises. But even if you are very clear about your targets and goals, don't skip these two exercises. Our aim is to help you get the *right* job—both in terms of making you happy now and positioning you well for the future.

Even if you can genuinely say, "I know exactly what I want to do next," doing the Seven Stories will bring your most important enjoyable accomplishments into bold relief, which will help in three areas:

- The *résumé:* Without fail, job hunters who faithfully work through the Seven Stories find new nuggets of information to make their résumés stronger. Sometimes the résumé will be altered dramatically.
- The *interview:* After all, if you've just recently reviewed 25 of your life accomplishments, you're bound to have more interesting things to say about yourself during interviews. The Seven Stories exercise is a refresher course about *you.*
- *Salary negotiations:* Although you will always do your best to deflect questions about money—and postpone the money *discussion* until the latest possible moment—salary negotiations begin *when you walk in the door.* From the very first moment you want to demonstrate what you bring to the table—and as the process moves forward—you will attempt to negotiate the job to make it appropriate for you. Being an expert on what you bring to the table means being able to articulate your life accomplishments and the Seven Stories Exercise gets you ready to do just that.

You're bound to have a flawed job search—far from a *perfect* one—if you skip or slight the assessment.

The Missing Ingredient: Your Personal Marketing Plan

What's the first thing you think of when you're gearing up for a job search? The résumé, of course. And there's probably a lot more work to be done on it than you think if you want to position yourself correctly (as opposed to just adding a few sentences about your most recent experience).

What's the next thing that might get a lot of your attention? The cover letter, naturally—

although this also probably requires a lot more work than people suspect, because it usually must be adjusted somewhat for each targeted company.

But you're not ready for the search until you have your *written marketing plan.* One of our reporting job hunters—a corporate controller— who attended the Five O'Clock Club by teleconference, recalls that his group coach said that he wanted to see his "map of 200 positions" *before* he started networking; he had planned to just get on the phone to call as many people as he knew. He was skeptical because he was pretty sure there *weren't* 200 positions in his targeted geographic area. But he followed his coach's suggestion, and, after a few days of Internet research, came up with 200 positions outlined in several targets—much to his surprise. "This was very empowering," he reported, "seeing the full scope of my whole search down on paper—and knowing very well that my next job was *there* somewhere."

Your marketing plan is constructed by

- outlining your ranked targets. This can easily be done on paper or on an Excel spreadsheet;
- then listing the names of the companies or organizations in each target, noting how many positions each may have (appropriate for you); and
- finally specifying *how* you plan to reach out to them. That is, which of the four ways for getting meetings will you use for each: answering ads, registering with agencies, networking, or making contact directly.

For example, someone aiming for a position as a financial planner at a hospital in Cleveland or Cincinnati will draw up a list of all of the hospitals in both cities, make an educated guess (i.e., based on research) as to the number of appropriate positions at each hospital, then strategize the best ways to get meetings at each, that is, which of the four ways to get meetings will be most effective?

With this kind of detailed marketing plan, you can see at a glance if you're aiming at *enough* positions. If you come up with only 25 positions, you've got to do more research, think outside the box, and brainstorm with your coach or small group about how to add more positions. With such a comprehensive marketing plan it's also easy to see at a glance, when you get up in the morning, *what to do to keep busy for seven or eight hours.*

And, by the way, when you go on networking interviews, you can take along a copy of your marketing plan. It's a great way to help people visualize what you're trying to accomplish, and it sends a message about *how serious you are about achieving your goals.* You can say, "You see, these are the 15 companies I'm planning to contact in my second target. What's your opinion of these firms? Do you have any suggestions about the best way to contact them?" You're more likely to come up with referrals into companies when people *see a list.* Known as "aided recall," this can be much more effective than asking, "Can you recommend other companies for me to approach?"

To paraphrase the commercial: "Your personal marketing plan—don't leave home without it!" People commonly have weak job hunts because they work hard on their résumés and cover letters, but stumble ahead for weeks and months, wandering into detours and blind alleys, because **they don't work from a written personal marketing plan.**

Don't Get Your Heart Set on Just One Job

Sometimes when folks arrive at the Club complaining about a "lack of traction," it turns out that they have been serial job hunting. That is, it's common to focus on one particular opportunity that appears ideal—with confidence that "they like me, they *really* like me." But then it turns out that they liked someone else more, there was a hiring freeze, or the boss hired his cousin! That is, the ideal opportunity vanished, and there's nothing else going on *because job hunting is something people hate to do* and it's easier to say "surely this will fall into place." But when it doesn't, it's oh so hard to pump up the energy and morale again, and the job hunt can drag on for months and months.

Five O'Clock Club research has demonstrated that the ideal scenario is to have six to ten things in the works, because five *will fall apart* through no fault of your own. Hence our advice is to *work your marketing plan furiously,* and don't ease up when you have several interviews scheduled. One Five O'Clock Clubber impressed his group when he arrived one night to talk about several second interviews he'd had—where offers appeared imminent. But they were even more impressed when he wanted to strategize about how to get *more* interviews, *more* companies, *more* opportunities in the pipeline. Having a lot going on gives you confidence, boosts your morale, and puts you in a much better position—when the time comes—to negotiate the offer that you really want. The perfect job search is based on having many options and choices.

Work Hard . . . but Work Smartly

Ironically, complaints from job hunters about "no traction" are usually accompanied by claims about a lot of job-hunting activity. That is, job hunters usually say, "Gee, look at all I've done, how hard I've tried: hundreds of résumés sent, perhaps hundreds of phone calls as well. I've been networking endlessly, not leaving any stone unturned."

We caution however that *volume does not equal quality.* To get a good search under way, the job hunters need to do more than keep busy and tally how much they've done. "I've sent out hundreds of résumés during the last three months" might sound impressive, but what if the résumé is poorly positioned and you're sending it to the wrong people? A hundred résumés sent to the wrong people is not so impressive.

To help job hunters work smartly, the Five O'Clock Club urges them to master our assessment tool, Stages 1, 2, and 3. (To learn about Stages 1, 2, and 3, see our book *Shorten Your Job Search,* chapter "How to Control Your Campaign," pages 187 through 202). This tool doesn't assess your skills, accomplishments, or potential, *it assesses the quality of your job-hunting efforts.* Exhausting yourself on practices and techniques that really aren't working very well doesn't win you any points—or job offers—no matter how much you feel you can boast at the end of the day about how many calls you've made or résumés you've sent. Here's a hint to help you understand what we mean by being in Stage 1, 2, or 3: memorize these four words: "***on an ongoing basis.***" If you have reached out, during a two- or three-month period, to 25 or 50 appropriate people in your target markets and are *not* staying in touch with them *on an ongoing basis,* chances are your job search will stall. And, chances are, you're not in Stage 1 yet.

A good job search is based on a realistic analysis of how effective the résumés and interviews are *while you're job hunting.* So it's vital to master Stages 1, 2, and 3 at the outset. With a job offer in hand, at the end of a grueling six-month job hunt, you may say, "Well, what I did worked. I got a new job." But if, *working smarter,* you could have found a job in just three weeks, the real lesson might be: What I did *didn't* work all that well after all. It's important to assess your efforts *during* the search. Pay just as much attention to Stages 1, 2, and 3 as you do to your résumé and marketing plan.

Work Hard, Work Smartly, *After* the Interview

The more you study and apply the Five O'Clock Club methodology, it will come as no surprise that we put a heavy emphasis on influencing decision makers in the days following an interview. We are fond of saying "the ball is always in your court," and this is especially true after interviews. Conventional wisdom has always recommended sending thank-you notes after interviews, and we hear from HR folks and hiring managers that even this is commonly neglected.

"What more can I do?" seems to be the attitude of so many job hunters. But there is so much more that can be done—much more than the thank-you note. Hence there is a heavy emphasis at the Five O'Clock Club on post-interview techniques and strategies: "What *can* you do to influence the decision makers?" So the perfect job search includes running the full race, instead of stopping when there may be several laps remaining. We usually say that the post-interview phase is the brainiest part of the search, which leads to the next point.

Never Go It Alone: Get Expert Advice

At the beginning we mentioned baseball pitchers, bowlers, and ice skaters. All of these, in their reach for perfection, have one thing in common: they rely heavily on *coaching* to get the desired results—even if they've been pitching, bowling, or skating for ten years! In other words, no matter what the endeavor, *benefit from the wisdom of others.* Since job hunting is an unpracticed skill, why try to go it alone—especially when it comes to such crucial steps as salary negotiation? How many people can say with confidence, "Yes, I'm really terrific at negotiating salary"? And how many can say, "I'll be brilliant when it comes to following up after my next few interviews"?

Because these can be the parts of the process that require the most imagination and creativity—where a lot of brain power can be really useful—we always urge job hunters to make full use of their Five O'Clock Club small groups. Here are the people who, over the weeks, have come to know you and your job search. They are peers who have been mastering the Five O'Clock Club methodology and are working through their own searches. Every week the group is there to brainstorm what to do next, suggest course corrections, and offer intelligent advice on options and alternatives. And, of course, the expert coach—certified by the Five O'Clock Club—is there to oversee everything and can be called upon for private sessions as well. You'll have a much better chance at a good search—at the *perfect* search—if you listen to others who have studied effective job search techniques.

Keep Stress and Weirdness to a Minimum

Being out of work can be disorienting. Job hunters commonly feel displaced, especially those who have worked at one place for 10 or 20 years or more. Hence we know that job hunters lose things, walk into walls, and have accidents. It comes with the territory.

We find that job hunters—even those who are still employed—commonly *act out* their stress. One man who'd lost his job was almost yelling into the phone when he called the Five O'Clock Club: "All I need is a job. I need one now." It turns out that he had also gone through a divorce, and he felt like his world was coming to an end. Chances are, when you're out of work, problems will multiply in other areas of your life as well. In other words, you might be a world of hurt on several levels as you tackle the job hunt process. It's important to keep things in separate compartments; work hard at being *calm and normal* when you network and interview. Obviously, when you're under heavy stress, this is easy to say, hard to do. Your small group at the Club will often pick up on the signs that you're bouncing off the walls and can help bring you back into line—*before* you say weird things during interviews.

And don't look for a quick fix—when the methodology *will* deliver for you. As we were going to press in the summer of 2005 with our four new updated Five O'Clock Club books, we spotted a newspaper article about a young man who decided to look for work by walking along 42nd Street in New York wearing a sandwich board with the message "Hire me, '05 MBA, Business Development." At the end of the day, he reported that he had "set up two interviews and been handed nearly a dozen business cards."

Did we call our publisher to stop the presses so that we could insert a few paragraphs about this wonderful new way to look for work? No, we didn't, because walking the streets with a sandwich board isn't new and isn't wonderful. It's *weird.* It won't even become a fad because it's *weird*—and we encourage our job hunters to avoid fads and gimmicks. Even if the young man got a job by wearing a sandwich board, this is not something that would work for anyone else.

The young man told the newspaper: "I've been trying the traditional methods of getting employment, but nothing so far has come up that's suitable. Almost every vacancy is advertised on the Internet now, and you have to apply for everything via email. No one wants to talk to you directly. It's impossible to make human contact, which makes it difficult to stand out in the crowd when you're trying to get a job." From this it is clear that he was unaware of *effective* job search methods—no hint here, for example, of using a targeted approach. Most likely his job search consisted of clicking his résumé into cyberspace. The newspaper even provided a link to his résumé—which looked like thousands of other cookie-cutter MBA résumés: no positioning statement, no bulleted accomplishments, no clear statement of what *separates him from the competition.* In other words, relying on the "traditional methods"—as understood by this recently minted MBA—he hadn't even really *begun* to job hunt effectively, but instead resorted to a sandwich board. "My wife and I came up with this idea and I thought, 'Wow, yes, that might work.'"

So if you read about someone getting a job by doing something weird, far from saying "Hey, maybe I should try this," the lesson is: stick to the research-based fundamentals. With the Five O'Clock Club books, coaches, and small group by

your side, you have a pretty good shot at putting together the *perfect job search.*

Are You Reading this Book When the Job Market Looks Bleak?

It was the best of times, it was the worst of times.
Charles Dickens

I've not yet seen a recession that Five O'Clock Club methods can't defeat.
Ellis Chase, Senior Five O'Clock Club Coach

When do people need the Five O'Clock Club the most? In times of recession or when things are booming? People even seem to worry that the Five O'Clock Club might be taking a hit because the economy is good . . . or bad. People ask us, "How's the Club doing since the economy tanked?"—or ". . . now that things have bounced back?"

Actually there's no time when we say at the Five O'Clock Club, "Where are the clients?" because people come to us when times are bad and they need help overcoming a rotten job market. They benefit from our methodology as well when hiring has picked up and there's lots of competition for good jobs. Because our retail rates are so low—*the lowest in the industry*—unemployed professionals, managers, and executives can usually afford to come to the Club.

But job hunters *do* need to hear a tailored message, depending on the state of the economy and the climate of the times. About a year and a half after September 11, we wrote the following to help job hunters cope:

Three years of a bear market, shaky consumer confidence, an economy struggling to right itself, Fortune 500 companies rocked by scandal, key industries in disarray or deep decline—job hunters will tell you that all of these are bad enough. Needless to say, applying bad job search techniques in this environment is deadly. To beat the odds—and the competition—your job search skills must be top-notch. The good news is that the Five O'Clock Club techniques work even now, *especially* now. As Ellis Chase, one of our senior coaches, has said, "I've not yet seen a recession that Five

O'Clock Club methods can't defeat." Our members are getting jobs *when they read the books, attend sessions regularly, follow the strategies suggested by their small groups, and do the assignments.* The good news also is that the overall economic picture isn't as glum as headlines would lead us to believe.

And, by the way, it's no good to keep reading the headlines if they depress you. Negativism will get you down, just when you need to keep a positive outlook: confidence in your skills—and positioning them correctly—can overcome a lot. A scientist once reported that, aerodynamically, it's impossible for the bumblebee to fly, given the shape of its body and the size of the wings. Of course bumblebees don't read negative headlines—and they continue to fly.

Five O'Clock Clubbers have achieved great results by ignoring bad news and exercising smart job-hunting techniques.

The
Five
O'Clock
Club

The Five O'Clock Club Way

"One organization with a long record of success in helping people find jobs is The Five O'Clock Club."

FORTUNE

Do not skip Assessment.

Even if you are rushed or know what you want to do with your life, the Seven Stories Exercise will help you develop a great résumé and cover letter, ace your interviews, and feel more confident. After you've done the **Seven Stories Exercise** and tried the **Forty-Year Vision,** your private coach can help you!!! These are a must!

CDs for Assessment:

How The Five O'Clock Club Works

The Five O'Clock Club Approach to Job Search

How to Develop New Targets for Your Search

Successful Job Hunters Report

ASSESSMENT: TARGET AND RÉSUMÉ DEVELOPMENT

Assessment helps you develop a career direction—and a good résumé. Go through *all of* the exercises in our *Targeting* book—*especially* the **Seven Stories Exercise** and the **Forty-Year Vision.** You will come up with job targets and be better able to focus on what you want to do next.

Assessment results in job targets, and a Résumé that makes you look appropriate to those targets.

A job target is:

- an industry or organization (e.g., banking)
- a specific position in those industries (e.g., marketing)
- a certain geographic area (e.g., St. Louis)

Do preliminary target research (Internet, networking) on your first list of targets. Refine your list. Use *Finding Jobs That Don't Exist.* Brainstorm as many alternative targets as possible in case you need more targets later on in your search.

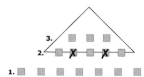

Target Development

- Segment your targets.
- Rank your targets.
- Measure your targets
  (Average number of positions per organization).
- Target 200 positions.

> **Target 200 *positions* —not job openings, but positions. It's okay if the positions are filled right now.**

"For profit" is not a target. "Not-for-profit" is not a target. They are too broad. For example, "not-for-profit" could include associations, hospitals, universities, the government – and all of those sub-targets are huge!

Break down your targets into sub-targets. Health care, for example, could include hospitals, home health care, HMOs, pharmaceutical companies, nursing homes, hospice care, health insurance companies, crisis intervention programs, congregate care facilities, medical billing, health-care consulting firms, medical device manufacturers, distributors, anything having to do with the aging of America, vitamin companies, health-care publishing, and more!!

MOST PEOPLE START OUT WITH TARGETS THAT ARE JUST TOO SMALL. THEIR SEARCHES ARE DOOMED!

Measuring Effectiveness of Your Search

You sent 100 résumés and talked to 75 people. But was it effective? *Measure* where you are.

- Stage 1 *Keeping in touch* with 6 to 10 people in your target area. Get feedback.
- Stage 2 is the core of your search. Keep in touch with 6 to 10 of the right people at the right level in the right organizations, AND when they say, "I wish I had an opening right now – I'd love to have someone like you on board," you have a GREAT search. Now, aim for 10 to 20 ongoing Stage 2 contacts.

If you're *not* getting positive feedback, your target is wrong or your positioning is wrong.

- Stage 3 will happen naturally: 6 to 10 *job* possibilities. *Aim for 3 concurrent offers.*
- Don't select the job that simply pays $2,000 or $20,000 more. Select the job that positions you best for the long term. You *will* have to search again.

Assessment results in a **RÉSUMÉ** that makes you look appropriate to your targets – so that you will be desirable when you go in for an interview. Remember, the average résumé is looked at for only 10 seconds. What ideas or words pop out? (It should *not* be your name!) Can the reader easily figure out your level? If you say I "install computer systems," you could be making anywhere from $15,000 to $200,000. Is your résumé accomplishment-oriented or just a job description? Work with your private coach and your small group to make your *résumé* stand out.

HAVING TROUBLE FIGURING OUT WHAT YOU WANT TO DO WITH YOUR CAREER? YOURPRIVATE COACH CAN HELP YOU.

If You Will Be Working with a Private Coach

in addition to your small-group coach: Prior to the first private coaching session, send your coach your current résumé, in whatever state it is in, and the results of the Seven Stories Exercise. You and your coach can address your thoughts about the Forty-Year Vision and brainstorm potential targets. Your coach may assign you other exercises or instruments that are right for you and will help you with your résumé.

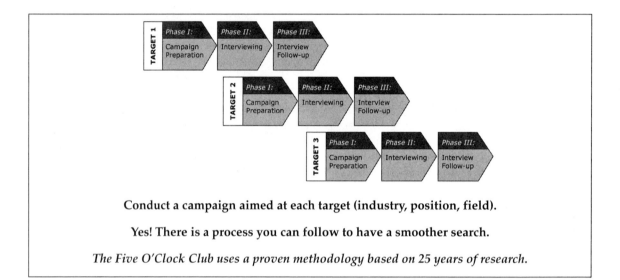

Conduct a campaign aimed at each target (industry, position, field).

Yes! There is a process you can follow to have a smoother search.

The Five O'Clock Club uses a proven methodology based on 25 years of research.

CDs for Campaign Preparation:

Your Résumé and the Two-Minute Pitch

How to Use Research and the Internet for Your Job Search

How to Get Interviews: The Keys to Effective Networking

How to Get Interviews Through Direct and Targeted Mail

Beat the Odds When Using Search Firms and Answering Ads

YOUR SMALL GROUP CAN REVIEW YOUR SEARCH PLANS AND HELP YOU PRACTICE YOUR TWO-MINUTE PITCH.

PHASE I: CAMPAIGN PREPARATION

- **Conduct research** to develop a list of all the companies in your first target. Find out the names of people you should contact in the appropriate departments in each of those companies.
- **Develop your cover letter.** Paragraph 1 is the opening; Paragraph 2 is a summary about yourself appropriate for this target; Paragraph 3 contains your bulleted accomplishments ("You may be interested in some of the things I've done."); Paragraph 4 is the close. (Lots of sample letters are in *Getting Interviews*.)
- **Develop your plan** for getting lots of meetings in this target.

Methods for Getting Meetings in Your Target Areas:

- Networking (40% of meetings),
- Direct Contact (40%),
- Search Firms (10%), and
- Ads (print and Internet) (10%).

"Networking" means using someone else's name to get a meeting ("Sue suggested I contact you."). "Direct Contact" means pursuing people whom you may have known in the past or people you have never met: association members or key people identified on the Internet, through newspaper or magazine articles, or from library research. (For entry-level people, it includes going from one human resources office to another in an office center.)

Segment Your Targets

Your A-list: organizations you would love to work for.

Your B-list: organizations that are okay.

Your C-list: organizations that don't interest you much.

Contact C-list companies first. Practice. Are they interested in *you* or not? You are researching. If C-list likes you, contact B-list. "I am already talking to a number of companies in our industry, but I didn't want to accept a job with any of them until I had a chance to talk with you." If B-list likes you, contact A-list.

Divide Up Your List

If you have a list of 60 organizations:

- Network into 5 or 6, if you can;
- Send a targeted mailing to 20 (requires follow-up phone call); and
- For the remaining 35, use a direct mail campaign (no follow-up phone call)

Condense Your Search

If Target #1 is hospitals, contact all of the hospitals. "Just yesterday, I talked to . . . " You appear interested in hospitals. Gives you credibility.

Segment your targets. The pitch that you use with one of these targets, say, hospitals, will be very different from the pitch you would use with a different target, say, health-care manufacturers.

The "Two-Minute Pitch"

—the way you position yourself—is used throughout your search

- at the top of your résumé.
- in your interview.
- in your networking meetings; and
- in your cover letters (2nd paragraph).

It is the answer to the question, "So, tell me about yourself." A great pitch helps people see you as appropriate for the kind of job you are going after. At the Five O'Clock Club we say, "If your pitch is wrong, everything is wrong." That is, if the way that you are positioning yourself is wrong, everything else about your search is wrong. It can't work.

The top of your résumé is your *written* positioning. Two-Minute Pitch is the *verbal* positioning of yourself. And they must correspond. So, the top of Wally's résumé could say:

> **Web Press Supervisor**
> **With 20 years' experience**
> **and an emphasis on quality**
> **and productivity**

In an interview, when an employer asks, "So tell me about yourself," Wally could start with the verbal version of that same pitch: "I'm a Web press supervisor with over 20 years' experience. I've always emphasized quality and productivity. For example . . ." And then he would go into examples of his ccomplishments, which would correspond to some of the bulleted accomplishments at the top of his résumé. When your pitch is correct, you will use it throughout your entire search.

CDs for Interviewing:

The Five O'Clock Club Approach to Interviewing

Advanced / Strategic Interviewing Techniques

How to Handle Difficult Interview Questions

How to Develop New Momentum in Your Search

Making the Most of Your Contacts

YOUR SMALL GROUP CAN HELP YOU PREPARE AND PRACTICE FOR YOUR INTERVIEWS AND NETWORKING MEETINGS, AND THEY WILL NOTICE WHEN THINGS ARE GOING WRONG IN YOUR SEARCH.

PHASE II: INTERVIEWING

Most people think interviews result in job offers. But there are usually a few intervening steps before a final offer is made. **Interviews should result in getting and giving information.**

- Did you learn the issues important to each person with whom you met?
- What did they think were your strongest positives?
- How can you overcome the decision-makers' objections?

Don't think like a job hunter. Think like a consultant trying to land a $40,000, $90,000, or $150,000 consulting assignment—whatever your salary is. What consultants do:

- Research beforehand.
- Dress and look the part.
- Prepare your 3" x 5" card including your pitch as well as your key points.

Find out:
- What is going on? What are their needs?
- How can I satisfy those needs?

Consider your competition.
- Ask how you stack up against others.
- Have all the information you need.
- Are they ready to decide?
- Try to keep in the running.

Plan your follow-up
- Get and give information.
- Don't try to get an offer right now.
- Get the next meeting.
- Consultants write proposals. So will you!

Conduct a campaign aimed at a company
- If Miss Gold is the hiring manager, don't try to see her just yet. *Surround* the hiring manager. Meet with others, so when you finally get in to see her, you will have a lot of advocates and know a lot about the organization.

Prepare for the interview
- Say to the person who set up the meeting: "I'd like to go in prepared. With whom will I meet?" Ask:
  – names and job titles
  – issues important to each of them
  – what they are like
  – tenure with organization

Uncover their objections
- Where are you in the hiring process?
- How many others are you considering?
- How do I stack up against them?
- Is there any reason why you might be reluctant to bring someone like me on board?

Have each person see you as the ideal
- Each should advocate having you on board. If anyone objects to you, handle it now.

Always have 6 to 10 possibilities going
- Try to get an offer (even if you don't want the job), or you'll never get 6 to 10 possibilities.
- Do *not* drop other search activities when an offer seems certain.

Mistake: Trying to get an offer too soon
- Instead, get that next meeting.
- Give and get information. Move it along.
- Address issues that concern *them* rather than what's bothering you (getting the job).

Questions to Ask

Responsibilities
- What is the most important part of the job?
- What is the first problem that would need the attention of the person you hire?

Resources
- May I meet other people who work in the area?
- What are the department's employees' experience, training, and tenure with the company?

Authority
- How is the department organized?
- What would be the extent of my authority in carrying out the responsibilities of this position?

Performance
- What are the short- and long-term goals of the position, and how are they established?
- How is one's performance evaluated? By whom? How often?
- What would you like to say about the person in this job one year from now?

Culture
- What do you find most satisfying about working here? Most frustrating?
- Who tends to get ahead here?
- How would you describe your management style?

Remember . . .
- You are being interviewed by everyone including receptionists and peers.
- They say they are going to call you back in 2 days. Do they ever? No, never.

> **Consultants don't expect to get the offer on the first visit. Neither should you.**

Handling Difficult Interview Questions

Your 3" x 5" card with the information you want to cover during your interview

? ? ? Off on a tangent
Questions that divert you from your main agenda

Handle them quickly and get back to the topic

Do not allow the interview to get off track. When the interviewer brings up something that takes you in a direction in which you don't want to go, briefly give a response that satisfies the interviewer, and then *get back on track.*

Give your answer, and then say, for example, "But I really wanted to tell you about a special project I worked on." It is your responsibility to get the conversation back on track.

CDs for Follow-up and Salary Negotiation:

How to Use the Four-Step Salary Negotiation Strategy

How to Turn Job Interviews into Offers

THIS IS THE BRAINIEST PART OF THE PROCESS. YOUR SMALL GROUP WILL HELP YOU TURN INTERVIEWS INTO OFFERS AND GET THE SALARY YOU DESERVE.

PHASE III: INTERVIEW FOLLOW-UP
(including salary negotiation)

Follow-Up After a Job Interview
- The brainiest part of the process.
- Takes as much time as getting interviews and interviewing.
- Keep things alive with 6 to 10 organizations.
- Don't write a silly "thank-you" note after a job interview. Instead, *influence* them.
- Tailor the follow-up to each situation.
- Build a relationship. Company says that they're not hiring until February. That's okay.
- Whether to call, write, or e-mail is not the issue. Uncover their objections to you.
- The best you can do: **If they were going to hire someone, would you be the person?**
- Your coach will want to know:
  - Who did you meet with?
  - What are *each* person's key *issues*?
  - Why would each want you there?
  - *Each* person's objections to you.
  - What can you offer vs. competition?
  - Problems *each* interviewer has.

- Decide the next steps, such as:
  - another meeting; meeting w/others
  - an in-depth review of documents
  - developing a few ideas and then meet
  - drafting a proposal
- State the "next steps" in your follow-up note. For example, "I'd like to get together with you to discuss my ideas on . . ."
- Influence the influencers.
- Be in sync with their timing, not yours.
- If unemployed, be open to consulting work.

Salary Negotiation
- Starts with your first meeting: position yourself so they see you at a certain level.
- Mantra: "Salary will not be a problem."
- Manage the process to get the right offer.
  - If original offer is too low, okay for now.
  - Don't try to close too soon and ruin deal.
- The Four-Step Salary Negotiation Process:
  1. Negotiate the job
  2. Outshine and outlast your competition
  3. Get the offer
  4. Negotiate the salary
- *Must* be done in this order. For example, don't negotiate salary if you have competitors.
- "Grow the job" to make it worth more.
- Find out what you personally are worth.
  - Network: "What would you expect to pay someone with my background?"
  - Salary.com and others. Associations.
- Make yourself in demand: 6 to 10 a must.
- Don't reject the offer—talk about the job.
- Keep process open; hear their best offer.
- Postpone salary discussion until offer.
  - Person who names a number first loses.
  - Talk more about the job.
- Discuss salary using a collaborative tone.
  - May take more than one meeting.

The amount of money you receive will always be in direct proportion to the demand for what you do, your ability to do it, and the difficulty of replacing you.

Dennis Kimbro, *Think and Grow Rich: A Black Choice*

You ain't goin' nowhere . . . son.
You ought to go back to driving a truck.

Jim Denny, Grand Ole Opry manager,
firing Elvis Presley after one performance.
From an interview on October 2, 1954.

Have 6 to 10 job possibilities in the works at all times. Five will fall away through no fault of your own.

With 6 to 10 things going, you increase your chances of having three good offers to choose from.

When you are in the Interview Phase of Target 1, it's time to start Phase I of Target 2. This will give you more momentum and insure that you do not let things dry up. Keep both targets going, and then start Target 3.

Research shows: those who regularly attend a small group, headed by a Five O'Clock Club coach, get jobs faster and at higher rates of pay than those who search alone or only work privately with a coach.

Remember . . .
- Get 3 hours of fun a week—like it or not!!
- Job search in summer and over holidays.
- "They" never call when they say they will, so follow up by being creatively persistent.

Follow-Up After Networking

- Immediate "thank-you" note.
- Then, at least every three weeks.
- Status report of search; send articles.

When You've Lost the Spirit to Job Hunt

They're all doing terrific! You're barely hanging on. You used to be a winner. Now what can you do?

1. **Put things in perspective.**
   You've worked 10 or 20 years, and you're not done yet. You *do* have a future, you know.

2. **Get support.**
   Join the Club! Relying solely on yourself is not the answer. Job hunters can feel vulnerable and uncared for. They walk into walls and have accidents.

3. **Remember that this is part of a bigger picture.**
   Learn from this experience and make some sense of it. Decide what is important to you now.

4. **Continue to do your job.**
   Sometimes you didn't feel like doing your old job, but you did it anyway. Job hunting is now your job. Get it done. Organize. Make that call. Have fun.

It's true that when God closes a door, He opens a window. But the hallways are hell.

Sol Wachler, former New York Supreme Court
Justice,
after serving time in jail.

Join Your Small Group

You will have help from:

- Your Small-Group Coach
- Your Job-Search Buddies
- Your Small-Group Team
- Hundreds of Five O'Clock Club Alumni
  The first week, listen to other members. Observe their search strategies. You can learn a lot from them. The second week, we start working on *your* search: help you figure out how to get more interviews in your target areas or how to turn those interviews into offers.

Study the Materials

- The books
- The audiotapes (or lectures at the in-person branches)
- **Web-site:** "How to Find a Job" Section and Worksheets in the Members-Only section

SEE YOUR PRIVATE COACH
USE *ALL* OF YOUR RESOURCES!

THE FIVE O'CLOCK CLUB
300 EAST 40TH STREET
NEW YORK, NY 10016

CALL 212-286-4500
FOR INFORMATION ON BECOMING
A MEMBER AND SUBSCRIBING TO
THE FIVE O'CLOCK NEWS.

OR CALL TOLL FREE: 1-800-575-3587
E-MAIL: INFO@FIVEOCLOCKCLUB.COM

WEB SITE:
WWW.FIVEOCLOCKCLUB.COM

CHAPTER TWO

The
Five
O'Clock
Club

"Not Another Boring Job, Please!": Embracing Assessment

A few times every week we get calls at the Five O'Clock Club from people who ask, "Can you write my résumé for me?" I usually take a deep breath, because I know what's coming. I explain that all Five O'Clock Club coaches can help with résumé preparation, but they don't usually *write* the résumé. I also explain, "The coach will help you with the assessment exercises to make sure that your résumé is really appropriate for your goals." If the caller says, "I don't want all that—I just need someone to write my résumé," I usually suggest doing a Google search for résumé writers. It's not hard to find résumé factories that will get the job done fast—and the résumé will *look* pretty darn good.

But beauty is only skin deep. "Looking good" is not really what it's all about. A really beautiful résumé can also be a very bad résumé! I take the deep breath because I know that the caller doesn't grasp a vital truth about one's basic marketing document: a *great* résumé requires hard work on the part of the person whom it represents. For many people, "writing a résumé" just means adding a few sentences about recent experience, getting the wording right about job functions, cleaning up the grammar and spelling,

making sure that everything is formatted properly—and having a hundred copies printed on quality paper.

The callers who just want a fast résumé don't know that the first step in an effective job search is not a pretty résumé. That crucial first step is assessment. This is a lesson that job hunters learn as soon as they arrive at the Club. For most of our members, the primary issue to not simply landing another job: The professionals, managers, and executives who come to the Club are eminently employable, although the process requires a full measure of focus and hard work. Despite the agonies and anxieties of job search, the next job is usually only a few weeks or, at worst, a few months away. The primary issue is getting *the right job*—getting the job that brings the most satisfaction and joy and that positions you well for the future.

Since almost all surveys of employees in the United States reveal a huge quotient of job dissatisfaction and unhappiness at work, those of us who counsel job hunters for a living are eager to help people escape from bad jobs and unrewarding careers. Naturally, if you're unhappy at work, the smart move is to *find out why*. Chances are, people aren't doing what they like to do (there are also bad bosses and toxic work environments, but that's another story for another book). Hence we counsel job hunters to avoid the quick fix and give a lot of thought to what should come next. This is what the assessment is all about: the "mental archaeology" that will reveal insights into what the next job should be—from the standpoint of job satisfaction and joy. The Five O'Clock Club tools for this are the Seven Stories Exercise and the Forty-Year Vision—or you can make it the Fifteen-Year Vision if this seems more attainable for you. As you will read in the stories found in this chapter, these exercises have been a revelation for job hunters who are serious about finding the *right* job. Who doesn't want to get up each morning and look forward to getting to work?

We have the wonderful success stories that inspire everyone, as you will see as you read this book. Not uncommonly we hear from job hunters for whom the Seven Stories Exercise is a wake-up call, sometimes even a shock. We always wince when we recall that one senior partner in a law firm confessed that his most recent *enjoyable* accomplishment—these are revealed by the Seven Stories—was in junior high school. This was an extreme case, but it is not uncommon for job hunters to discover that most of their enjoyable accomplishments did not take place at work. This outcome may prompt a person to consider a career change or at least a course correction of some kind. But it is also very common for people to have a lot of work-related accomplishments, and this is very affirming. Either way, it's a confidence booster to move forward with a very clear idea of what the past means.

And what about going forward? The Forty-Year Vision—or the Fifteen-Year Vision—is designed to get you hooked on a vision of what your life can be like. If you are reading this book in 2006, it may seem like a pipe dream to plot events that will unfold in 2021, 15 years out. That's *so* far away. But what was your life like in 1991, 15 years *ago*?—that may seem like yesterday. My . . . how time flies, which is just the

point. The year 2021 will get here, and the scheme of your life at that time should have evolved as much on your terms as possible. And this will only happen if you are *thoughtful and careful now.* Make job and life decisions based on strategy. That's what assessment is all about.

Here are job hunter stories from people who embraced assessment and used it to change their lives.

Listening, Once Again, to the Seven Stories

When Roberta attended nine sessions of the Five O'Clock Club a few years ago, "it was a real eye-opener for me to learn the strategy and the tactics. I found it so logical—it made much more sense than other job search advice I'd been given." When she found herself in the job market again, she headed back to the Club. "I started networking again, I rewrote my résumé, but I also redid my Seven Stories—and that, for me, was the real key.

"Doing the Seven Stories a second time helped me focus once more. I had a lot of additional accomplishments. It actually opened up my thought process. I had always worked for big companies—the perks and the prestige were very appealing. But now I saw that I should be thinking outside the box more, and I realized I should be targeting smaller companies. So revisiting the Seven Stories helped expand my targets."

Roberta stumbled across the website of a new company in one of her possible new targets, nutrition. She called the owner directly and assumed the role of a consultant from the outset: "My marketing mind started going. What are you doing now for promotion? How many customers do you have currently?" The owner hadn't even hired a marketing person yet—he'd been trying to handle everything himself. He suggested that they get together, and during the first meeting she helped him rewrite the ad he had placed in the newspaper for a marketing person. "But he started calling me every day for advice." The newspaper ad drew responses, but Roberta had already beat the competition. She was the one who landed the new position to direct marketing, sales, public relations, and business development.

She reflected on the broad impact of the Seven Stories Exercise: "It helped me target personal goals as well: getting in shape, feeling healthy, and feeling good about myself."

Roberta's second visit to the Five O'Clock Club lasted three sessions. The leader of her small group points to one of the main lessons to learn from her experience: "Anyone who says "I can't create a job for myself" should pay attention to this story."

A False Start, at $4000

Larry was worried about his future when he lost his position as director of retail operations for a consumer products company. "I was 54, and the prospect of a job search and possible career change was a real challenge." So much so that he followed the suggestion of a friend and enrolled at an outplacement firm, despite the sticker-shock fee of $4000. "I found it somewhat helpful, but after three months I was still without direction in my job search."

When Larry found the Five O'Clock Club, he discovered at the outset that he hadn't really done proper assessment. He booked a private session with his Five O'Clock Club coach and put full energy into doing the Seven Stories. "I discovered that I had significant experience and skills to transfer to my new objective, which was to move from operations management to product design." With a refashioned résumé and a clear understanding of targeting by geographic areas, Larry focused on generating interviews at companies near his home. After years of enduring a three-to-four-hour daily commute, he wanted to improve his situation in that respect as well.

"I was able to interview confidently, and the Five O'Clock Club approach to negotiating

money helped greatly. I ended up with significantly better salary, stock, and benefits package." Larry's coach commends him for "applying Five O'Clock Club principles from the very start. He has a very diverse background, so it was crucial to really focus on the assessment and rewrite his résumé to reflect the themes that emerged."

Larry attended the Club for eight sessions. "I'm profoundly grateful for all the help you've given me. The Five O'Clock Club techniques are the best that can be found anywhere."

Career Change: Trusting the Seven Stories Exercise

Judith was a corporate tax lawyer with a large firm and decided a career change was in order when she faced pressure to increase billable hours—even though she was already working 12- and 13-hour days.

Assessment at the Five O'Clock Club prompted her to build on her legal expertise, but to shift focus and environment. She decided to aim for a position in immigration law, but also kept a second interest in mind: could she somehow combine this with a marketing-related role? Her group coach at the Club commends Judith for the serious attention she devoted to the Seven Stories: "Her new direction didn't come as a flash. It came through putting a lot of time, effort, thought, and hard work into the Seven Stories. She's a living example of someone who took the time to do an in-depth assessment, and it paid off for her."

Speaking up during the "information exchange" at the Club also paid off. She was put in touch with an immigration attorney who was not only willing to meet with her, but who ended up asking her to help on a project—which turned into her new job. "The project was a way for him to check me out, and vice versa. I've started to specialize in employment-related visas, especially extraordinary ability visas and national interest waivers. It's my job to convince the INS that people are so talented that we have to let them stay. So, in a way, I'm integrating my marketing aspirations, because I'm marketing people to the INS."

During the first few months of her job search, Judith admits, she was too cautious and afraid to move ahead because of uncertainty about her future. Part of the cure for that, she suggests, is "to take action, even if you're not sure. Once I started taking action, revising my résumé, and calling people, I felt more sure. I waited for months to be sure, but it really doesn't work that way. Talk to everyone, raise your hand during the information exchange."

As is sometimes the case with career changers—especially someone coming out of corporate tax law—Judith took a step back on money. But she feels that she took a step forward in terms of the quality of life: "I no longer need to buy so many massages and martinis to make up for being so miserable at work!" Judith attended eight sessions.

Discovering What You Really Like to Do

After more than a decade with a major investment bank, doing quantitative analysis in fixed income, Roger was bored. "I like to be intellectually challenged, and my job really wasn't all that interesting. I felt trapped." He came a few times to the Five O'Clock Club, but really wasn't committed to work the method as much as he should have.

He thought he'd found the way out of his dilemma when he was asked to be the CEO for an Internet start-up. Although he eventually ended up "turning out the lights" when the company collapsed, he recalls it as a "great learning experience. I put the business plan together, and I found it interesting to partner with people who were creating something new. Unfortunately I hadn't done enough due-diligence." Despite the positives, Roger admits, "the failure of the company took a big emotional toll and I lost a lot of money."

Roger returned to the Five O'Clock Club and, this time around, decided to put full energy into making the methodology work for him, starting with assessment. "The Seven Stories Exercise requires a lot of soul-searching, but that's what it takes to discover what you really like to do. Any way you can get yourself to do that is quite wonderful. You only live once—you don't have to work in a job you don't like. And the Seven Stories is the best way to put together a good résumé."

In his role as CEO of the Internet company, Roger had developed a long list of contacts in the world of angel investors and venture capitalists. Networking intensively with these people, he was able to generate job interviews, and ended up with three job offers. He accepted a position at a small firm structuring global real estate investments, requiring travel to Europe and the Far East.

"I didn't do any Internet résumé posting," Roger points out. "You have to meet people, and be persistent about it. Get over your fear of talking to people you don't know."

Roger attended eight sessions at the Club and found the small-group sessions a great stimulus. "The people in the groups have great experience to share, even if they're not in your field. And they're very helpful with résumés and cover letters."

Turning Down Offers—with the Forty-Year Vision in Mind

Rose discovered the Five O'Clock Club in 1997 and has been using it ever since to help keep her life on course. She feels that the Seven Stories and Forty-Year Vision provide a solid foundation: "My approach and my decisions should always be aligned with these exercises." And she followed Five O'Clock Club procedures throughout the process. She recalls that when she was job searching in 1997, she found one major opportunity by answering an ad and another through a headhunter. When she answered the ad, she used the two-column approach to demonstrate that she was a match, and she did her best to outclass the competition by "getting in" through contacts; she recalled that a former teacher used to work for the company and called him for help in reaching decision makers. And she did thorough follow-up. "I wrote letters to each person I met with; I really tried to address each person's concern. I reiterated their expectations and showed how I was qualified."

Rose received the offers she'd been working so hard for, but as she reviewed her Forty-Year Vision, she realized that neither one would position her correctly for her long-term goals. Her self-assessment, in fact, was pointing her in the direction of setting up her own business. In pursuing this dream, she affirms the value of Five O'Clock Club methodology. "I have found several Five O'Clock Club techniques to be very valuable in many different applications—whether it's a job search, selling the services in my consulting practice, or looking for partners and sponsors. Always play the role of the consultant: get information, assess needs, find out priorities, discover what skills and talent are in demand, then make a proposal."

The first step in our Four Steps Salary Negotiation method, that is, negotiate the job, holds true for the consultant: "Make sure," Rose advises, "you know what they need. Let them know you can fulfill that need, then you talk about money."

And the fundamentals for finding interviews through networking apply to building a consulting business. Rose is the first to admit that research is crucial, but, above all, "network, cultivate relationships, and keep in touch."

Rediscovering His Love Through the Seven Stories Exercise

Greg had been in a frustrating 10-month job search. Relying primarily on ads and agencies, he had developed "four waves of promising things,

with five or six opportunities in each wave"—but everything had fallen through. He acknowledges that the Five O'Clock Club methodology proved to be the key to turning things around. In fact, he says, my experience "is the story of the enduring principles you learn here and the perils when you ignore them." The Seven Stories Exercise, he says, "is the essence of my success story." It helped him rediscover his love for working directly with people and handling personal transactions. And following the Five O'Clock Club advice to use all four ways of getting interviews, he launched his networking in earnest. His group counselor noticed the impact: "Greg got momentum in his search when he started to network . . . by answering ads he had been going where all the competition was."

Greg realizes furthermore that it probably had been his own fault that the "four waves of promising things" had fallen through. He praises the Five O'Clock Club interviewing techniques especially:

"I was vastly unprepared when I started. Had it not been for the Five O'Clock Club homework, I never would have succeeded in any interview. I commend the Club interview method, both for preparation and follow-through, especially the follow-through."

Greg secured a position in private banking; he attended 14 sessions.

An Experienced Five O'Clock Clubber

Amy knows the power of the Forty-Year Vision, and she's a good example of a career-minded member of the Five O'Clock Club. She had attended club sessions in a prior job search, so was no stranger to our methodology when she returned. In fact, after only one session, she landed a new job. She admits that it wasn't what she was looking for—or so she thought when she showed up for the interview. But she adopted the "consultant mentality," and the interview turned into a five-hour marathon with the senior entertainment executive who would be her new boss. She found that the position had all the ingredients that her Forty-Year Vision told her she was looking for—except the title. It would position her brilliantly to move in the direction she wants to go.

Amy had kept up with the Five O'Clock Club methodology, primarily because it teaches basic life and career management skills, not just job search techniques. As her Five O'Clock Club group counselor attests, she is proof of "the power of the process."

Repeat After Me . . .

Nicholas suggests that "all the phrases in the Five O'Clock Club methodology bear repeating . . . they are extremely powerful." He says that he found it "extremely liberating" to go into an interview with the "consultant mind-set." He argues that this approach goes a long way in shifting the "psychological balance of power." The consultant always must be thinking ahead, anticipating new assignments. With this in mind, the question "Why do you want to leave your current job?" is not so intimidating; it is natural for a consultant to reply, "I'm assessing opportunities." And Nicholas heaped praises on the other members of his small group at the Five O'Clock Club for their skills in critiquing his Two-Minute Pitch—since everyone had read the books and mastered the methodology.

Nicholas's counselor at the Club praised him for coming into the group with "enthusiasm, discipline, structure, and focus"; he was a natural for applying Club methodology to his job search. For Nicholas the process was an enormous positive in his life: "The search is not drudgery. The search is a great opportunity of personal growth . . . you'll get unbelievable benefits."

Nicholas landed a position as VP at a marketing firm.

From Low-Tech to High-Tech Career: Using Assessment and Targeting

Ian attended 11 sessions of the Club before finding a new career in electronic commerce retailing. Having spent many years in food import/export, he was stumbling to find a new direction. "For a few months I did the antithesis of a good job search, even looking in a field that I really didn't want." At the outset with the Club, he found that assessment played a crucial role in turning things around. "My biggest issue was making peace with the past," and *writing down* all the *good things* he had done helped him to do that. He also credits his success to the concept of targeting and conducting an organized campaign. By "spreading the net very wide," he developed targets in Internet marketing.

Coming out of what he identifies as a low-tech field ("We had just discovered the fax machine"), he had to learn a lot to begin to sound like an insider. He was careful to get networking interviews with companies that really didn't interest him, and then "attacked all the real positions in my major targets at the same time." At the urging of his small group at the Club, he wrote to 16 second-tier companies, which resulted in seven responses, considerable new momentum—and his new job.

"I really want to say how much the Five O'Clock Club helped me and how much the format helped. Going every week made me feel more empowered. Especially when you don't feel like coming, come to the meeting."

From Academia to Corporate— After 25 Years

"I don't think if I'd come in with white hair it would have made any difference," Karen claims. "I don't think I encountered age discrimination. I find that the baby-boomer generation has a different attitude toward age. When my mother was 50, she felt old. I don't feel old, and the people around me don't feel or act old." She recalls the remark of Gloria Steinhem to someone who said to her, "You don't look fifty"—"this is what 50 looks like."

Karen was much more concerned about her attempt to move from academia to the corporate world—after almost 25 years at a college. She accomplished the leap to the for-profit world because she positioned herself well, stressing her management skills especially. "I did the Seven Stories Exercise before writing my résumé; it helped me get focused. I had a lot of experience that was all over the place. I recommend the Five O'Clock Club to everyone I can. It was very good for me because I'd never looked for a job, and I found a job within a month."

Being in a high-tech field, Karen is not about to let her technical skills slip, and her daily routine includes the homework required to remain current. Her long commute gives her a lot of time to read trade literature, but she also attends conferences, takes classes, and subscribes to several Internet discussion lists.

Karen doesn't believe her career has peaked and looks forward to many more years on the job. "I can't imagine the idea of retiring. Even if I won the lottery, I wouldn't want to give up working. I find it very satisfying and fulfilling. I couldn't retire and pamper myself." But her vision of the future does allow for a more relaxed pace: "At 70 I would like to work part-time on project management. When I was in academia, I took consulting jobs for the United Nations and had the opportunity to go to Africa. I wouldn't mind taking it easier—but I don't want to stop working."

Karen attended the main branch of the Club in Manhattan.

Overcoming a Two-Year Bad Job Search

Angela's passion in life is jewelry design, and she is the first to admit that job searching in this field can be daunting. "I conducted a two-year job search, by which I really mean I would look for a job for a week, then get very discouraged and put it all away for six months. But I'd be carrying the job hunt with me even though I wasn't actually doing anything about it other than feeling depressed."

She began attending the Five O'Clock Club at the suggestion of a friend and discovered the structure and format for a good job search. "It gave me focus. I read the books and did the Seven Stories—I got clear on what my real talents are." But Angela had not been idle in her "depression" months; she had been savvy enough to know that her marketability depended on state-of-the-art skills as well as on talent; she learned computer design software and studied package design. After she discovered the Five O'Clock Club, she used the self-assessment exercises to visualize and target her dream job.

She landed a position in jewelry design, working three days a week. "I got my dream job, although not my dream salary. But now I will build my portfolio and be able to move on. I give all the credit to the Five O'Clock Club because it gave me focus; it clarified things for me. I felt empowered." The woman who once was too discouraged to job hunt claims a new outlook: "Nothing is going to defeat me now."

Getting the Target Right—with the Forty-Year Vision in Mind

In her attempt to move from corporate finance to strategic planning, Connie came to appreciate our warning that if your targets are wrong, everything is wrong. She had targeted smaller firms, which didn't have the flexibility to accommodate her background—and couldn't afford her. When she finally did get an offer nine months into her search, she made the brave decision to turn it down and reevaluate the search. To get an offer was gratifying—and accepting it as a triumph was tempting—but the money was a disappointment, and she had the gut feeling that it wasn't the right match.

Connie took a fresh look at her goals and, following the advice of one of her networking contacts, shifted her focus to major firms. Her small-group coach says that Connie "went through a great deal of soul searching. She knew, based on her written Forty-Year Vision, that the job she turned down really wasn't the right one for her. So she managed not to get waylaid by the wrong offer. She pulled herself together, retargeted, and kept her Forty-Year Vision in mind. Approaching her new targets, she managed to get where she wanted to go."

Three months later Connie landed an offer from a major firm at 40 percent more money than the job she had turned down. She attended the club for 15 sessions.

Letting Assessment Point the Way After 40!

Tom Lewis can tell you that 1975 was a bad year for college graduates. In the middle of a recession, he was one of many students left empty-handed when campus recruiting was over. With his BBA from Ohio University, he managed to land a job at a Goodyear Tire & Rubber retail outlet in Parkersburg, West Virginia, just across the river from his hometown of Belpre, Ohio. He changed tires and helped service cars.

An Old Lead Pays Off

Within a couple of months he came to the attention of Goodyear management. He was tapped for training to be a credit manager and was assigned to the office in Princeton, West Virginia. While he welcomed the chance to get onto a career track, Tom was reluctant to stay in Appalachia. "A lot of people in small towns max out early. My goal was to go much further; I wanted to be able to achieve all I could. And I

wanted to see what the rest of the country was about."

Fortunately he got a call from a lead he had pursued months earlier, and it proved to be an opportunity he welcomed. He was hired by Kaufmann's department store in Pittsburgh for their management-training program. He remained with Kaufmann's for five years as it built more stores, progressing through the ranks and learning all aspects of merchandising and store operations. He learned as well that he had a natural talent for sales. I like dealing with people and helping them. I like the satisfaction of meeting people's needs."

The Move to Industrial Sales

But while retail was a "hot trendy place to be"— Nieman Marcus was also on the rise at this time—Tom was looking for a way to increase his earning power. "I had always heard that the big money was in industrial sales." He was also looking for a way to get to see more of the country.

Through a friend he was able to secure a position at a company that manufactured complex machinery for factories and steel mills, Mayfran International. Mayfran traditionally had hired degreed engineers, but was now looking for sales and marketing talent. Tom was hired as district sales manager based out of Pittsburgh and serviced a clientele of steel mills in western and central Pennsylvania, developing an expertise in the sale of waste-handling conveyor systems. He was also charged with the role of purchasing dealerships to sell the Mayfran product line, which required even more travel. Eventually transferred to Chicago, Tom was able to pursue his MBA at Keller Graduate School of Management at night; he graduated in 1985.

Tom's next career move came when one of the distributors he had worked with, Paul Riley, asked him to come on board and help grow the business. "I found that my strength was in starting something, getting it going, taking a concept and putting it into reality—or taking an existing setup and altering it to fit changing market conditions." Tom leveraged his knowledge of conveyor systems and, for the next five years, helped the new firm sell industrial shredders, bailers, and compactors. More people were hired, and new products were offered.

In the search for new industrial products to promote, a European product that was virtually unknown in the United States came to Tom and Paul's attention: high-speed doors. These fabric roll-up doors are used in very large plants that manufacture cars, tractors, and planes; opening and closing very rapidly, these doors are used to protect environments that would be compromised by heat, humidity, or dust. They launched a new company, Ritek, with the challenge of educating the American industrial marketplace—and manufacturing, marketing, and selling the new product. Tom enjoyed this assignment and was able to fulfill his dream of discovering the country.

He traveled widely in the United States, Canada, and Mexico during the next several years, promoting the high-speed doors and helping to build Ritek to a $12 million company. But as much as anything else, he relished having his curiosity satisfied. "Industrial sales allowed travel and the opportunity to see many different plants. I got to see how cars and trucks are built." He also assumed the roles that he found rewarding: building something from scratch—starting with a concept and turning it into a reality—and at the same time helping to satisfy the needs of customers. "I'm a problem solver. I like to get something done, then move on."

The next "move on" was prompted when Ritek was sold in 1994. The new owner didn't need Tom's start-up expertise, but another company did. Megadoor, headquartered in Sweden, had sold high-speed doors in Europe for some time and was looking for someone to build its business from scratch on this side of the Atlantic. So Tom spent the next four years repeating the pattern of building a new company, growing the business, and promoting it throughout North America. And Dynaco, USA, a high-speed door company based in Belgium, used Tom to build its business in 1998–1999.

The Decision to Start Career Planning

By this time Tom was in his mid 40's and realized that it might not always be so easy to fall into the next job. One start-up after another had been a great challenge, but it might not look all that smart on the résumé if this pattern kept repeating. And as his daughter was getting older, the heavy travel was beginning to be a concern as well. He had been traveling almost every other week, now to Europe as well as widely in North America.

"Life had been very good. I'd been very fortunate—opportunities had been presented to me. But I'd never really sat down and said, 'What do I want to do when I grow up? What do I really want to be and where do I want to go?' It wasn't a midlife crisis, but I realized I'd better start to do a more formalized career search—a more formalized way to trying to stay employed."

Tom heard a radio advertisement for Korn-Ferry, the national executive placement company, and went to their website, FutureStep.com. He soon discovered the link to the Five O'Clock Club and was pleased to discover that there was a physical branch in Chicago. He called the branch manager, Joy Muench, and signed up for sessions.

For DuPont: Big Ticket Floor Sales an Opportunity

Having had "no luck with headhunters," Tom decided to follow the Club's suggestion to use all four ways for getting interviews and began networking aggressively. He soon was in touch with a friend who worked for DuPont, which was rethinking and retooling its approach to floor sales. DuPont was looking for entrepreneurs—people who could pursue new marketing techniques and sell directly to major accounts. After "many interviews and meeting many people," Tom was brought on to service northern Illinois national accounts and to go after multimillion dollar deals, including the flooring for federal and state office buildings.

Tom acknowledges that he landed the new position quickly, but credits the Five O'Clock Club with far more than teaching him the value of networking. "High school, college, and graduate school really don't teach you how to take care of yourself career-wise. I was searching for a way to educate myself so that I could be in charge of my destiny, as opposed to letting it be more of a random act. The Five O'Clock Club gave me the education I needed on how to do a proper search. It gave me a framework and a game-plan for managing my career."

And he is confident that the Club helped get him ready for the lengthy interview process at DuPont. He admits that he balked initially at the assessment part of the methodology. "I didn't want to do the Seven Stories Exercise and the Forty-Year Vision. But they were great; you have to start from scratch and do it right. I did everything. It's a formalized, structured way of doing it the way it should be done. After I finally gave in and decided that the Five O'Clock Club was right, I was spending 10 to 12 hours per day doing research, thinking, getting things lined up. Doing what the Club says allowed me to get focused and move in the right direction quickly. I was a much more powerful candidate when I went to DuPont for the interviews.

The Best Is Yet to Come

Looking back at where he's been—as well as forward—Tom believes that his "most important accomplishment has not been made yet. I want to be successful on a much broader scale. I'm still aspiring and I have a plan. I'm working the Forty-Year Vision."

He credits his success so far to determination and curiosity to see the world beyond the Appalachia where he grew up. Launching start-ups and selling have taught him the value of self-motivation. "When you're in sales, you're actually unemployed every day. When you get up in the

morning, it's up to you—no one is going to hand it to you. That's the motivation: it's 100 percent up to you."

Ten years out Tom sees himself "still working, growing, and moving, very much involved in sales with a major corporation—trying to do better things better ways." And retirement will be a high-energy affair for Tom: "I will still have a job. My idea of retirement is working at something I want to do. Perhaps a farm with gardens and horses requiring manual labor outside—and being able to play golf *during* the week."

Tom feels that the Five O'Clock Club has given him lessons for life. "I now have the toolbox. If I am ever in the job search situation again, I can get started much more quickly. I have recommended the Five O'Clock Club to 20 to 30 people. A lot of people like to moan, groan, and complain about their lives. It startles them to find out that it's up to them. It's easy to complain—it's hard to move forward. Even if you're not really searching for a job, the Five O'Clock Club is great to go through to prepare yourself."

Designing a Career: Architect Michel Franck

"I want to expand the firm domestically and land more projects in the global marketplace as well," says architect Michel Franck, speaking of his role over the next five years at his new firm, Owen & Mandolfo.

The firm had specialized during the prior 20 years in high-end interior design, primarily for leading financial institutions. Clients included Goldman Sachs, Commerzbank, and the Dime Savings Bank. "At Goldman, for example," Michel points out, "we do about 20 private offices for partners at a time, at offices throughout the country. We are responsible for all interior installations, including technology requirements, furniture, custom cabinetry, and artwork selection.

We oversee the process from inception to finish, putting together all the documents for the contractors. For Commerzbank, we prepared and implemented the standard guidelines for offices in Los Angeles, Chicago, Atlanta, New York, and Paris. A half-million square feet of office space altogether."

Michel signed on as principal at Owen & Mandolfo in October 2000, managing a staff of 30. He brought a wealth of experience to his new role. The previous year-and-a-half he had worked as principal for a corporate design firm, but the previous 15 years he served as CEO for the architectural company he founded, overseeing six to eight architects and support staff. A native of Luxembourg, Michel earned his first Master of Architecture from École St. Luc in Brussels. Looking for a two-year postgraduate study program, he won a full scholarship to Miami University in Oxford, Ohio. In 1983 he graduated there with a second Master of Architecture.

In recent years Michel has contributed articles to *Interiors, Oculus, Real Estate Weekly, Revue Technique de Luxembourg, Architectural Record,* and *The New York Times.* He addressed the ninth annual conference of Attorneys and Executives in Corporate Real Estate on the topic "Environmentally Responsible Development, Architecture, and Interior Architecture Installations."

Michel looks back with pride on more than 70 projects that his firm brought to fruition. These included design of the eight-acre *Place de l'Étoile* in the City of Luxembourg, the Luxembourg Consulate and Permanent Mission in New York, and facilities for Guardian Life Insurance Company and RCA-Columbia Pictures. But reflecting on the decade-and-a-half in his own business, he sees that his true calling is business development and building client relations, for which he would have more opportunity at a larger firm. "I'd gotten ahead of myself. I had the ability to work on large-scale projects and secure large-scale clients, but my firm did not have the necessary infrastructure."

Expanding the Client Base and Maintaining Quality

Hence winning—and keeping—the clients is Michel's primary role with his new employer. "I'm here to focus on business development strategy and expand the firm. I will lead the front-end effort to increase volume and secure more projects, while maintaining the quality of design. But I also bring a layer of knowledge with regard to design and project management." Having deep product knowledge in addition to selling savvy should help Michel with another primary objective. "I want to assure long-term relations with clients, focusing on repeat business from a strong client base."

Throughout his career, Michel has drawn inspiration from architects who combine artistic brilliance with an understanding of how business works. "I have looked up to architects for the quality of their design and the integrity of their work, but also to those with good business sense, a business-oriented approach."

Positioning to Win Clients

In his first three months, Michel put together extensive documentation on the firm's history in order to develop presentations highly customized for individual clients. He feels that lessons from job search apply to winning clients. "It's much the same approach that the Five O'Clock Club recommends in pitching yourself to the target. When we go to a presentation to potential clients, we can't just say how wonderful we are. We've got to show how wonderful we are for them. We must address the needs of the clients as specifically as possible."

Michel developed his five-year plan for leading Owen & Mandolfo forward, and while attending the Five O'Clock Club he managed to flesh out a 20-year personal vision as well. "This was a very good exercise. I had not done something like this before. I didn't do a Forty-Year Vision," he laughed, "because I would have been planning my own funeral!" Still in his 40's, however, Michel grants that a 40-year outlook might not be such a bad idea after all: "My father is 82 and he just bought a computer!"

Michel came to the Five O'Clock Club through a friend's recommendation. He attended for nine sessions over a four-month period before landing his job. "It was helpful to talk to others about my search—it boosted my confidence. Doing the Seven Stories was very valuable because it gave me insight into what I really like to do and who I really am. I benefited not only from the end result of getting a job, but from the process itself."

Michel affirms that approaching the search *like a consultant* is the key. "Looking for a job is a very humbling experience, whether you do it because you have to or want to. The Five O'Clock Club prompts people to look at things differently. It's the candidate who has to be the leader, rather than just sitting back and letting things happen. I worked to get 6 to 10 things in the works and got to the point where I was having four to five networking meetings and interviews per week. The methodology and the rigor were very good. I have been referring other people to the Five O'Clock Club."

Planning Semiretirement

What does Michel think his life will be like 20 or 25 years out? "My goal is to semiretire at age 72, at the level of being a consultant. My father still works a little, and I don't want to stop working. Especially for people in my generation, it's important for people to keep getting educated, keep growing and participating in the world."

Fluent in English, French, German, Luxembourgish, and basic Italian, Michel sees himself spending more time traveling when semiretired. "I will enjoy different aspects of life. Take walks, play golf, hang out, and visit the world—it's a very good way to keep on learning."

Michael Dunaway: Exchanging the Navy for Homeland Security

"How do I continue to serve after I've taken off the uniform?" This was the question that Michael Dunaway faced as his 27 years of active duty with the U.S. Navy were coming to an end. His distinguished career included tours of duty on U.S. Navy destroyers and commands of a guided missile frigate and a patrol hydrofoil. He also taught at the Naval Academy and National War College and served as a strategic planner on the staff of the Chief of Naval Operations.

"When you're in the Navy, you're used to being handed a set of orders," Michael reflected on the process of taking charge of his future. "You can negotiate orders and manage your career to a degree, but orders are orders. This was my first real career transition."

A friend at the National War College suggested that he look into the Five O'Clock Club, and Michael began attending the branch in Rockville, MD. Our coaches there, Harvey Kaplan and James Dittbrenner, specialize in helping people transition from military to civilian careers. "It was worth investing the time and money in the Club. I had attended a couple of seminars offered by the Navy, but I really had to learn how to do a transition. I came to look upon the Five O'Clock Club program as a graduate course for minding my career."

With "how do I continue to serve?" foremost in his mind, Michael was struck by the Club's emphasis on analyzing what you already know and love and applying it to the future. "The approach is about learning about yourself, learning about the market, doing proper research, being persistent, working hard, doing the networking." When he did the Seven Stories, Michael noticed that there were a lot of things in his career that he had done well—but didn't especially want to do again. "You put these things into a separate basket—skills to fall back on if you have to—but which you don't necessarily want to rely on again." The Forty-Year Vision appealed to him especially as he was "trying to figure how to contribute to society and make my future life meaningful. Figuring out how to serve a higher cause, orienting your life to what's important," Michael notes, "is right in line with working out your Forty-Year Vision."

His role as strategic planner for the Chief of Naval Operations was one he enjoyed, so trying to build on this made sense as he began targeting a civilian career. At a job fair he visited the booth of an engineering and strategic planning consulting firm in Arlington, VA.

He was soon in the door there for a series of interviews. He knew he had competition, so he followed the basic Five O'Clock Club rules about trying to get "6 to 10 things in the works" ("I actually had about three or four") and following up smartly. He wrote "influencing letters" to the president of the company, the executive director, and others he'd met with. "I was impressed with the president's positioning of his company," Michael notes. "He told me, 'We provide a service to the nation, we do high-quality work, hence we have a good reputation and get good customers.' I liked his priority of putting 'service to the nation first.'"

Michael saw the process through for five or six weeks, but got the offer he wanted and was assigned to work on scientific and technology projects for the Office of Naval Research.

On the morning of September 11th, 2001, from his office he could see the smoke rising from the Pentagon. Within a matter of weeks the focus of his role shifted. From November 2001 through March 2002 he served on a homeland security task force involved in designing a bioterrorism response plan for the Philadelphia region. This focused on interagency planning and mass casualty response during "worst-case scenarios." He has continued to assist in community preparedness, most recently establishing a nonprofit organization to assist businesses in emergency preparedness and business continuity planning. The focus of his work at the Office of Naval Research, using virtual reality systems for military training and planning, has proven valuable. Using the skills he most wants to use, Michael found his answer to the question "How do I continue to serve?"

Seeing where Michael landed, it might, at first blush, look like an easy answer and an even easier transition: a captain in the Navy ends up with a company that does scientific and technical work for the Navy. But that would minimize the complexity of a major life shift. Such a move—even one that seems so obvious—shouldn't be made on a hunch. Michael values the discipline of doing the Seven Stories and the Forty-Year Vision, as well as the camaraderie of the 10 weekly Five O'Clock Club meetings he attended. "The association with a group—one focused on more than simply following the routines of a job hunt—was important. It helped to develop relationships with other people who were facing the same process. And we weren't all getting together to pool conventional wisdom—we were applying what we learned in the Five O'Clock Club books."

Didn't Get Fired After All, But Moved on Anyway

When rumors are flying about layoffs, many people prefer denial: "It won't be me." Gwynne assumed, however, that it would be her. After working for a large corporation for more than a decade, she assumed that her role in the corporate philanthropy department was anything but secure. "After all, we're not exactly a profit center." Although Gwynne liked what she did, she was unsure that she really was being true to herself in terms of being on the best career path. She asked a headhunter for suggestions about a career coach and was referred to the Five O'Clock Club. "The Club matched me with a coach who specializes in helping women with career change.

"I read the books and found the Seven Stories Exercise especially helpful. I had been in the same job with the same company for 12 years, yet a lot of the things I'd loved doing had come earlier in my life, such as leading projects and working with young people in the arts. Looking at these accomplishments gave me a whole different sense of direction and a different sense of self-confidence. I got informational and networking interviews that wouldn't have happened if I'd not done the Seven Stories."

As is often the case when a person networks intensively and generates informational interviews, Gwynne didn't find a job that existed, but stirred enough interest that a job was created for her—based on her experience and enthusiasm. She had targeted properly, positioned herself well, and secured a management position at a large community music school. "This is exactly what I wanted to do—creative work with young people."

Gwynne counsels patience and persistence for anyone working at a career change, especially if it means the creation of a new position. "It turned out to be an amazing process for me. It's important to talk with people broadly and go with their time frame instead of yours—it takes a while to create jobs that don't exist. Just remember that delay doesn't mean lack of interest." And Gwynne's approach from now on will remain anchored in the Seven Stories. "You have to follow your gut in choosing a job. Even if you take something now that's not the ideal job, just remember that you have to keep on the right path as much as possible."

As it turned out, Gwynne's job in corporate philanthropy wasn't eliminated, but she was pleased that the prospect of unemployment prompted her to be proactive in managing her career. She encourages others to search for the best possible fit: "It's important to know you're in a place where you can thrive, contribute, and grow."

Start with Assessment, Then Follow the Method

With more than 15 years in business consulting roles, Clayton admits that he was no stranger to job hunting. But he decided to take the advice of a friend who suggested that he give the Five O'Clock Club a try—and he did so with the hope that he could use it to give a boost to his networking efforts. He found, however, that the Club did much more—it got him grounded in the fundamentals of the job search process.

Although he had completed assessment exercises in the past, he did the Seven Stories and affirms the value of always revisiting this part of the process: "Do not neglect any part of assessment. Every time I come back to such exercises I learn something new about myself that I can then exploit." And he applauds the focus that the Five O'Clock Club books bring to assessment. "The entire process is well thought out. If you follow it, you know yourself, your strengths and weaknesses. You also know how to approach the market to maximize your strengths and downplay your weaknesses. In the consulting business I have come across far too many people who don't know themselves—that's where the Seven Stories are important."

Heavily focused on computer consulting, it was natural for Clayton to use the Internet to hunt for appropriate openings—and it worked for him. He cautions, however, that Five O'Clock Club research on this technique is accurate, namely, that only 7 or 8 percent of job-hunting executives land key interviews this way. "I'm an exception. The vast majority of Internet ads won't pay off. You can assume that every ad you see will draw 500 résumés—because it doesn't cost 39 cents for postage to submit a résumé."

In his case, however, he found a match made in heaven—a perception that was helped, no doubt, because Clayton was careful to craft his résumé according to Five O'Clock Club standards. "Review your résumé with a hypercritical eye," Clayton recommends. "The résumé must be eye-catching. Be sure to highlight what you want *them* to notice and ask about. That made the difference for me. I know people with extremely good credentials, but who present themselves so poorly on their résumés.

You really have to dig to understand what they do. When I'm looking at résumés of friends I make the effort, but hiring managers don't have the time."

Clayton found that the Club was helpful beyond assessment and résumé writing. "The books are excellent, and I also always want to keep the tapes in my professional library. Everywhere I went on a drive I listened to them, especially the tapes on networking, interviewing, and the use of direct and targeted mail. Repetition is very important. You're trying to internalize the message, so that it becomes an automatic part of you when you're in an interview."

Clayton attended his weekly Five O'Clock Club group just five times and credits his coach with helping him stay focused, but his dream job happened almost overnight. After submitting his résumé on line, he was called in for a meeting with the president of the company he works for now—on a Wednesday. He was called back for a second interview on Saturday, was made an offer on Sunday, and started the job on Monday! He works for a consulting firm that assists small businesses, thus he gets to use his expertise in computers, operations, and finance. He finds it very satisfying in helping small firms to survive. "Some are asset rich and cash poor," Clayton points out, "and they wonder why they're sinking. First we stabilize the cash situation, then figure out what needs to be done."

Assessment and a Major Course Correction

"I thought I would be instantly marketable. Luckily for me, I wasn't." This admission comes from John Ratliff, who didn't realize that he was destined for a life-altering career change.

After 14 years with one company that did government contract work, he stayed on for seven months after the company was sold in 2001. He had served as COO/CEO, and in May 2002 began what he describes as "a very unfocused campaign" to find a new job. "I had a fairly blah résumé and fairly poor interviewing skills. All this helped keep me unemployed." While sitting one day in his CPA's waiting room, he was flipping through an accountancy journal and saw the Five O'Clock Club listed as a "reasonably priced outplacement firm." He visited our website and began attending the weekly Club meetings. "The *effective* phase of my career search began," John says.

His first discovery at the Club was that he had skipped the assessment phase of job search, and he set about carefully working his way through all of the exercises in *Targeting a Great Career*. "I discovered that I hated what I'd been doing the last two or three years—and here I had been searching for something just like it! I did my Forty-Year Vision and measured my life up to that point against it. I found gaps." John decided he needed to forge a career with social impact and targeted leadership roles in a nonprofit environment.

He began a campaign to educate himself about the world of nonprofit, which included arranging informational interviews, teaching himself not-for-profit accounting, learning about nonprofit boards, and—since he hoped for a visible role of some kind—he joined Toastmasters to overcome his fear of public speaking. At the suggestion of his career coach, he even contacted the author of an article in the *Harvard Business Review* on competitive corporate philanthropy.

After only about a month into this new "effective phase" of his search, John spotted an ad in *The Washington Post* for a position with a well-respected not-for-profit. He was careful to structure his response to the ad in the format suggested in our book, *Shortcut Your Job Search: The Best Ways to Get Meetings.* "I had several interviews, one of which was a panel interview. I relied heavily on the interview book and all went well. I received an offer in October."

Unfortunately, the offer was not all that he had hoped for and he attempted to "negotiate the job—I gave it my best shot." Although a meeting of the minds failed, he didn't want to close doors: "I offered to help out on a temp basis in the months ahead. Since I was now pretty well aware of their needs and issues, that might make sense for both of us." And in January 2003 he was called back again—the number two candidate had not worked out either! John began as a consultant, but they soon achieved the meeting of the minds that had eluded them in October. John was hired full-time as vice president of operations and his career in nonprofit was under way.

In reflecting on the lessons learned at the Five O'Clock Club now that he has used the techniques for an effective job search, John suggests a few fundamentals for job hunters to keep in mind:

- I can't say enough about assessment. Do it seriously, do it completely; what comes after will be easier and more logical.
- The people you meet during informational interviews can be a resource for the rest of your life. Take time before meetings to come up with good questions about their organizations—that way, later, you can repay them with information as you come across it. The more you help them, the more everyone will benefit.
- Contact writers of books and articles. Most people don't think of taking this next step. You will sound more like an insider if you can quote from these conversations, not just from the articles.
- Remember that you're in this for the long haul. It's very easy to get focused on that next job, but keep your eye on what you need to do with your Forty-Year Vision in mind.
- Read the Five O'Clock Club books—don't skip anything.
- The experience with your Five O'Clock Club group is invaluable. It's nice to have the support of family and friends, but they can be helpful and sympathetic only up to a point. You need to be involved with, and share resources with, other job searchers. The focus here is careers.

A Career Lawyer: Renewed Grounding with the Seven Stories

"When I entered the job market in 2003 I was general counsel at a health-care firm," Paul Lubetkin points out, "and when the dust had settled, I ended up as general counsel for another health-care company." Which was perfectly fine with him—but even so the journey was interesting and gave him a renewed understanding of his objectives.

A 1976 law school graduate, Paul worked initially in the Division of Enforcement at the U.S. Securities and Exchange Commission. But throughout the 1980s, he worked as a trial lawyer for the prestigious law firm of Kelley, Drye & Warren, ending up as partner in the Chicago office by the middle of the decade. He opted for a major change in 1990 when he accepted an offer from a friend to join a start-up biotech company in Westchester as general counsel. "One year after I joined the company, it went public. I was lucky to be exposed to new challenges and opportunities." With a full decade of biotech experience on his résumé, Paul responded to another opportunity at an Internet health-care company that anticipated going public. "If you're allergic to risk," Paul points out, "you shouldn't be in the pharmaceutical business." The new company experienced "tremendous rapid success," he says, "followed by tremendous rapid lack of success. I managed to survive the first three or four waves of company shrinkage, but, when one-third of the management team was let go, I was among them."

The company's head of organizational effectiveness was included in the downsizing, but shopped for outplacement help and identified the Five O'Clock Club as "a cost-effective and effective service." Living close to New York, Paul chose one-on-one career coaching with Jim Borland in Manhattan, but for the regular weekly group meetings was assigned to Phil Ronniger, facilitator of a Tuesday night telephone group.

Although Paul used all four ways to get interviews, the payoff for him came through networking and through recruiters who specialize in placing senior attorneys. He was actually brought to their attention through a combination of working with other general counsels and by his use of Internet websites geared to the needs of corporate counsels. Within three or four months of the launch of his search, he reports, "I had about a half dozen interesting prospects—but, as we all know, five will fall away through no fault of your own—and I was eventually down to one. And after six or seven interviews—and strong follow-up letters—he received an offer to be general counsel for a pharmaceutical company in Bucks County, PA. He accepted the position in September 2003—despite the company having trouble finding a new CEO and being involved in several lawsuits. He moved from Westchester to Princeton, New Jersey in December.

As he was moving into a new house, however, he received a call from one of the companies that had fallen away from him, Pliva, Inc. "Not wanting to close doors, I pursued the conversation. There was more potential challenge and upside in their situation." Paul remained with the Bucks County firm for a few months—long enough, in fact, to help the new CEO get into place and assist in settling several of its lawsuits. In February 2003, he signed on as senior vice president general counsel for Pliva, Inc. The latter is a wholly owned subsidiary of Pliva, d.d. of Croatia and became the general counsel of Pliva's global proprietary pharmaceuticals group, known in the United States as Odyssey Pharmaceuticals, Inc. Although Paul had no doubts about his career direction when he arrived at the Five O'Clock Club, he nonetheless followed Club advice and did the Seven Stories Exercise. "It was very helpful for me to go through the process of thinking about what skills I enjoyed using, what settings I enjoyed using them in, and where I found satisfaction. The exercise also helped me think about other things I might do. It gave me much clarity and focus—I hadn't done an assessment exercise as a grown-up!

"I referred to the books throughout my search," Paul says. "I used them as references and resources. I listened to the assigned tapes every week. They help with focus and motivation." He also attended the group nearly every week for three months during his search. "They were very fine people doing very interesting searches. And I really liked working with Phil Ronniger." By the time he began working with a weekly group, he had already hammered out his Two-Minute Pitch in his private sessions with Jim Borland. "That experience with the coach one-on-one was very good. Jim was very helpful. I always looked forward to those meetings. I got a lot out of them."

Paul has a new perspective on career satisfaction after his experience with the Five O'Clock Club and feels that he is in a better position to advise others. "I get inquiries from people in job search, but very few of them know what they really want to do. They have a vague feeling that their current role isn't where they want to be. So it's incredibly important to have clarity about what's going to make you happy. It's clear to me how many people are unhappy where they are—and they assume that the next job is going to make them happy. But they really don't know what will make them happy, and they don't know how to think about what will make them happy—other than that they want to get away from where they are. So it's a lot better to do the Seven Stories before you start looking."

In a Hurry . . . in the Wrong Direction

Alex was more than happy to do the reading assignments, but bauked at assessment. "I read the Five O'Clock Club books, but skipped the Seven Stories Exercise. I was in a hurry. I got thirty informational interviews with private equity folks, which is tough to do." He didn't land a job, but he got some good advice. Several people said, "Alex, you're looking in the wrong place. Check out Internet opportunities."

Being in the wrong place is often what happens when you slight assessment. So Alex did the Seven Stories; he realized that he had been rushing—which didn't help much if he really didn't know *where* he should be rushing. "The Seven Stories got me to think about what I'm good at and helped get me in sync with what's in the market."

He also took to heart one of the Club's mantras: If you don't have experience, go get it. "I talked three companies into giving me consulting projects where I didn't get paid anything." Within a couple of months he had developed a business strategy for one of them, a private equity group "that was morphing into an Internet B-to-B." After a few months he headed to California to talk to as many dot.coms as he could and attended as many seminars as he could. The consulting experience and all the informational interviewing were making Alex an insider—so much so that a university professor asked him to write an article on Internet market makers.

In July Alex got a call from people he had met at a seminar in March. After a series of interviews, he was offered a position as "entrepreneur in residence" for a business development firm specializing in wireless applications. Building on assessment, Alex rapidly learned a new field, acquired the experience he needed—and through vigorous networking generated leads that paid off. Alex's coach confirms that "he was rigorous. Alex worked hard at identifying options and was receptive to trying new things."

Getting a Boost on a Short Job Search

Anyone who lands a new job quickly may also be tempted to think that job searching is easy—but when job search time comes again in a year or two, there may be a rude awakening. However, unseen preparation commonly is a key even for the brief job search. Camilla was sent to the Five O'Clock Club for outplacement, but found it difficult to get to meetings because of her school schedule. Happily, a combination of networking and a few Club techniques paid off fairly quickly. "I attended one session," Camilla acknowledges, "and that one group meeting was so helpful. I got to see the interaction, I saw everyone giving feedback to everyone else. That was invaluable. I went home that night and sat up late with my résumé. I saw that there was a lot to be done to fix it."

She also booked private sessions with her coach, Ruth Robbins. "She was very helpful with the positioning statement on the résumé—what was important, what to position where." Camilla also saw the truth of the Five O'Clock Club rule that a good résumé can't be done without the Seven Stories. "I found this exercise really difficult. It was a challenge to look at my accomplishments and figure out what I am good at."

Camilla's lucky break came from an early networking contact, so she recommends networking—but properly, as the Club recommends: "If you're going to hit someone up for a job, forget about it. I simply told a colleague that I would be moving on and that it had been a pleasure working with her. She responded that she would let me know if she heard of anything that might be of interest." When the interview from this connection did come to pass, Camilla was conscientious in applying what she had learned at the Club: "I addressed all of their concerns in my follow-up letter." As it turns out, Camilla was hired for a position that was new—and that was likely to evolve. Ruth points out that Camilla was concerned that the offer came very early in her search. "So we went through all the pros and cons of the situation. I was impressed with her energy and focus. She was very methodical." And because Camilla was assigned to the Five O'Clock Club by her employer for outplacement, she is entitled to work with her coach and group for a full year—in case she runs into any problems on the new job.

After 13 Years, Redirected by the Seven Stories Exercise

Cynthia had been the director of the research library for an educational television station. She was laid off after being with the station for 13 years. In her 50's, she felt she'd better play it safe and look for a position in the large city library system. But after several interviews and no offers—even for entry-level positions—she enrolled in a local university to strengthen her librarian credentials.

Her self-confidence was eroded when she joined a weekly group at the Five O'Clock Club. She was disillusioned about her prospects of getting reemployed as a librarian. After doing the Seven Stories Exercise, it became clear that she had a passion for teaching; many of her stories revealed the enjoyment she got from helping her colleagues at the television station find information they needed for their productions. Her library role had almost been that of a teacher.

Her small group challenged Cynthia to look higher. With all her experience she was selling herself short by pursuing positions in the city library system. She expanded her search to university libraries and even managed to arrange to shadow the librarian at the university where she had enrolled. It became clear to her that she was more than qualified to handle a university librarian position and began to expand her search to college libraries.

She felt confident that she was about to get an offer at an Ivy League institution, where she was called back for two rounds of interviews; she was devastated to learn that she came up second. But one of the members of the search committee suggested she expand her search to some of the colleges who were trying to start libraries to obtain accreditation and gave her several leads. She met with one, where she was well received—and got an offer. Not only did the college want to start a library for accreditation, but they also wanted a librarian who would be willing to teach a core course in information. Cynthia ended up realizing her ideal revealed by the Seven Stories.

Paying Attention to the Seven Stories—Finally!

By Renée Lee Rosenberg

When I first met Gloria she was a recent MBA graduate. She was looking for a marketing position in a large cosmetics or hair product company. She followed the Five O'Clock Club methodology closely and within two months was delighted to land a marketing job with a major hair product company.

Gloria and I met again, three years later, when she returned to the Five O'Clock Club and was placed in my group. As it turns out, her delight with the job had faded. She wanted to leave but couldn't understand the source of her unhappiness, especially since she'd done very nicely. During her three years with the company she had been promoted twice. She was well liked and respected by her managers and her team, traveled a great deal for her job (which she liked), had use of a company car, and had a nice office with a big window. Yet with all this she wasn't crazy about the job. She didn't look forward to going into the office each morning.

Gloria and I met privately and decided that she needed to revisit the assessment exercises, especially her Seven Stories Exercise. Her assignment was to start from scratch, even extending to *putting aside* her old Seven Stories Exercise. Even as she labored over the exercise, she attended her group regularly—which normally isn't the best place to pursue assessment. Each week she came in with her spiral book and her evolving stories. She read them to the group. With the help of her peers she delved more deeply into accomplishments that made her happy. The accomplishment that topped her list three years earlier—obtaining an MBA—had faded away.

Another story surfaced to take its place. The theme that began to develop involved *mixing dyes and developing new colors*—a far cry from corporate marketing!

Redoing the Seven Stories represented a major "aha!" for Gloria. Her stories had changed dramatically. She realized that her stories three years ago *were not hers.* They belonged to her family and friends. She was living their dream, not hers. That's why we say that only things *you enjoy doing* can be included in your Seven Stories. As she continued to analyze her *new* stories she discovered more about herself. She really wanted to work hands-on with clients: advising, consulting, and directly *using* hair products—not marketing them. She wanted to use hair products and see immediate results.

Gloria moved on now to the right target and looked for positions in hair salons. Within four months she left her corporate job and became a hair colorist at a major salon. She makes a good living and is thrilled each morning to go to work. That was six years ago and she's still doing it with passion and enthusiasm.

One-on-One Career Coaching: Why, When, and How

You may think of the Five O'Clock Club as a source of help for getting a new job—and you're right about that—but you should also think of the Club as a "research lab." Our methodology works so well because it's based on more than 20 years of research on the job search process. Nothing goes into our books that's not based on research—and the group process we've worked out for clients to follow also rests on research.

However, job hunters sometimes have complex or delicate situations that cannot be covered adequately in the small groups. In this case, they will speed up their search if they occasionally meet with a coach privately, in addition to attending their small group. Why is this the case? Why is this combination of group and one-on-one so powerful and so effective?

Just You and the Expert

A career coach has helped hundreds or thousands of people through the entire job search process and knows the common mistakes that people make. Why not tap into this wisdom and save yourself missteps and grief? A coach can also help you "figure out what to do with your life." Assessment is the step most commonly skipped by job hunters, yet it is the true foundation for an effective search *in alignment with long-term goals.* Why go after jobs that don't point you in the right direction? Five O'Clock Club coaches are trained to make assessment pay off. That is, our assessment exercises are designed to help you figure out what to do—not just merely tell you what you already know (i.e., you're good with people, you like to initiate projects, etc.). Huddling privately with a career coach is like conferring with your accountant or attorney—you're looking for expert advice in a key area of your life.

The Company of Expert Peers

But six people usually have more energy than one—which is one of the reasons that brainstorming works: six people can come up with more ideas. If it's "just you and the expert," a lot of good advice may be overlooked. When you join a Five O'Clock Club group, you're surrounded by peers who bring considerable life experience to the process—and they've been reading the Five O'Clock Club books to deepen their understanding of our system. Six or seven brains tackle your issues and strategize your job search. You may take issue with a piece of advice from your coach one-on-one, but it's harder to ignore suggestions coming from several peers. There's a dynamic to the group that helps drive you forward—it's hard not to do the assignment when your peers have suggested it *and* are expecting your report on results next week. The focus of the groups is: "This is what you must do this very next week to move your job search forward." Joining a group, by the way, doesn't mean that you give up seeing a coach for private sessions; you can continue with those as you see fit.

How to Get Assigned to a Coach for One-on-One Sessions

It is very common for new members of the Five O'Clock Club to sign up for a group at the outset, either at one of our in-person branches or in our popular Insider program by teleconference (anyone in any time zone can participate). These clients have a pretty good idea of their tentative targets and are ready to hit the ground running. But they may also feel the need to see a coach privately for a session or two (e.g., for help with the résumé or intensive interview coaching). In this case, they simply ask their group leader for a private appointment, and they pay the coach directly at his or her hourly rate (the Five O'Clock Club takes no percentage of this fee, by the way).

But it's also very common for clients to call the Five O'Clock Club not knowing what they want to do next. They are not ready to "hit the ground running." They may be very unhappy at work and in search of a "way out." They may be contemplating a specific career change, or they may be well along in the job search process and need private coaching to help with interviewing or salary negotiation.

In this case we refer clients to coaches before putting them into groups. As soon as Club membership for one year has been paid ($49/year), we do our best to match the client with two of our coaches; that is, based on

- the reason the person wants to see a coach
- the client's income level (current or recent)
- the client's industry or specialty (or target industry or specialty)
- the expertise or specialization of the coach

. . . we suggest two appropriate coaches for the client to call. We maintain a large database of information on our coaches—who is an expert in what and who has worked most with clients in specific industries. For example, some of our coaches are experts with Wall Street executives, others have specialized in working with lawyers, government workers, not-for-profit professionals, IT specialists, health-care workers, biochemists, bankers, artists, career changers, or returning housewives, for example. We have the capability of putting our clients into the best hands possible.

We don't expect the client to use both coaches that we recommend; we suggest two so that the client can have a choice. And our experience has been that clients appreciate having the option. Once the process has been initiated, we ask clients to try to reach both coaches within two business days. We send an e-mail to the client suggesting the best ways to "interview" the coaches and a few basic "do's and don'ts" to be observed. These include:

- Try to keep the initial "shopping call" to 10 minutes (in other words, don't try to get a free session lasting 20 or 30 minutes).
- Keep focused on interviewing the coach about his/her skills in the areas of coaching that you need help with ("How are you qualified to help me prepare for interviewing?").
- Don't ask coaches to negotiate fees (their fees are at fair market rates and are based on their years of experience and areas of specialization).
- Please be prepared to pay the coach at the time of the coaching session (if it's by phone, mail a check within 24 hours).

After a client has decided which coach to use, we suggest the courtesy of sending an e-mail to the coach who wasn't selected. This can be a one-sentence message and does not need to be an explanation of the choice. We also ask the client to notify the Five O'Clock Club home office as to which coach was selected. This should be done by e-mail and should include a brief explanation as to why one coach was chosen over another (this helps us improve our client-coach referral process).

Speaking of Fees

Our coaches who provide one-on-one sessions for Five O'Clock Club clients are asked to follow strict guidelines on fees, in line with the Five O'Clock Club doctrine of always doing what is in the best interest of job hunters.

- They may not ask you to commit to a minimum number of sessions (with a huge up-front fee).
- They may charge you on a per hour basis only.
- They cannot ask you for prepayment (unless, after an initial session, several short sessions seem likely, in which case the coach can ask for "an hour's fee" up front, and the short sessions will be deducted from that prepayment).

Many of our competitors in the career-coaching field charge thousands of dollars, asking clients to put $2,000, $7,000, or even $10,000 on their credit cards, or helping them take out loans. Our rules are designed to protect you, the consumer, from such practices.

We cannot ask our coaches to work for free, even to the extent of offering a "sample session" of a half hour or an hour, but with our "charge on a per hour basis" rule, you are protected against significant loss. If you walk away from an hour session with one of our coaches and feel that you really weren't helped all that much, you still owe the coach, but you're only out for one hour of coaching—not several hundreds or even thousands of dollars. Going back for the second hour is entirely up to you. And it's very rare, by the way, that clients do walk away disappointed from that first hour.

The Real Reason for One-on-One Coaching

At the time we refer people to our coaches, we make it clear that the purpose of meeting with a coach initially is completing the assessment; this is, *getting ready for weekly strategizing with a group of peers.* As was stated at the outset: our research shows that clients who use group sessions get better jobs faster and at higher rates of pay. When you are assigned to a private coach, you should think of him or her as your tutor—getting you ready for the group.

We should point out that cost is one of the factors that make group participation a wise move. Private coaching sessions can run from about $100 to $200 per hour—even more with some of our most seasoned coaches. While group sessions must be purchased in blocks of 5 or 10, the cost per session works out to be about $35 to $54—by far the best bargain in the industry!

To get assigned to a private coach, contact David Madison at David@fiveoclockclub.com or 212-286-4500.

CHAPTER THREE

The Heart of the Five O'Clock Club Process: The Small Group

The
Five
O'Clock
Club

It's not uncommon for people to be skeptical about using a group for job hunt. Most people have never taken this approach before, and the first reaction may be that "joining a group" sounds a little too touchy-feely. In fact, a lot of job hunters have had experience with networking or support groups at churches, synagogues, libraries, and government-sponsored employment services. In such settings people commonly get together to swap business cards and war stories. And, just as commonly, if there is no structure or goal (other than networking and support) there may be a lot of venting and complaining, with too much of a negative tone. Hence we often say: go to a support group if your morale gets a boost, but don't go if you're surrounded by negative people. It's possible to attend such groups for months without any practical results in terms of making progress in the job search.

The Five O'Clock Club groups are different. We often say: these groups are *not* for venting, support, networking, complaining, commiserating, or therapy. Obviously people do get support and they network when they come to the Club, but we try to keep the terminology precise: our small groups are for *strategy*. The reason you attend every week is not to get more business cards or meet new people (although that does happen). People show up every week to brainstorm *what to do next* to move their job searches forward. This is done with the five or six other people in the small groups—monitored and guided by the certified Five O'Clock Club coach.

But just exactly how is it that *this* small group can come up with appropriate, effective strategies? Just think about this: imagine picking out five or six people on your commuter train to form a job hunt group. You don't make your selection recklessly. You look for those who strike you as the brightest and best—those whose demeanor, bearing, and dress bespeak success. What a group that would be! But guess what? Chances are you'd end up with a lot of the tired conventional wisdom and muddled advice on job search. This is true because job search is an unpracticed skill, and even highly successful professionals aren't very good at it.

You need a group that is committed to studying a proven job search methodology. That's what people get when they come to the Club. We say, "This is like signing up for a course in job search, so read the books as if you were in graduate school." Hence the process of weekly meetings with peers is informed by the proven methodology. This is a graduate course that requires careful study of our four books. It's not hard to see why our groups can have high impact. Via the books and weekly lectures, people master the research-based techniques for success in the job market. On this basis job hunters at the Club hammer out smart strategies for the coming week and *leave with assignments.* The contrast with traditional support groups—or the theoretical group of your better-than-average commuters—could not be more dramatic.

Just how do we do it? That is, how do we create and maintain *strategy* groups? One key is the coach. We recruit the best in the business, but the other key here is our training. All of our coaches are trained in our group management techniques that took more than a decade for us to perfect. Ironically, watching one of our small groups may lead an observer to say, "Well, that's not all that hard to do"—because it may *look* easy. How many times have you heard a television commentator remark, "Wow, she made it look so easy"—after an ice skater swirls through the air and executes a perfect landing? It only took a few thousand hours of practice to get it to look easy.

As the director of the Five O'Clock Club Guild of Career Coaches, my responsibilities include recruiting and training our coaches, and I always caution those who want to be considered for leading our groups: "This will be the hardest hour of your week." I sometimes hear from prospective coaches—who mean to reassure me of their skills—"Oh, I've led groups for years." My response is, "But you've not led *these* groups." We would be letting our clients down if the weekly session turned into a discussion about a general job search topic—or if the coach allows complaining and venting. One-on-one coaching in a group setting is the goal, resulting in concrete assignments. To make sure that the group sessions remain *strategic,* we focus heavily on getting our coaches up to this task. There are four chapters in our *Coaching Training Manual* on

how to run the groups the Five O'Clock Club way—yes, *four* chapters on how to make sure that a lot is accomplished in an hour. Our coaches-in-training are also required to observe or audit 10 of the one-hour sessions to complete the Five O'Clock Club certification; they are expected to do far more observations or audits if they want to be considered for a group.

Now with more than two decades of experience running our small groups, we know that we have a system that works well in moving people forward in their searches. The overwhelming testimony of the job hunters has been that the small group provided the important boost that they needed. After all, what's the point of going it alone—making blunders or allowing competitors to get the edge—when there's a group of informed peers to help keep you on track every week?

As you will read in the reports that follow, Five O'Clock Club members make the most of this asset.

The Small Group as Steering Committee

Brad had worked for several years at a strategy consulting firm and he found the Five O'Clock Club after six months in the job market. He reports that the Club process was helpful in a number of ways, but stressed that the Club method of choosing and prioritizing targets helped him achieve focus that had been missing. "It's easy to get involved in all this garden of opportunity of different things out there . . . it's easy to get distracted."

Attending weekly sessions with other professionals committed to the same methodology actually provided a familiar context. "The Club gave me a steering committee. In consulting assignments we typically formed steering committees, which are basically peers who give you feedback." His small group at the Club provided that role in guiding his job search. "I described my process and objectives and got feedback on things I was doing well, things I wasn't doing well."

And as the process neared the end, he was able to rely on the "the coach and her team" for "input on negotiating strategies, on how to postpone offers so I didn't have to accept them immediately while still trying to get others and keep up the energy."

The Club gave him a fresh perspective for the long run. "It's common to say, 'I need a job, so I'm going to target this particular position,' and leave it at that. But you should look at it as an opportunity to meet new people and develop new relationships, so that you can go back to people on an ongoing basis. The methodology helped me develop longer-term horizons."

Brad attended six sessions.

A Dynamic Career: Anchored in Five O'Clock Club Method

"I'm trying to earn money to go to Norway. I'd like to come by your house and collect newspapers and aluminum cans once a week." This was Linda Hardy's pitch at age 13, as she went door-to-door in her California neighborhood. Of Norwegian heritage, Linda was fascinated by the idea of visiting the faraway homeland and was determined to find a way to get there. The neighbors were glad to help. "I got so many customers I had to go running back and forth with the wheelbarrow." It wasn't long before her dad saw that the one-wheel vehicle wasn't adequate. "Can I get my pickup and help you there?"

Linda got her trip to Norway, and the recycling business was so successful that she kept it up for almost four years until the family moved to the East coast.

In the Beginning: Retail

Linda had learned that there was money in talking to people face-to-face and filling a need, and she enjoyed doing it. During her last year at Pace University in White Plains—she graduated cum laude with a B.B.A. in marketing in 1986—she was hired by a local store that sold Scandinavian gifts and clothing. "I loved buying, managing, and creating store displays." Linda stayed with the store for seven years and helped with the opening of two stores in Manhattan.

She realized, however, that there was potential for more money in wholesale, and through a friend she got a job with a firm that sold women's accessories to retail stores. She assisted the sales manager handling 650 store accounts in the northeastern United States, helped coordinate trade show appearances for the firm, and generated publicity in more than two dozen trade and consumer magazines.

But the trip to Norway had only heightened Linda's interest in travel and discovering other cultures. Now married to Mark, who has a keen interest in British history, she decided to take a break from work for a two-month trip with her husband to India.

Finally Learning the Computer— and Selling Neckties

Back in the United States, they decided to settle "out West," this time near Linda's parents in Las Vegas. Although opportunities were limited, she found a position with a wholesale neckwear company that specialized in fashion and novelty neckties. This job helped to build Linda's skill base. "I didn't know computers, so I had to learn; I was on a fast learning curve for six months." A few months later Linda and Mark moved back to New Jersey, and the company hired her in their New York office as assistant to the vice president of sales, with responsibility for handling her own accounts as well. She eventually moved into sales full time, selling ties to 350 retail stores of a large national chain; she exceeded quotas while covering a territory previously handled by two account representatives.

But Linda couldn't see herself selling neckties—for either the long or short term. She saw that the Internet offered huge potential and wanted to see if she could forge a career in marketing. She also sensed that it would be a good idea—and this was the right time to get professional career guidance.

Keeping a Brochure for Six Years

Six years earlier, Linda had heard a report on television about the Five O'Clock Club and had sent for a brochure. The brochure was still in her file, and she put in the call.

Linda's Five O'Clock Club coach assigned her to do the Seven Stories and the Forty-Year Vision and to do preliminary research in potential target markets. Linda did the assessment exercises and the research; the initial targets that she investigated were travel and direct marketing companies.

But before she was very far into the process, she got a call from a school friend—with a promising lead. A major direct marketing company with a heavy Internet focus was looking for someone to offer its services to retail store accounts. Linda was skeptical since she had limited work experience either on the Internet or with direct marketing. But her background working with retail accounts proved to be what the firm valued the most.

Linda had attended sessions at the Five O'Clock Club when this opportunity came up and was well along in her grasp of the methodology. She had done extensive industry research and had learned that job hunters should remain proactive in the interview; she was prepared for the unexpected. "I was offered the job at the end of the first interview. But I really had not had a chance to explore the market yet. I wanted to follow the methodology—I wanted to have 6 to 10 things in the works! I felt that things were happening too quickly, I wanted to slow it down. I said, 'This is very sudden, I have other things going on. I have to digest what we've spoken about and weigh my options. I'll get back to you.'"

The Group Helps Her Buy Time

First she wanted to get back to her group. "You can ask your friends and family—everyone will have an opinion. But people at the Five O'Clock Club have been through it and know what's going on. The coaches are trained and everyone in the group has read the books." Linda brainstormed with her small group how to buy time; it was not only a matter of exploring other options—she wanted to make sure that this option was really the right one. "I wrote a follow-up letter to the man who had offered me the job. I told him I was very interested, but I needed to meet the whole retail team before I could make my decision." The company agreed and flew Linda to their out-of-state headquarters to meet five people. The more she heard, the more excited she became. Buying time had worked—in the sense of giving her confidence that she would be moving in the right direction.

"Following the Five O'Clock Club methodology, I wrote five letters—a different one to each person—covering the key topics that each had raised. I e-mailed the letters the next day." Within a week Linda had a formal offer that included five weeks of training at corporate headquarters.

Linda's Five O'Clock Club coach, Ruth Robbins, assured her that waiting to have "6 to 10 things in the works" wouldn't be necessary this time around! Linda accepted the job and became an account manager servicing retail stores. "I do consultative selling. Our clients, retail stores, need help figuring out who to target for ad campaigns and catalog distribution. Through market research and computer modeling, we help them understand their customers."

Linda points out that direct marketing will have to become more sophisticated in the years ahead. "The malls won't die. People like to shop—but the consumer will expect to use all channels as they please: shopping at retail stores, using the Internet, and browsing through catalogs."

Learning to Listen

Linda ranks listening as one of the most important good habits in her line of work; it is crucial for serving the clients who turn to her for very sophisticated information. "Sometimes when you're talking to clients, you're actually formulating your response—I've been working on *not* doing that. I've got to clear all the noise out of my head and listen. I must find out what they're trying to accomplish, what their goals are, what their challenges are. If I don't get it right, I can't figure out what products to sell them. I have to be very focused every time I'm in a meeting with them. I have to be able to articulate what they want. I have to be able to tell other members of my team what they expect of us."

Determined to Stay Ahead of the Curve

Linda recalls that not too many years ago she was a novice at the computer and playing catch-up taught her a valuable lesson. "You really have to keep up with the world, whether or not you have a job. If you don't have the resources at your present employer and the world is passing you by, it's going to hurt you. I won't let that happen again. The world is moving too fast not to keep yourself marketable." Hence she tries to keep as much information flowing in her direction as possible; she subscribes to a multitude of e-mail newsletters—"I sign up for everything." She also joined the Women's Direct Marketing Group and took a course at NYU on direct marketing.

Now Working the Plan

The inflow of information can play a role in long-term career and life planning. Linda can see herself in business for herself someday, perhaps after she and Mark have started a family; working at home would be the ideal. "But I haven't had 'the Big Idea' yet, and unless I expose myself to everything, how am I ever going to know, or have that come to me? But it might not happen until I'm 60."

Linda feels that the assessment exercises at the Five O'Clock Club have helped her look more creatively at the future. "I keep looking at my Forty-Year Vision. You need a plan; executing it takes listening and learning. You have to plan and at the same time be open enough to know that not everything can be planned. Something can come into the picture that wasn't expected. You have to be smart enough to know if it's still taking you in the right direction."

Retirement on the Go, With a Camera

Linda loves what she's doing now and can't imagine remaining in any job or career that isn't fundamentally fun and rewarding. "I like marketing, I like being creative. I like working with people selling ideas. Since I was 13, I was always pitching something to someone. I was able to convince people that they should come along, that they could become involved in something too."

Thinking ahead to retirement, Linda says, "I see myself working. Whatever I do will be so much a part of my life that I would do it until I couldn't do it anymore." But there will be more time for her hobbies—traveling and photography. "I am an amateur photographer—I don't do my own developing—but I just love photography. My working retirement will give me the flexibility to say, 'I'm going to Brazil to take pictures for a few months. Hold the fort'."

Discovering that a Job Search Isn't a Job Search

Anthony was grateful to have a group to bring his issues to every week. A not-for-profit COO in Connecticut who discovered the Five O'Clock Club through FutureStep, Anthony had been job searching for a year and a half. "I *thought* I was doing job search, but I realized I wasn't after reading the Club's first book. The books helped me come to grips with reality. I saw that I needed to be more proactive in the search, more focused, more targeted. I'd simply been sending my résumé to ads for months on end."

And he came to look forward every week to the Insider Branch session, which is done by teleconference. "It was helpful to have the other people hear what I was doing. The job hunt process can be very intimidating and lonely, and hearing what the others were struggling with was useful. There were a couple of people trying to make decisions around new jobs and new fields, very similar to what I was going through.

"I learned to push more than one opportunity at once, which I hadn't been doing prior to the Five O'Clock Club. It was helpful to get the assignment every week from the counselor—it would have been very easy not to have a focus for the week."

Anthony got his job after only four Insider Branch sessions. He believes that another aspect of Club methodology proved to be the key in landing his new job as COO of a much larger not-for-profit, which he was led to through networking. "The president of the organization that hired me told me that my follow-up letter was what did it—it differentiated me from two competitors."

Benefiting from the Methodology in a Hot Market

Irene, an IT consultant from Oklahoma, had a fairly short job search that was wrapped up after only three Insider Branch sessions. "The group was helpful from an emotional standpoint. Knowing that there are people in similar situations, being able to listen, talk, and brainstorm—that was useful. It boosted my confidence to help others in the group who were just getting launched in the process."

Irene feels that key aspects of the Five O'Clock Club methodology played a role in shortening her search. "The books were a great help. The targeted approach to a job hunt helped

me organize what I was doing—otherwise it was a random walk without much structure. And the Two-Minute pitch was very helpful."

Having valuable knowledge and skills in a hot field helped Irene land so quickly. "I contacted only about ten companies based on referrals from friends and got eight interviews. But structuring the process according to Club methodology was very useful." Irene secured a consulting position with a small information technology firm and has no intention of abandoning what she learned at the Five O'Clock Club. "I'm going to apply that structure to my consulting business—the objectives are the same."

A Christmas Story, 2000: From Homelessness to a Vision Fulfilled

Ask Mary Margaret Cannon about obstacles—she has quite a story to tell. More than most of us, she has known the trauma of opportunities "falling away through no fault of your own." Indeed, a series of dramatic setbacks resulted in her being homeless for twenty-five months. Today Mary Margaret considers it part of her mission to share her story and celebrate her good fortune as she surveys her life today.

Born and raised in Washington, DC, after college she jumped into government service, first at the Department of Energy's Congressional Affairs Office, and then later at the Congressional Liaison Office of the White House during the Carter administration. When Jimmy Carter lost his reelection bid in 1980, Mary Margaret worked in a variety of capacities for both the Democratic National Committee and also in assorted state and municipal races. In 1986, she accepted a position in the administration of New York's Governor Cuomo. But on April Fool's Day, just 48 hours before her first day on the job, the position was eliminated when a line in the budget was deleted.

Giving Up the November Elections for December 25

But Mary Margaret believes that a door closing means that another is opening. It just took her a while to grasp that the new door led to an entirely different field, namely, the retailing of Christmas decorations.

Having worked in retail on and off during high school and college, she was aware of the difficulties of retail. She worried that her lack of formal training as a buyer, merchandiser, or marketer would seriously hinder her efforts. But Irish persistence and an unwillingness to back down in the face of challenge proved invincible.

Cannon sought out innovative and unique handmade American and European Christmas ornaments to represent. By advertising these products in such publications as *Smithsonian, Town & Country, Connoisseur,* and *New York* magazines, she developed a following and went on to design and produce a color catalog. And she designed a line of limited edition ornaments painted in the manner of Russian lacquer boxes entitled the "Noel Angels."

Mary Margaret was thoroughly hooked on being an entrepreneur, and she had become something of an expert on handcrafted Christmas decorations.

All of this came to an abrupt halt, however, during a traumatic divorce—an event that spawned a much deeper meaning to her faith and turned her new journey into a wild roller-coaster ride.

Ornaments with an Attitude

Now on a spiritual journey as well as charting a new course for her future career-wise, Cannon hit on a new idea. The convergence of expertise in the Christmas business and her deepening spirituality sparked a passion to convey a message of substance through ornaments. For some time, she had been alarmed that *Christian* had somehow become synonymous with the religious right in the minds of many: "It bothers me deeply that people hear 'Christianity' and they automatically associate it with something that is punitive, judgmental, and dictatorial," she said. "I frankly don't think that's the message. The Gospels are filled with stories of mercy, love, peace, justice, and forgiveness—and I wanted to incorporate those on the Christmas ornaments."

Mary Margaret faced challenges on two fronts. First, she had to find artists willing and able to convert her sketches—her vision and message—onto the ornaments. She had never considered herself artistic (she had never pursued formal training in painting because she believed her efforts would be inadequate). Certain color combinations presented a serious challenge to her—she knew she was color-blind for all practical purposes. Still, friends had often complimented her on her "artistic flair." It required many hours carefully articulating to artists what "her mind's eye" envisioned, requesting and receiving revisions until the ornament designs were "just right."

Second, she had to find venture capital. Before she even had a product in hand, she presented her business plan to an angel investor who was willing to invest "month-to-month." The offer was not ideal, but it enabled her to start operations.

And so, the Sacred Season Christmas ornaments were born. In January 1997, the new ornaments made their debut at the Atlanta Merchandise Mart's International Gift Show. Her business plan was structured so that the growth of Sacred Season was enabled by representing other American and European artists.

Buyers flocked to her showroom, and she realized sales of nearly $500,000 after just three trade shows. Customers ranged from small gift shops to Marshall Field's and Asprey & Garrard, purveyors to the queen of England. In 1998, Disney awarded Sacred Season the Rising Star (one of just six such awards that year) at its First Annual Christmas Collectible Convention at EPCOT. Sacred Season ornaments were used as set decorations on several television shows and found their way onto the trees of movie stars. Sacred Season was a hit, and the entire business model was working. The future looked golden and full of promise.

When the Bad News Overwhelms the Good News

But May 1998 proved to be a fateful month. Throughout this entire period of growth and promise for her business, Mary Margaret's personal trials were increasing as a deadline approached for her to leave her home (finally lost in a court battle with her former husband). She found out in early May that she could no longer continue the legal battle. She would have to vacate the house on May 22nd.

However, on May 15th, she received spectacular news when she was offered the worldwide Vatican Museum License for ornaments, angels, and Christmas decorations. Furthermore, the master license holder said that the Sacred Season ornaments could be sold in the Vatican Gift Shops and in other Cathedral gift shops worldwide.

"I felt like I'd won the lottery. We were jumping up and down, laughing and crying, celebrating our great good fortune. I can still hear my associate Kathy Cox saying to me, 'See, you're losing your home, but just look at the window God has opened for you!'" But just four days later, Cannon received a stunning blow. Her angel investor was pulling out—totally disinterested in the Vatican opportunity. He insisted there were faster ways to make bigger returns by investing elsewhere. He could not be swayed.

"None of us could believe it. One of my friends thought I must have misunderstood somehow, because the decision made no sense. We were successful. How in the world could this be happening?" The bleak reality was that her operating capital was nearly dried up. There was no money to produce the new line for the Vatican or to continue Sacred Season operations.

On May 22nd, she left her home for the last time and checked into a seedy motel. "I just sat and cried. Within one week, we had tumbled from an unbelievable high into a shocking loss. There

are just no words to describe the disbelief and pain we all felt." But Mary Margaret had no intention of letting her vision and her dream die, even though her friends, deeply concerned about her situation, were urging her to "give up and get a job."

She tried to find more venture capital, and, of course, she looked for work. "That experience was a huge shock. People told me I was 'unemployable' because I had been on my own too long. Or people saw my White House experience—from 20 years ago!—and assumed I would be bored with anything they had to offer. Telling them there was nothing boring about paying one's bills had no effect. I tried to find secretarial jobs, but was told over and over that I was overqualified. I was also told that entrepreneurs make poor employees."

The Night in the Wilderness, May 1998 to June 2000

"I never in my wildest dreams imagined I would wind up effectively homeless for 25 months. Thank God for the spectacular friends and extended family who hosted me and encouraged me and for the parish community that was so wonderful to me. But still, there were times I slept in cheap motels, in my car, and even on the floor of my showroom in Atlanta. There is no way to articulate the devastating effects of not having one certain place to call home."

Throughout this long ordeal, Cannon explored various other options to relaunch her ornaments, including licensing the ornaments to major corporations. All of the deals offered were very one-sided—in favor of the corporations. She even offered to give the ornament business away to charity, but the offer was turned down, due to the charity's lack of experience in the field.

"It's for Your Own Good"— And It Really Was

It was during these negotiations that Mary Margaret showed up at the Five O'Clock Club— reluctantly. Her friend, Bruce Robertson, was a member of the Club. "For a year, Bruce was Johnny-one-note about the Five O'Clock Club," she said. "I told him, 'I'm not going to sit around and wring hands with people.' But Bruce kept telling me, 'You don't understand, this is a fantastic program—it can help you.' But for a year I balked—I was very stubborn."

Robertson wouldn't take "no" for an answer. In the spring of 2000, he gave Mary Margaret the money to buy Five O'Clock Club sessions. "I'm making an investment in your future. I believe in you, you're very talented, but you're floundering because you need to learn how to target yourself."

"When I arrived at the Five O'Clock Club," Mary Margaret said, "I was at the end of my emotional rope. I had been without a home and solid footing for two years. I'd landed a couple of small consulting jobs, but I was sure I was never going to find the right niche for myself ever again. Most of all, I was devastated that I had not succeeded in relaunching the Sacred Season, because I knew in my heart it would be a success."

"I was floored on my first night at the Five O'Clock Club. I heard the coach lecture and thought how wrong I had been to dismiss the Club so casually without checking it out. It was like going to graduate school—I knew I'd better pay attention. I felt so foolish for not listening to Bruce sooner."

Mary Margaret read the Five O'Clock Club books—and the Seven Stories Exercise proved to be a revelation. "It was a lightbulb going on for me. I'd spent the better part of those last two years trying to fit myself into categories, depending on what was available. By doing the Seven Stories Exercise I found out what I was really best at, what my real natural talents are, what was going to make my heart sing. And I did it at just the right time. I was contemplating a licensing contract that would have meant, for all practical purposes, abandoning Sacred Season. The Seven Stories helped me realize I should stay the course. I saw that I am an entrepreneur, I am extremely creative, and can take a project from

concept to fruition. I can handle crisis situations and do very well with them."

Getting a Grip: The Group Talks Strategy

Her small group at the Five O'Clock Club also helped her stay the course. "I broke down one night in the group. I was depressed and very tired. I told them I was facing a painful decision about whether or not to license the product and I asked if I could bring the ornaments in the following week to get feedback. Everyone was so tremendous. They couldn't have been more terrific—and not in the sense of it being a hand-holding, hand-wringing counseling session. Rather, the attitude was, 'This is a severe crisis. How are we going to tackle this? What's the best strategy?' It was all about getting a grip, figuring out the best steps to take."

Looking back, Mary Margaret is able to articulate what happened. "I got focused again. I'd really become so scattered and emotional, telling myself that Sacred Season was a lost cause. The confidence I got from a careful evaluation of the facts came at a pivotal moment. The group wasn't saying to me, 'Hey, you're a good guy'—it was saying, 'This is where you're strong, don't give up.' The group helped me believe in myself again—that I did indeed know my business and this market niche and that I wasn't just a cheerleader for myself with no substance."

With her renewed determination, everything did begin to come together again. Networking brought her in touch with a new angel investor, and she was able to establish her office in Manhattan. She also found an apartment in New Jersey—two-and-a-half hours away—but she doesn't complain about the commute. "I pray I will never again take for granted having a home. Every day I marvel that I have my very own place and cannot believe how fortunate I am to enjoy it."

Mary Margaret traveled to China in the fall of 2000 and saw the rebirth of the Sacred Season ornaments, which brought tears to her eyes. "I'm sure the Chinese artists must have wondered what in the world was wrong with this woman who was so emotional over ornament samples! But I could not believe that it was happening once again— that so many prayers were being answered."

In August 2001 Mary Margaret received the first container of ornaments from China, and her warehouse in Maryland started shipping product to a growing number of stores around the country, including Saks Fifth Avenue and Fortunoff. She designed new ornaments for introduction the next year and prepared a custom order of "private label" ornaments for a large customer. Through the good offices of the Five O'Clock Club media team, in December 2001 her story was published in *People* magazine.

Another Major Focus: Helping Others

Mary Margaret remains passionate not only about her ornaments and their message, but also about helping people realize their full potential. "Millions of people go through life in a coma. They never think, 'What are my talents? What am I really good at?' When you figure that out, and if you've got the guts and the support, you're going to make your life fuller and happier—and you're going to help other people become happier too."

Mary Margaret doesn't look back at her two years in the wilderness with bitterness. There were so many people who saw her pain and potential and offered their help. "Gratitude really has to suffuse your life," she insists. "And the Five O'Clock Club is a blessing—it's a gift. If anyone comes into the Club and just goes about the program haphazardly, they are brushing off that gift. Some people are sprinters, and others are long distance runners. I'm a long distance runner. God has blessed me greatly with so many wonderful people and opportunities. The Five O'Clock Club is one of those blessings for which I am very grateful."

And now she plays the role with others that Bruce Robertson did with her. "I talk about the Club to anyone I meet who is looking for work or seeking a different career. There are two guys I

see on the train—they're out of work. I keep saying to them, 'Have you called the Five O'Clock Club yet?'"

No Lazy Days of Summer

Alicia was downsized by her company early in June and accepted the offer of Five O'Clock Club outplacement. "On the day I was let go I was upset and sad, but, at the same time, I must admit that the thought of taking the summer off was very appealing." But after the first meeting with her private coach she realized that a summer of relaxation was probably not such a good idea and got down to the serious business of job search.

The first line of attack was to e-mail her résumé to her primary industry contacts, which paid off after just a few weeks. One of the vendors with whom she had worked brought her in for interviews, and she landed in a job that she is confident positions her well for the future. Eventually, Alicia sees herself moving in an entrepreneurial direction, and her new assignment is the creation of a new division for the company. This gives her a great deal of independence and will add to her skills for being in business on her own one day. Alicia attended her small group at the Five O'Clock Club regularly, a total of eight sessions, and credits the group with keeping her on course: "The small-group discussions were really important. I got great advice and feedback."

Launching a Career on the Business Side of Academia

Environmentalist, land use specialist and master's graduate in public policy from the University of Chicago, Christopher Theriot adopted Chicago as his hometown in 1994. His career there has included positions with the Department of Environment, the Project for Violence Prevention and his own consulting practice, ERC (Environmental Research and Communications).

In the summer of 2002 Christopher took his career in a new direction when he accepted a position with the Chicago Public Schools, where there appeared almost unlimited potential in this setting for his varied interests and passions. The CPS is the third largest school district in the country with more than 40,000 employees and an incredible array of projects and cutting-edge initiatives. For example, Christopher had applied originally for a coordinator position in a new real estate development project designed to increase teacher retention. Employees of CPS are supposed to live in Chicago, but the high cost of housing makes this impossible for many—hence, the need for the CPS to take a lead in developing affordable housing.

While interviewing for this role, Christopher became aware of another opening that appealed to him even more—on a grant-writing team— and he landed this job. "I was hired to join a group of people with heavy educational backgrounds and strong experience writing grants, to develop concepts, grants, and arguments. The CPS must go after incredibly competitive federal dollars." Christopher spent a year and a half with this team, then applied for a position in another start-up situation. In early February 2004 he moved to a project focusing on charter schools and new schools. "The CPS is revamping existing high schools, building new facilities, and developing charter schools. These are new educational products with real estate and finance components. This is where my new job is—which brings me back to my original interest."

Christopher considers the Five O'Clock Club a companion on his career journey. He originally learned about the Club during a job interview, when the man with whom he was talking showed him one of our books. He later bought the books himself and signed up for 10 sessions at the Chicago Loop branch headed by coach Joy Muench. He landed the grant-writing job at CPS

just as his sessions were up. "But I right away bought 10 more sessions. I knew I would need to redefine my pitch and my direction continually." He made a practice of dropping back in to use his sessions from time to time. "This was a great value to me in terms of focus, developing momentum, and accountability. The group was the prime mover for me." But Christopher understands as well the crucial role of learning the methodology. "The ABCs of job search are so well captured by the Five O'Clock Club. I love the books, and I've bought quite a few copies of the *Targeting* book to give to friends." And unlike most people who hear the weekly lectures in person at a physical branch, he also purchased the lectures on tapes to help master the methodology.

Christopher's introduction to the CPS came through a networking contact, and he took to heart Joy Muench's reminder that the Five O'Clock Club advises pursuing organizations, not just positions—especially appropriate advice as he was interviewing with a 40,000-employee organization. After he was in the door for his meetings with CPS and developed relationships with the people, he learned about other options. "I had noticed a listing for a position as a grant developer on my grad school posting. I asked one of the CPS people I had interviewed with about the role." And he put to use lessons learned at the Five O'Clock Club: "When I began meeting with the grant-writing team I used the consultant mode to find out what their needs were and made an argument for their hiring me."

Christopher testifies that the Two-Minute Pitch and the 3×5 card were the most powerful elements of the methodology for him. "The discipline required for these was important. Also making careful notes and writing influencing letters. The clearly defined steps help you separate yourself from the competition."

But for Christopher the group remains the fundamental element of the Five O'Clock Club program: "*You* verbalize what you're trying to accomplish, and you hear the others. It's a lift. Be sure to engage with fellow job hunters and put in the hours that they expect of you. It's such an emotional journey. A positive frame of mind is essential. I tell people about the power of the group and the support you get from it. I came away from the Club meetings saying that momentum is everything, and it needs to be fueled. The Five O'Clock Club is the high-octane fuel."

Aim for the Company, Not the Job: Stay in Touch

We've always encouraged job hunters to attend their groups consistently, because skipped sessions can mean losing momentum. Although Walter lost his job as a publishing production manager in a downsizing in January, he didn't put his search into gear until April. But then he did attend 10 sessions in a row, and met as well with his private coach, Ruth Robbins. After the tenth session he was able to return to report on his successful search.

"When I finally got down to business in April," Walter says, "I met with Ruth and we charted what I was aiming for. In the beginning it was hard to push myself to meet people. I spent more time in the library then I ever wanted to—it's very quiet there." Walter confesses that with "traditional channels, ads, and the Internet, I had no luck at all. So I got to work networking. I have lots of contacts."

And he found that the Club's advice "aim for the company, not the job" paid off. He was encouraged by a networking contact to interview for a job he knew he wasn't qualified for at a major publishing firm. This interview, indeed, was a flop, but he stayed in touch with the company and was invited back for another interview when an appropriate job in production came along. After a series of meetings, he landed the job, which gives him visibility and the chance to work with people.

Ruth valued Walter in her group for his consistency and sense of humor: "It was wonderful having him take part every week."

Walter points out that "everyone goes through the peaks and valleys. The great thing about the whole Five O'Clock Club experience is the feeling that there's continuity. You're not out there by yourself. If you have some uncertainty, you can always bounce it off the others." He also now values networking more than he did before: "Stay in touch with the friends in your network. This is a life skill to help you carry on."

His 10-Session Course in Job Search

"I'm a media planning warhorse," Paul Greenberg admits, "this is my chosen field." Hence the agenda was not career change when Paul approached the Five O'Clock Club for help in 2004. His was the classic case of the job hunter who is looking for the next step up—doing what he loves to do. He had been working on consulting assignments after leaving a prior job, but was looking to secure his next on-payroll position.

"I had read about the Five O'Clock Club in the press and in professional journals, but I hesitated to check it out because I thought I could do it on my own." After a year of the on-my-own approach, Paul visited the Five O'Clock Club website, made the call, and began attending the Penn Station branch in Manhattan on Wednesday evenings.

Most warhorses might doubt the need for assessment—after all, when you don't need to figure out what to do next, why bother? But Paul approached the job search process with the Club as a college course. "I bought all four books and studied them and found that they were a great source for learning about myself. The Seven Stories Exercise and Forty-Year Vision turned out to be very important to me. They helped me to diagnose myself—it had been a long while since I'd done anything like that. This assessment gave me a fresh perspective. I learned more about my strengths and weaknesses and what I bring to the table. I found this very encouraging. It made my strong points very clear to me—seeing it all down on paper made such a difference."

With his assessment done, Paul purchased 10 sessions and began attending. "You can't get better training at $40 per session. I learned so much from my fellow students. You hear many different viewpoints. That's experience I would not have been exposed to on my own. That was fascinating." With everyone using the Five O'Clock Club books and methodology as foundation, "the group kept us honest." And the books "helped me fine-tune what I needed to communicate in my cover letters and follow-up letters." The Two-Minute Pitch proved to be a crucial tool as well: "I did manage to distill my pitch down to a couple of minutes. This discipline helped me cut through the fat to the most important core aspects about myself that I needed to communicate."

While Paul used all four ways to get interviews, he feels that the networking paid off the most for him. One of his networking contacts tipped him off about a recently opened position at a major advertising agency that he had already been trying to penetrate. In fact, two or three times during the prior 12 months he had attempted to contact the person who turned out to be his new boss. Since his name was already in the air, getting in for the interview was not difficult. He ended up having a couple of interviews with three people. Since the tip about the position had come from a contact who had been approached by a headhunter, Paul knew that he had competitors. "So I followed the Five O'Clock Club approach to follow-up. I sent correspondence to all three reiterating my strengths and stressing what I could bring to the situation."

Having been in consulting roles for about a year, Paul was not discouraged when the company offered to bring him on as a consultant for a month—as a trial. He was hired full-time at the end of the month, and he actually welcomed the opportunity to test the waters. "There are good employers and there are bad employers. This gave me a chance to find out if the marriage was going to work!"

At the end of his 10-week "course" at the Five O'Clock Club, Paul had his new job. He lauds the assessment, the books, and his group, but also credits the coaches who played a role in his success. "Coach Dwight Clarke was terrific," Paul points out. "He's a tough taskmaster. He expected you to perform—I needed that." While he was in the process, Anita Attridge took over Dwight's role as group facilitator. "She was great. I couldn't have done it without Anita."

Keeping Crisis Out of Sight

If the eleventh commandment of interviewing is "Thou shalt not speak ill of a former boss," perhaps the twelfth would be, "Thou shalt not talk about personal problems." When Juliet arrived at Five O'Clock Club, her group coach, Roy Cohen, sensed that she might have a hard time not telling people all about the things that had been going wrong in her life—which included being the single mother of a toddler (because of a recent divorce), ongoing court battles, losing her apartment and having to move. The misfortunes included a flood at her parents' home, where her clothes were stored, ruining her suits for interviewing. "I was waiting next for the locusts," Juliet admits. "While Roy was sympathetic, he also was realistic. He said, 'When you're out there networking and interviewing, you can't make them into therapy sessions. It's not someone else's responsibility to find you a job.'"

One of the things that helped Juliet get balance was the Seven Stories and the feedback she got at her weekly group meetings in terms of how she was presenting herself. "It's not just about inventory, it's about fit—you've got to communicate fit." Juliet is a high-energy, outgoing person, and it is not surprising that networking paid off for her. In her case, the payoff came fairly quickly. She had arranged a luncheon with a former colleague. "I just decided to treat this as a test-run interview," she says. The result was a phone call from the company that turned out to be her new employer. Her luncheon friend had passed on the information that Juliet was looking for a job and was probably a good fit. Juliet went to meet with the company, . . . "and I treated it as a test-run interview as well." But a few days later she was offered a job.

In reflecting on the rapid conclusion of Juliet's search, Roy saw the role that the group had played: "She came in a moment of crisis. This was an anchor. The group encouraged her to do the exercises and try to calm herself. During a crisis we sometimes can be too hasty. We want to take immediate action. But we held Juliet back. We wanted her to think through her approaches and her decisions."

Getting Back on the Stage

"I was shot from a cannon," is Candida Canfield's self-description to account for her energy and enthusiasm. And anyone who has been in her presence for even a few minutes can see why she usually achieves what she sets out to do. So it's all the more surprising that Candida's early career dreams in the theater didn't come to pass.

With a B.A. in fine arts (theater major), Candida had given it a hard try. But when she was in her late twenties, after doing summer stock, off-Broadway, bit parts in soaps and commercials—and waitressing—she realized that the theater career had become a long shot. "You've got to have an extraordinary amount of drive and be able to handle rejection," she points out. "The number one ingredient before talent is self-confidence, which I didn't have. I have a lot more of that now. I struggled to find work. I would have done much better if we'd had the Five O'Clock Club back then!"

Being on her feet hours on end as a waitress became too painful physically—Candida had been a ballet dancer when she was a child—so she arrived at the point that "let's think career" became an imperative. When a fellow actor bragged on the set one day about his big paycheck at a telemarketing job, Candida decided to check it out. This led to a job with Ziff Davis, then at Sureway Air Traffic, where she used her management skills to build a telemarketing department.

By 1985 she had moved to the *New York Daily News,* where she spent seven years, ending up as manager of retail/national advertising. Then, after a decade with *The Journal News* (1997–2002 as director of advertising), Candida became vice president of advertising and marketing at Manhattan Media; in December 2004, she accepted a job as online marketing consultant for a professional association.

With two decades of a "real career" behind her, Candida had demonstrated that she possessed determination and self-confidence in full measure. But the reservoir of talent— theatrical talent—had only lain dormant; her great love and passion is singing. "So I started taking singing lessons again at the Westchester Conservatory," initially with an opera coach because of her large vocal range. By this time, luckily, her networking contacts included her son, who pointed her toward an organization called Lagond Music School, Inc. that is dedicated to finding and cultivating talent and helping its students find performance venues (www.lagondmusic.org). Here Candida found the training and help to boost her aspirations, to breathe new life into her vision that she could find an audience as a singer. By the spring of 2005 she was part of a program at CB 313 (also known as CB's Gallery) in lower Manhattan. She sang four standards: "If I Were a Bell" (from *Guys and Dolls,* "one of my favorite shows," Candida points out), "I've Got a Crush on You," "The Look of Love," and "They Can't Take That Away from Me"—although Candida prefers an alternative title from the lyrics, "The Way You Wear Your Hat," because of her fondness for hats. She is building her book of songs for future performances.

During the years she pursued her career, Candida became a veteran Five O'Clock Clubber, returning to it for group and private sessions. "An old business associate gave me one of the Club's books in about 1996. I regret that I didn't look at it for almost a year! But I called to get involved, and the Club gave me a great foundation for my personal quest: what I wanted to do and where I wanted to go." Her most recent stint with the

Club was in late 2004, when her private coach was Cynthia Strite. "I had a very good experience with Cynthia," she says, and the group played a key role for her as well. "The small group is invaluable. They told me to redo my marketing plan, and I refined it. Then another group member spotted one of my target companies and said, 'I might know someone there,' which led to the interview that Candida turned into a job offer. "You usually don't get a hot lead like that from your group," she points out, "but the lesson is, when you have a good marketing plan, you should show it around."

She believes in showing the Five O'Clock Club around as well. One morning on her commuter train she was sitting next to a young woman who was working on her résumé. "I'm sorry for intruding," she said, "but you should bullet those points, and that summary statement about yourself needs to be positioned in bold at the top. You should get a copy of *Building a Great Résumé* and follow the résumé formats there."

This is a reflection of Candida's enthusiasm: "I have taken the Five O'Clock Club methodology into my entire life—my personal life and business life. The whole philosophy makes sense."

The Peril of Ignoring the Two-Minute Pitch

By Dwight Clarke

When I lead my small group each week at the Five O'Clock Club, I ask every member to begin by saying his or her Two-Minute Pitch. This helps keep the pitch sharp and stimulates feedback from the `

group. One client, John, didn't like to follow this protocol.

He joined our group *knowing* what he wanted to do for a living and who he needed to talk to to get it. He did not feel that repeating the pitch to *us* was necessary because he was aiming for a niche target—*something* to do with precious metals. He had done a lot of research, had developed a robust list of contacts in his target, and for the first few weeks in the group talked about all of the stage one meetings he was getting and how well his search was going.

But then John came in one night discouraged; he wasn't getting any stage two meetings. Someone in the group asked, "What are you saying when you go on the interviews?" John's response was unclear and jumbled. If, in the safety of the small group, he couldn't clearly articulate his pitch, imagine how he was presenting himself during meetings! The group suggested John get on track with the process and stop calling and meeting people until he had his pitch and other marketing materials in place (his cover letters and résumé were no better than his Two-Minute Pitch). Over the next few weeks—this was like watching a baby take its first steps—John practiced his pitch and helped us understand: He was a marketing professional with 13 years of business development experience in the precious metals industry. He had worked for some of the industry's largest firms and was looking to make a transition from the sales side of the house to the strategy areas where he could combine his passion for research with his sales/marketing savvy to produce business results. John resumed interviewing and landed a job about four weeks later.

For some people, talking about themselves and their accomplishments does not come naturally. The more comfortable you get with this process, the more relaxed and confident you will be during interviews. From my experience as a coach, I can see that there is a direct correlation between mastering the Two-Minute Pitch and conducting effective stage 1 and 2 interviews. Obviously there was a happy ending for John, but he must cringe when he recalls the interviews that he botched because he hadn't mastered the pitch. So the lesson here is to *use your group* to master the pitch before you meet those who have the power to hire you.

The Small Group: Helping Survive the Worst of Times

By Roy Cohen
with David Madison

Jennifer is perhaps one of the most distinguished alumna of the Five O'Clock Club. Today she is a top marketing officer at a Fortune 100 company, and if you look at her résumé you might say her achievement is a natural progression for such a very smart, poised, and articulate person. But when Jennifer arrived at the Club and was assigned to my small group, she probably would not have given great odds that the next step for her would have been a wonderful move forward. She might have told you that her career had derailed.

As a marketing officer for a well-known industry association, Jennifer had seen that really bad things can happen when senior management takes a turn for the worse. In her case, she didn't lose her job—which might have been a blessing—but she was saddled with an ineffective boss who got *his* job through blatant cronyism and proceeded to cause considerable damage. Of course, such damage can take the form of crippled operations and impaired services. But there's also the human toll, and Jennifer was among those who were bruised by the rampantly incompetent boss. She was not only frustrated by the deteriorating scene, but she was demoralized and came to doubt her own capabilities.

Jennifer was accustomed to being a top performer, and she sensed that she needed to reconnect with the best that she had achieved. There was a need to rebuild and reestablish confidence. In years past, she had been a Five O'Clock Club participant, and she decided to return to the Club.

There were three elements in the effort to get Jennifer back on course. At the outset, it was important for her to do the Seven Stories Exercise. By surveying her history she was reenergized by the knowledge of all that she had accomplished which had become clouded by the experience of working with the boss from hell. The Seven Stories helped her put the bad *recent* past in perspective and enabled her to see that, moving forward, she had choices. She could *choose* to be terrific again!

The second element was the Club's weekly small group, which was made up of respected peers—and me, the coach. We all saw her as an accomplished, impressive, well-spoken, powerful person, and we were able to help get her back where she needed to be psychologically—even as she was *still* toughing it out at work. The small group was also a safe place to test market herself. She practiced with us as she prepared to approach and meet with industry leaders.

The third element was the focusing on a few realistic, manageable targets. In her case, because of the heavy demands on her time, we didn't set unrealistic goals for her. It was best to go after three or four companies at a time. But the tangible targets made a better future seem within Jennifer's grasp and helped her set aside distractions that came from several directions because of her many interests. Once the targets were well defined and her morale was on firm ground again, Jennifer came out swinging to get a new job. She networked impressively—and her group was astounded at some of the very high-level executives in corporate America that she managed to get in to see.

Jennifer ended up with two concurrent offers and negotiated for the best possible deals in both situations, not relenting until one of the offers was firmly in hand. It was quite a transformation to witness. She had come to the Club deeply wounded and in a crisis of confidence, but emerged—thanks to the Club's methodology, the backing of her group, and her own remarkable resources—to secure meetings with the leaders in her field and to land a high-profile position with one of the country's brand-name companies.

CHAPTER FOUR

The
Five
O'Clock
Club

Small Groups by Telephone: How Job Hunters Who Never Met Helped One Another

"I found the Five O'Clock Club books at my library in Minneapolis and I'm wondering if you have a branch near me." "My uncle in Maryland attended the Club there, but I'm in Ohio and need to find out if you hold meetings in the Columbus area." "I heard a Five O'Clock Club coach on the radio. I live in central Florida. Do you have branches in this area?"

We can answer *Yes* to all these inquiries—which we receive frequently at our home office in New York—because of our Insider Program, launched in 1999. If you want to advance your job search by attending a Five O'Clock Club meeting, you need go no further than your telephone.

People are sometimes disappointed that there are no "actual meetings in my neighborhood," but several years into the run now, we have found no difference between the *effectiveness* of our group meetings face-to-face and those conducted by telephone.

People sometimes wonder how this can be. Since we are, generally speaking, social creatures, we like to press the flesh and mix in person. But the unprecedented growth of cell phone usage demonstrates that we have become accustomed to doing all manner of business by phone, in

almost all conceivable settings. Professionals, managers, and executives—the core constituency of the Five O'Clock Club—usually don't give a second thought to the idea of phone career coaching.

The coaching experience by phone *is* different. But in some ways the Insider Program—as put together by the Five O'Clock Club—is better than face-to-face coaching. And, in fact, the outcome is what everyone wishes for: people find the jobs they want.

But You Don't Just Pick Up the Phone

If you were to select, at random, six or seven people you see on your commuter train every night, and you suggest: "Let's have a conference call tonight to talk about how to find better jobs," it's a fairly good bet you'd make new friends, but you wouldn't make much progress on job search. Or even pick out a half dozen people whom you know from your church or synagogue and make the same suggestion. The conventional wisdom of such a group could carry you only so far.

Five O'Clock Club group telephone coaching works so well because we don't just say, "It's great that you've joined the Insider Program, so call this number on Tuesday night." *You've not just joined a group, you've joined a Club.* We help you take the steps to get you *ready* for group, so that it will be a productive experience with a fairly predictable outcome—namely, a new job!

First of all, we want to make sure you're ready for strategy, brainstorming with four or five peers every week to arrive at an assignment to move you forward in your search. It may turn out that a new job hunter is too unfocused—she may think she's ready for the group process, but actually she doesn't have clear targets and objectives. "Getting a new job," by the way, is too vague—it doesn't reflect strategic thinking, so it is not an adequate objective!

If this is the case, we recommend that clients arrange for one-on-one sessions with one of our certified coaches. This is typically for assessment, initial résumé review, and selection of tentative targets and generally takes no more than two to four sessions. The Five O'Clock Club, by the way, does not make money when clients hire a coach for one-on-one work. The fee is paid directly to the coach by the client. There are strict fee guidelines for the coaches to follow, to insure that clients are charged fairly.

For clients who are impatient to get started with their telephone group, we suggest that they take their first "listening" session right away. Insider Program sessions are purchased in blocks of 10, and newcomers always are asked to simply listen the first time they take part: pay careful attention to how the process works and to how the others are strategizing their searches. For people who are still in the assessment process, this provides an incentive to "get their act together" and arrive at tentative targets as the preliminary step for joining the group. New enrollees in the Insider Program get a call, usually several days before the meeting, from the group coach. This call usually lasts about 15 minutes. The coach wants to get a good reading on new clients, as well as let them know what to expect during the first meeting. We want new attendees to feel that they already have a friend when they call in for the first time.

The bottom line: the Five O'Clock Club telephone coaching groups work well because we make the effort to prepare clients for a process that goes well beyond having a chat with friends and that has precise weekly goals and objectives.

More a Graduate Course than a Chat

We have seen the explosive growth of college classes by teleconference in the last few years, and the Five O'Clock Club Insider Program also works so well because it actually follows the model of a college course: clients are expected to study in preparation for the telephone sessions. Just as the in-person group experience at the Five O'Clock Club would not be effective if participants just "showed up," successful Insider Program participants have found that the payoff is based on *careful study* of the books and the CDs. In the example cited above—commuters selected at random to have a teleconference on job search—there is likely to be little reward because there is no anchor, no foundation. The Five O'Clock Club methodology is the main reason teleconferencing succeeds.

Clients don't just call in every week for hints, tips, and encouragement. Clients call in to report on assignments done and brainstorm the strategy for the coming week, based on where they are in the Five O'Clock Club process. We always stress that the groups are not for support, networking, chatting, venting, general discussion, or therapy—although networking and support are byproducts of what we do. The groups are for hammering out strategy based on the whole group having mastered Five O'Clock Club principles. The Club's methodology for an effective job search is based on 25 years of research—and clients find dramatic results when they learn the Club strategy, techniques, and terminology and apply them in the real world—based on the guidance of the coach and group. It is not uncommon for job hunters to arrive at our doorstep many months into a frustrating and demoralizing job search. They've not been following a methodology; they've simply been pushing résumés out the door—usually résumés that don't represent them very well. They become reenergized when they discover a research-based methodology and realize the mistakes they've been making. Once they begin following the methodology and commit to working it from A to Z, the issue of "should it be done by telephone or in-person" becomes a nonissue.

Economy, Convenience, and Flexibility

A job hunter in the Chicago suburbs was pleased to hear that he could connect with his group by phone: getting into the Loop for the weekly meeting would have been a two-hour round trip. Clients who have 5¢ or 6¢ per minute long-distance phone rates find that they can spend an hour with the group for less than $4.00—typically far less than a commute costs. And the Five O'Clock Club charges less for blocks of sessions in the Insider Program because we don't have to pay for rental space. In fact, we were able to *reduce* Insider Program rates a few years ago because we found cheaper teleconferencing rates.

Insider Program participants also don't have to worry about cancellations due to weather and sessions missed because of out-of-town travel. Clients have called into their groups from hotel rooms, airport lounges, and hiking trails—location and distance simply are no longer a barrier. For a while one of our Insider groups included an executive in Vancouver, BC and another in Munich, Germany—who, unfortunately, had to stay awake until 2:00 a.m. to take part. Some of our coaches, who can't sign

up to facilitate our in-person groups because they're on the road so much, can be assigned to our Insider groups. For a while, one of our Insider coaches led her group from England and Belgium. And fitting an hour phone conference into a busy schedule can sometimes be done, while having to travel across town or into town to the brick-and-mortar branch would be impossible.

Protocols: Conducting the Business of Job Search

Of course, coaching by telephone—with the absence of visual cues—requires that participants exercise listening skills on the keenest levels. It also means that the session must be *treated absolutely as a business meeting,* despite the fact that participants may be sitting in their living rooms or have papers spread in front of them on the dining room table. Eating while on the phone, or making comments aside to a spouse who is putting kids to bed, or doing dishes will irritate others in the group. One of the huge advantages of participating by phone, obviously, is that you can stay at home. But during the hour on the phone, the at-home frame of mind has to be suspended.

Leaving the group early, for instance hanging up after you've had your turn and not sticking around to help others brainstorm their searches, is bad manners. We also ask that Insider Group participants inform the coach ahead of time—a simple e-mail is sufficient—if they can't join the call as scheduled. And when you've landed your new job or consulting assignment, join the next session to report the good news to the group. If you wait too many weeks, the people who helped you perfect your strategies will have moved on too and won't get to hear your story. We are a Club, and sharing good news with one another is a morale booster. You are not charged for a session when you "come back to report."

Counseling by Teleconference: A Report Card from the Telephone Branch

The Five O'Clock Club launched its Insider Program—small groups by telephone—in 1999, in response to increasing demand from around the country that our weekly strategy sessions be made available to job hunters everywhere. Professionals, managers, and executives anywhere in the country can dial into their small-group meetings each week to brainstorm with peers and receive guidance from certified Five O'Clock Club coaches.

About a year after the launch of this program, we asked three of our telephone group leaders—highly seasoned members of our Guild of Career Coaches—to comment on this experience of coaching clients "long distance." Helen Scully headed one on the West Coast, Louis DiSclafani directs an East Coast strategy session, and Ellis Chase facilitated a group that spanned the continent.

"One fellow," Helen recalls, "reported to the group a few weeks ago that he was on the verge of a major offer. What was his strategy at that point? He told us, 'I really need to get a few more things in the works. I've got 5 . . . I'd like to get that up to 6 to 10'—even though he was confident he was about to get an offer. I thought, 'Now, that's the Five O'Clock Club attitude!' He wasn't just going to sit there, waiting to see what happened."

There is no question, therefore, that Five O'Clock Club methodology is the backbone of the telephone branch experience. "If we were trying to do this without the backup materials," Louise observed, "I don't think it would work. The methodology validates what we're doing."

The First Hour Lecture: In the Car or at the Gym

For the clients who participate in the Insider Branch, a set of recorded lectures provides a vital anchor to the methodology. When the telephone groups were launched, it was felt that a two-hour teleconference was too unwieldy. Would people really want to listen to a 45-minute lecture on the phone? Hence the recordings were produced: 16 talks by Kate Wendleton (now available on eight CDs) on all aspects of the Five O'Clock Club methodology. Before dialing into the weekly teleconference, people are expected to listen to the CD for that week whenever they wish.

"The world of the telephone branch," Helen points out, "is commuting, working, fitting things in. For the last few months almost everyone in my group has been job hunting while employed. For these folks the recordings are really good."

"The people in my group master the concepts," Louise says. "They listen to the CDs over and over, and, of course, they refer to the books as well."

"I start the weekly session," Ellis notes, "by asking 'What did you get out of the lecture? What was new to you that you've never heard before?' I want one minute from each person in the group. This helps get everyone engaged. Everyone has a take on it." Helen asks at the start of her sessions, "How is the CD relevant to your search right now? How are you using the information?"

Moving the Job Search Forward

The weekly strategy sessions are all about *momentum.* Whether at the physical or telephone branch, the groups are not for general chatting about job search topics. It takes an average of only ten Five O'Clock Club sessions for people to land new jobs because they receive proactive coaching based on the methodology. Ellis's question to everyone is, "So what have you done during the last week to *make it move*?" Louise finds that after the quick review of the CD, "no one is hard to draw out. We move to the individual reports. People are read to jump in."

The medium of the teleconference seems to present no impediment to jumping right in to coaching. Any initial reservations about career coaching working by this method were soon dispelled. Managers and executives are accustomed to doing business by teleconference, and the business of managing a career or getting a new job is no different. "I find that virtual branch coaching is very focused," Ellis says. "We stick to business. It's very intensive strategically. We have tasks to do and we're getting them all done." "Most clients have worked hard at it between sessions," Helen observes. "The notion of having to report about doing something and receiving another assignment is welcomed. They understand that they're supposed to stay focused."

Benefiting from the Wide Perspective

"And it's actually a plus that people are from different geographical areas. They're getting different perspectives," according to Louise. "Right now there are people in my group from New York, New Jersey, Illinois, and Wisconsin." Ellis's strategy sessions included executives from Vancouver, Denver, southern California, Texas, Ohio, and New Jersey—one client even joined the call from Munich. "It's fascinating. The diversity makes it very interesting." Helen also senses that the long-distance aspect actually adds to the dynamics: "Being a thousand miles apart can facilitate the process. People share networking contacts that the others are very unlikely to have accessed. To those who are making long-term plans, making contacts with people outside their regions is very beneficial, and it's a plus for those who are looking to relocate."

Forging Friendships

"Although the people aren't meeting each other face to face, they're extremely supportive," says Ellis. "One guy in my group had a search that was far too narrow. But he pursued the

methodology, he started working at other targets—he was disciplined and relentless—and was finally able to generate more action where he wanted it. The group was very helpful in helping keep his morale up." "I find that members of my group bond right away," Helen added. "They phone each other outside the sessions. They're very anxious to give each other help." "The people remember one another as much as they would at a physical branch, even if a person has missed several sessions," Louise says. "And if someone is looking for a resource, others dive right in with suggestions."

Why Does It All Come Together?

Helen notes that the typical Five O'Clock Club client is highly motivated and goal-driven. "The folks in my strategy sessions are looking for immediate and long-term solutions to their careers. They're very concerned with doing work that suits their natural talents and will position them well for future opportunities."

The small group supervised by a career specialist provides an ideal setting for moving forward. As a consultant, Helen has advised corporations on team-building, and she sees parallels between the Five O'Clock Club Virtual Branches and high-performance teams. All of the necessary ingredients are present. "Everyone knows what the core values are and what the shared mission of the team is. There is also a defined way for new members to become acclimated to roles and responsibilities, to share the mission and the vision. And you have a leader who is an expert."

In Search of "Best Practices"

As a data-warehousing executive, Charlotte found a certain appeal in the Five O'Clock Club stress on following a proven system. "I'm a methodology person. I like to develop a plan of action." All the signs pointed to a downsizing at her company, and with good progression in her career at American Airlines, KPMG, and IBM, among others, Charlotte wanted to take the initiative to keep things moving in the right direction. From her home in Texas, she found the Five O'Clock Club, after a little bit of Internet research, and signed up.

"I was a little disappointed when I found out that I would have to participate by teleconference," she admits, but the experience turned out to be exactly what she had hoped it would be. Headed by one of our Chicago coaches, Ann Brody, "the group provided moral support and good ideas for expanding my network right here in Texas. I rate Ann very highly for her ability to get the team to drive the process and for encouraging us to work together." The geographical spread of the people in the group proved to be an asset as well: "This was an added value. We got different perspectives and a broader understanding of the job market."

Wanting to follow the Five O'Clock Club "plan of action" from the beginning, Charlotte did the Seven Stories and the Forty-Year Vision, and, at the urging of the group, reworked her résumé according to Five O'Clock Club principles. "Basically I tried to make my résumé look like one of the examples in the book, and I know that the new format got me more calls and interviews than anything else."

Always on the lookout for "best practices," Charlotte read the books and listened to the CDs, and, for her, the CDs were the best way for absorbing the methodology. "I listened to all the CDs multiple times, while I was in the car or on the treadmill at the gym." She decided to use all four ways for generating interviews and came close to getting her "6 to 10 things in the works." And she never turned down an interview: "Even though you think you don't want a position, the interview is good practice. Until you truly know what a position is all about, you should keep going on the interviews. In fact, the position I ended up taking was one I thought at first I wouldn't want."

Networking brought Charlotte in touch with a recruiter who referred her for interviews at a major brand-name beverage company. Following nine interviews—after which she always sent letters stressing "how I would add value"— Charlotte received the offer she was looking for and became the director of data warehousing. She had attended the Insider Program for nine sessions.

"Follow the methodology," Charlotte recommends to others. "Be true to yourself in following it. Utilize every part of it you can."

Finding a Job in the Desert

By his own admission, Bob Wells was in a tight spot in late 2001 in Las Vegas—and it had nothing to do with gambling!

With 16 years in banking behind him, he'd taken an entrepreneurial leap that didn't work out as he'd hoped, and he was looking for work. September 11th had made the difficult job market even worse. A friend urged him to join the Five O'Clock Club, with the observation that her friends who took this advice ended up with jobs. Those who ignored her were still looking for work the next time she ran into them. Since Bob made occasional trips back to New York in his search of banking positions there, he joined the Club, bought the books, and attended a session at the main branch in New York. But since he wasn't in New York most of the time, "the teleconference made a lot of sense," and he was assigned at first to the West Coast Insider Group led by Terry Pile. As his focus shifted more to exploring the East Coast banking opportunities, he shifted to Ellis Chase's group in the eastern time zone.

"I was eager to be on the phone with the group," Bob says. "It was important to have the weekly contact. The group gave me a timetable and kept me on track. The assignment and the accountability were worth it ten times over." But he admits that assessment done the Five O'Clock Club way was crucial to his eventual success. "I did the Seven Stories and the Forty-Year Vision, and they were the key to identifying myself and what I really want. I had been looking for CFO positions, and I came to see that I was barking up the wrong tree." And the methodology kept him on course. "The books are phenomenal, invaluable—and I like the CDs a lot. I listened to them all several times. This absolutely changed my entire search methodology. I learned that networking is so much more than telling everyone you know that you're looking for a job."

Bob intensified his efforts both in New York and Las Vegas, using all four ways to generate interviews, and eventually was referred by the friend of a friend to a major bank in Las Vegas. Having his Two-Minute Pitch perfected didn't hurt when, in a social setting, he ran into the man who would be his future boss. Bob was called in for interviews and was hired as a client manager in the Commercial Real Estate Group. Having Five O'Clock Club wisdom at hand as he closed the deal was vital: "Without the salary negotiation process, I would have blown it."

"I had to reorient my thinking about who I am and what I want and what it means to network." And he sees the value of having a trusted career advisor. "When I got depressed, Ellis was great at pumping me up and telling me how valuable I am. I will keep in touch with him forever."

Bob attended nine Insider Program sessions before landing his new job, and he has much the same advice as the friend who urged him to join the Club: "Follow the system, keep reading, keep doing, keep attending."

Working the Five O'Clock Club Method in London

"When you need a shot in the arm, it's great to put on one of the CDs and hear someone say, 'Get up out of your seat, just go do it, make another call.' Energy, enthusiasm, and optimism come through on the tapes. You need a bit of cheerleading." In the London job market in the

fall of 2002, Jewell found it helpful to keep plugged into the Five O'Clock Club via the CDs, books, and Insider Program group. "I was delighted," she says, "when I found out about the coaching by phone. I had already taken courses by tele-classes."

A media consultant who helps companies with marketing strategies—especially new market entries and product development—Jewell had been aware of the Club for some time. But at the urging of a friend, she joined during the summer of 2002 as she was intensifying her efforts to land a position in England. She was put into one of our senior groups headed by coach Mary Anne Walsh, a seasoned international consultant herself. "It's great to have a coach with more international experience than I do, who has worked with a lot of senior executives. I didn't have to bring the coach up to speed on what I am trying to do. She's someone I can look up to in that respect." Since Mary Anne is herself in London frequently on business, they have been able to meet for one-on-one sessions on both sides of the Atlantic.

"But the London market is pretty thin right now," Jewell points out. "In my target market, you just don't hear about full-time openings and people getting hired." Hence she is pursuing two tracks, working on projects week-to-week or month-to-month, while scouring the market for the rare full-time openings. "You keep working the process, calling the same people, networking—it's continuous, it has to be nonstop."

This includes checking in with her Five O'Clock Club group. "There are people in the group from Texas, Canada, and the New York area. There's good diversity job-wise too—all executive-level people in marketing and finance. We relate to one another, we help each other with résumés, suggestions, and even leads." Jewell draws a parallel to the experience of going to the gym and using a personal trainer. "With the coaching I'm more likely to push and drive myself. Having to report every week is a driving mechanism, knowing that there are expectations placed on you, knowing there are deliverables and milestones."

"I'm very structured about this kind of thing," Jewell points out, and she finds the books appealing for that reason. "They're great. They put you right into the process, they're very systematic." And she has words of counsel for others who may be searching in tough markets: "You have to adjust your expectations appropriately. Work to keep your head above water, find the right things to do, and stay in conversation with people."

Mastering the Method Between Rounds One and Two

Claire is a senior marketing executive in the financial services industry. She lost her job when key roles at her company were transferred to another state and remembers her fear in the months following September 11th. "I did the round of headhunters. I had cultivated relationships with quite a few of them, and they were more desperate than I was. Some had lost their own jobs, and others had no searches to work on."

Claire came across the Five O'Clock Club on the Internet and ordered *Targeting a Great Career*. "I fell in love with the process. I became a real fan. The style of the books was very appealing, a combination of hope—the inspirational quotes on almost every page—and practical advice: 'Do this because it works.' I joined, got the tapes and books, and followed the method religiously." She also signed up for 10 teleconference sessions. "It was nice to know that there were people just like me going through the same thing. The hardest part of the search is that feeling, 'I will never get another job.' But when you're working with great people you realize that this is a business process, it's a method. If you work through it, you'll get to your goal."

Early in 2002, one of the headhunters who had introduced Claire to a bank in the spring of 2001 called with the surprising news that there

was still interest. She had gone on several interviews in April and May, but had failed to "outclass the competition." Claire went back and knows that her coaching by the Five O'Clock Club paid off. "I was much more on the ball about doing research and interview follow-up. If I'd followed up as I should have back in the spring, I might have landed the job then!" The new round of interviewing was much shorter, and she got the job offer.

Claire has a new perspective on job hunting. "I found out when I came to the Five O'Clock Club that I had never really done a job search before. You have to think of it as a strategic campaign. How do you get in? Who do you have to follow up with—and how thoroughly?" And the assessment was a revelation as well. "The Forty-Year Vision helped me zero in on my 'outside of work' goals. In fact, I am now giving serious thought to turning one of my hobbies into a 'retirement' career."

Claire received her job offer after attending 10 teleconference sessions; she combined these with several one-on-one meetings with the group coach.

On the Phone from the West Coast: A Longtime Fan of the Five O'Clock Club

"Sometimes interviewers ask me where I see myself in five years. They are always amazed when I tell them I have a forty-year plan." Tom had been getting used to the Five O'Clock Club way of doing things for a long time—since finding out about the Club several years ago from the *Fortune* magazine video that features the Club's main branch in New York.

Tom loves his work as an international logistics specialist, coordinating the shipment of cargo by air and sea worldwide. And after a couple of downsizings in his industry, as a resident of California he was pleased to discover that the Club conducts sessions by teleconference. "I was delighted when I found out about the coaching by phone. I'd already taken courses by tele-classes." Getting into the group was a morale booster. "The thought of revisiting my network was a bit daunting, but when I got into the group, I found that there were other professionals in the same boat. That helped get me energized to get to work. It helped my self-confidence, which I wouldn't have had without the group."

Early on in the process Tom landed a job—one of three offers, in fact—but concentrated work on his Forty-Year Vision had prompted him to begin thinking more seriously about eventually setting up a consulting practice. "It made me realize that there were a lot of things I'd taken for granted that I would do someday. But by saying, 'this year, at this age, I've done only a few of them,' I realized that I'd better get going. And doing the Seven Stories helped me see the skills I've not really tapped into yet."

Tom's payoff interviews came through direct contact, but he says that networking was the other technique he used the most. And he used all of the Five O'Clock Club support materials. "The books are phenomenal. I refer to them constantly, and I listened to all of the CDs several times. Especially right before interviews I listened to key CDs. It's so important to keep in mind when you walk in the door for interviews, 'It's a game!'"

Tom's advice to people who are actively in job search: "Do all of the exercises, read the books, and when you get into group, don't be shy about asking questions. You can enter the process knowing that everyone wants to help. My coach was Sylvan von Berg. He always went the extra mile with his follow-up. It made me feel like I had a personal coach even within the group setting."

When the Group Won't Take "No" for an Answer

Jack, a senior bank operations manager from New Jersey, switched to the Insider Branch after attending a few physical branch sessions. He wanted to avoid a commute to get to the meeting, but didn't want to give up the group. "There were nights when we were all down, but it was a good group, and our coach was a good cheerleader and advisor. It kept me on a positive road. It was a great experience all the way around having the weekly group to check in with. It gave me momentum. I wanted to have things to report, to see what other people thought about what had happened."

Jack landed with a major investment bank managing Internet strategy, a role that he feels positions him well for the future. The lead that paid off came from networking with an old colleague, and it took several months to get to the offer stage. But the group helped him keep other things going. "At one of the Insider nights I said I was going to give up on one company. The group came after me and persuaded me not to give up. I wrote to the company again, made the follow-up phone calls, and got the right dialogue going."

The Five O'Clock Club in the Middle of the Night

"I had been looking for over a year and a half and easily had sent out 500 résumés." After 15 years with an investment firm in Switzerland, Al was conducting a long-distance job search, looking for the right niche back home in the United States. The Internet made the mass distribution of his résumé possible, but it also led him to the Five O'Clock Club, which proved to be the key for conducting—at long last—an *effective* job search. "When I first heard about the Five O'Clock Club, I thought it was just for people in New York. Then I found out that the Club has the Insider Program by teleconference."

Al called to sign up for 10 sessions, despite the fact that his small group started at 7:30 eastern time—he would have to stay up until 1:30 in the morning in Switzerland! Since he joined just before the Christmas–New Year break, he had time to do serious homework before his first group session. "I went through all the books and tapes. I tried to take all the lessons to heart. It really became kind of a religion for me. And learning the Five O'Clock Club method brought about a night-and-day change in my job search. During that year and a half of sending out résumés, I had a few interviews, but then when something fell apart, I'd not do anything for the next six weeks. The Five O'Clock Club is always pushing you to *do something.*"

As with most successful job hunters, Al discovered that proper assessment had been a missing ingredient. "What really helped was the Seven Stories and the Forty-Year Vision. About a year earlier I'd actually had an offer for a job in New York, and I saw now that it didn't fit anywhere in my Forty-Year Vision. I wasn't suited for it at all. The money was okay, but it didn't play to my strengths."

After completing the assessment, Al took his cues especially from the tape on effective networking. While previously he had sent out the 500 résumés "applying for everything under the sun," now he sent a targeted mailing to fellow members of a professional association. He crafted a cover letter with bulleted accomplishments and began with a simple question: "I'm thinking about moving back to the United States. I'm interested in your organization. Can you steer me to someone who might be interested in my background?"

"I got lots of responses. By my fourth or fifth session with my telephone group, I was talking with five companies." With his laptop and a box of stationery, Al made a trip to the United States after getting several interviews lined up. He was in touch will all his targeted companies by e-mail and was able to hand-deliver polished follow-up letters during his week of interviewing stateside.

"I learned from the Club not to write 'thank-you' letters. Instead, in my letters I suggested solutions to problems. I made specific legal and portfolio management proposals to people I'd met. I never talked about applying for a job. I always talked about what needed to be done." Within a few weeks, and by his ninth session with the

Insider, Al had the offer he wanted. He booked a private session with his coach to discuss salary negotiation. The insurance firm that eventually hired him, by the way, had called him in for an exploratory interview ("we don't have anything right now, but we'd be pleased to talk to you").

Looking back over the whole Five O'Clock Club process, Al values the Two-Minute Pitch especially. "I practiced it to death. At the Insider teleconference sessions, every time someone new joined the group, the counselor had us recite our pitches. And I really got a lot of practice because all my first interviews were on the phone. When it becomes second nature, you're much more prepared. You come across as a different kind of person."

Coming to the Five O'Clock Club after a long and unproductive job search, Al was pleased to discover a methodology. "The Five O'Clock Club process forces you to do everything systematically. You're expected to figure out what you do well—and enjoy. You're expected to figure out where you want to go and then to work out the possibilities to get yourself there."

Boosting Quality of Life for the Elderly: A Five O'Clock Clubber by Serendipity

Nobody's Forty-Year Vision includes ending up in a nursing home. While we all know that we may not enjoy the best of health in our later years, we all deeply hope that we will be living at home when we're 85 or 95. Five O'Clock Clubber Steve Hansen landed a job with the company whose mission is to grant that wish to as many people as possible.

Comfort Keepers, with hundreds of U.S. offices, is dedicated to keeping the population in nursing homes down by providing the support that the elderly need to remain in their homes.

Steve's quest for a new job began in the wake of a buyout that reduced the headcount at another health-care company he worked for. Since the pink slip had not really been all that much of a surprise in the summer of 2003, Steve headed off on a planned one-week vacation. While passing through the airport in Oregon on his way home to San Diego, he settled for a copy of the *Financial Times* when a newsstand didn't have *The New York Times.* "This was serendipity," Steve declares, "and I believe in following through when that happens." The issue of the *Financial Times* that he perused on the flight happened to have an article about the Five O'Clock Club. He visited the Club website and joined the Insider Program.

"I have a lot of discipline and a lot of energy. But a job hunt is about strategy, coaching, and group support." And Steve saw from the outset that taking stock and setting goals were the key to it all. "I spent five weeks on the assessment before I made a call. It drove me nuts. I was so eager to get out and talk to people. Sometimes I thought, 'Hey, I am not doing my job.' But I was absolutely doing my job." For Steve this included doing the Seven Stories Exercise. "This helped me get more grounded in who I am, what I want, and what I'm good at—things you do not think about deeply all of the time. This was very important." Steve then relied on the books for the next step. "They helped me create a search strategy about which I knew very little, and they helped me with the interviewing process." He cautions people not to ignore thorough preparation: "Don't talk to people until you've done your assessment, know your targets and strategy, and have your résumé and Two-Minute Pitch ready."

When his five weeks of assessment were at an end—coinciding with Labor Day 2003—he pursued networking intensively. "The Club helped me develop the strategy of networking by organized targets and aiming for the right people. I did very little networking at the peer level. I was always shooting for one or two levels up, so I was trying to reach COOs and CEOs." And he also took the principle of 6 to 10 things in the works seriously. "I used to be in sales, so I know the importance of feeding the pipeline. What you do today won't come to fruition for three to four weeks, so stay focused to keep your calendar full a month from now."

One of Steve's first ventures after Labor Day was to attend a networking meeting of an association of home care professionals, where he met a local Comfort Keeper franchise owner. He realized that he had skills that he could offer to the local owner, and Steve adopted the consultant mentality that the Club recommends, which led to a lengthy telephone conversation with the president of Comfort Keepers franchising. Two months later he was invited to meet with the COO to discuss a position as regional manager, one of the six that the company was creating. The process culminated in a six-hour interview with seven people at the company headquarters in Dayton, Ohio. Steve was offered his new job early in January, just four months after wrapping up assessment and launching his networking campaign.

In his new role he works with Comfort Keepers franchisees, advising them on operations, marketing, networking, and hiring care providers. He makes sure everything is done according to Comfort Keepers' brand-name standards.

Throughout the process Steve relied on his Five O'Clock Club group and was just at the end of his package of 10 sessions when he got the offer he wanted; he was weighing two other offers as well. "It was really great having a forum to say what's going on. There's a difference between thinking something and saying it out loud and getting feedback. People would say, 'You are being too hard on yourself,' or 'This is what I did when that happened to me.'" The CDs also played a role in keeping him on course. "When I was feeling lost or down in the dumps, I found the CDs to be very helpful. They are great for review and for some of the subtleties that you can't get from the books."

Hence Steve is a great believer in getting support for the complex process of job search. "Don't be afraid to ask questions and ask for help. Use a coach and rely on your Five O'Clock Club associates. "From all this comes the attitude necessary for doing well: Be confident. The only way you can create a buzz about yourself is to have confidence when you're sitting in front of someone. Work on it—don't fake it—work on it, be it." Although they live on opposite coasts, Steve hopes one day to meet with his group coach, Mary Ann Walsh, whom he describes as "incredibly supportive."

A Doctor Comes to the Five O'Clock Club

One of the most important doctors in your life might be one that you don't even see. Dr. Kathryn Francis, for example, is very much involved in patient care and treatment, but has spent her career behind the scenes. She is an anatomical pathologist, which means she studies tissue in the laboratory, helping family doctors and specialists make diagnoses that are critical to patient treatment.

The growth of computer technology in health care proved to be a key factor for Kathryn's career, although this was barely on the horizon when she finished her residency in 1984 and began her work as a laboratory physician. But as this workplace was revolutionized—along with almost all other professional environments—she found her role evolving. "As we became computerized," Kathryn says, "as things became more complex and more integrated, I was doing more and more of it. I became the de facto laboratory information officer, and I liked it. I liked conferring with other specialists and helping to figure out their needs and managing the transition to computer applications."

But after more than 15 years in the lab, Kathryn found that doctors can fall prey to career turbulence as much as any other professional: not only banks, entertainment companies, and law firms merge—hospitals do too. The expertise that she had developed, however, proved to be a solid foundation in moving her career in a new direction. In 2003 she was hired by a health-care software and services solutions vendor. "I switched from being a full-time anatomical pathologist to managing health-care information. This was not really such a jarring thing when you stop to think about it. In the laboratory all those years I was creating data and information. And I provided this information to physicians in order for them to take care of patients."

Kathryn is a senior clinical consultant with her new company. "I confer with customers. They may be hospitals, physician groups, integrated delivery networks, and other health-care organizations. My background is key, because doctors like to talk to doctors. Our business is software and business transformation systems, but it's much more than that. We're really dedicated to finding solutions. In such complex environments, you can't just say, 'Here's the software, install it.' We partner with health-care providers to create improvements. Data and information have to be used to yield outcomes that are better. I assess their needs, help with the redesign of workflow, and optimize the products that they're purchasing."

One software product enables the creation of sophisticated electronic medical records for each patient. It captures information for storage and retrieval to make the doctor's job easier. This represents a vast improvement over the old system of file drawers filled with scrawled notes. Such software plays a major role in advancing the understanding and treatment of disease as well. Patient data can become part of a huge database fed by thousands of physicians, so that the impact of various techniques and treatments can be gauged more accurately. "We can make much more robust predictions," Kathryn points out.

While she is very pleased with the new direction her career has taken, Kathryn admits that she didn't relish the idea of looking for a new job after 15 years—especially with her background. "Since I'm a doctor, I always assumed I had a track. So I really had no idea what to do to find a job." Her sister told her about the Five O'Clock Club, and, at the outset, she signed up for ten sessions in our teleconference program, the Insider Group. But she took the Club's advice about completing assessment before plunging into job search. "I read the books and did the exercises. The Seven Stories and the Forty-Year Vision can be emotionally wrenching, but they give you a written framework for going forward—they help get you focused. If you don't do this, I don't think you're going to do as well. You're not going to come up with a good marketing plan and get the job you really want." She also made full use of the recorded lectures. "The CDs were excellent. You need to keep hearing the methodology."

Kathryn turned to the Internet to do research on her targeted areas and came upon the website of the company that eventually hired her. In the section on its management team, she found the photo of a man she had met when she worked for the lab. "I put in a call to him and got on his calendar. It was a good thing that I was prepared with my résumé and marketing plan. I had also worked on my Two-Minute Pitch. I could explain what I wanted to do." As a result of this meeting,

her documents were forwarded to the chief medical officer, and her marketing plan proved to be the key for driving the interview process forward. "Most people aren't used to seeing a well-thought-out marketing plan—but you have to do the Seven Stories and the Forty-Year Vision before you do the marketing plan."

Altogether Kathryn attended 13 sessions of the Insider Program with coach Phil Ronniger. "The group was useful. You know you're not alone, and you can listen and understand how other people are presenting themselves. I give Phil a lot of credit. He didn't overcoach. He was kind and supportive; he gave the guidance and the nudge." She also turned to Phil for one-on-one sessions. "He gave me good advice about the real world."

Because of her highly specialized niche, Kathryn relied very little on ads and headhunters. She knew that direct contact was the technique most likely to pay off for her, which, in fact, is what happened. "But you can't be afraid to make the phone calls. Once you have your list in front of you, it's not that bad. It's hard, but what's the worst that can happen? People say 'no'."

But Kathryn is a very firm believer in making your case with absolute clarity. "If you can concisely state what you want in your marketing plan, with your résumé to back it up, you will make progress. Employers want to know what you want so that they can match your needs. "One of the most frequent questions I heard— maybe because I'm a physician—was 'Are you sure this is what you want to do?' They don't want to invest in you if you're not sure. Don't think that nobody wants what you have to offer, but don't think either that they're going to understand what you have to offer. You have to articulate this very well. Believe me, someone out there is going to want it."

Getting a Job Hunter Under Control!

By Louise DiSclafani

Arthur was elated to tell his "strategic partner"—by which he meant *me*—that he had landed the job he wanted, and at higher pay than his previous job, six weeks after his downsizing from a major pharmaceutical company. In light of the way that Arthur launched with the Five O'Clock Club, I found it amusing that he had come to consider *me* his strategic partner.

Arthur described my role in this process as his strategic partner because I held him accountable for his job search tasks. He decided it was in his best interest to put aside his ego, not go off on his own, but look at the job search from another perspective—namely, that of the Five O'Clock Club. It was a difficult choice since Arthur had been hiring people for many years and thought he knew everything. Arthur ended up working hard applying the Five O'Clock Club methodology to his search.

He found the job (that turned out to be his) posted on the Internet, but then used personal networking to influence events and nail down the offer. After the first interview, he realized the hiring manager knew one of his former bosses. Immediately, Arthur contacted his old boss and got the right wheels turning. He was asked back for more interviews and then got the offer he had dreamed about, regional sales manager for another pharmaceutical firm.

Throughout this process, Arthur was mindful of the Five O'Clock Club process; in fact, surrounding the hiring manager is a classic Club maneuver. He read the books, listened to the CDs, and participated in the Insider group. He gave good advice and supported his peers in the group. But at the outset we did have to overcome his I-know-everything attitude. Asking for my guidance was a big step for him since, as he confesses, "I was fast out of the gate." He was eager to land a new job and had started to network and search before his end date with the pharmaceutical firm. We reviewed what he'd been doing, and I knew some changes were needed. We revamped his résumé and recast his targeted letters, which got him a few more responses. He accepted my interview advice that helped him get more second interviews. Most gratifying for me personally was helping Arthur identify the habits he needed to change to move forward. He wrote to me: "You were there to prod me when I needed it, kept in touch with my progress, and made me submit assessments and progress reports."

Now that Arthur has learned the Five O'Clock Club approach, he says that he will hire differently: "I'll be looking for Five O'Clock Club résumés and interview techniques."

CHAPTER FIVE

The
Five
O'Clock
Club

Mastering Targeting and Pushing for 6 to 10 Things in the Works

How many times have you heard this one? Perhaps the most common nugget of conventional wisdom in job search is, "It'll take you *one month* for every ten thousand dollars that you earned to find a job." Maybe in some perverse way this comforts people who want to manage their expectations: they're trying to prepare themselves for a long stressful search. Or maybe they've just heard the stories of all those people who have been through the agony of a 6- or 12-month job search . . . so it must be true that professionals and managers deal with the reality that every ten thousand of salary equates to a month of punishment in the job market.

When you come to the Five O'Clock Club, however, you'll hear nothing about this formula, for the simple reason that it's *wrong.* Of course, people often do have very long job searches, and the correlation between the months of unemployment and what they had earned seems to be confirmed by experience. But this is not because there is an immutable law—written who knows where—it's a consequence, rather, of a *bad job search.*

During the last twenty years many people have arrived at the Club with their tales of woe and were ready to recite in great detail all of their

hard work in the job market for many months. The first question that we pose to these folks reveals that one of the crucial foundations for a good job search, almost without exception, has been missing. We ask, "What are your targets?" and usually receive an uncertain and confused reply. They may be able to name the general fields that they're aiming at and even specific areas they've been digging in for interviews, but these long-suffering job hunters aren't really sure what we mean by organized targets. One of our Five O'Clock Club coaches, who worked for a while at a traditional outplacement firm, reported with chagrin that clients usually left the three- or four-month outplacement program without being taught what it means to search by targets.

Next we ask to see their personal marketing plans, because an organized, well-researched campaign by organized targets *is written down* in the form of a personal marketing plan. To be sure, many of the people with long job searches do have lots of documentation about all of their hard work, but this is usually a paper trail, recording what has happened. What's lacking is *the master plan by organized targets.* We have always counseled that getting a good job, getting the right job—that is, not *settling* for an offer because it represents, at long last, a paycheck—depends on *targeting 200 positions.* Initially this sounds very scary. Indeed it will appear far too daunting *unless* the job hunter is working on the basis of organized targets in a written format. In fact, once these are all written down so that they can all be seen at a glance (an Excel spreadsheet is one good way to do it), the personal marketing plan is very empowering. On the first try, the job hunter can see how close she has come to having those 200 positions in the cross-hairs.

For example, a fund-raising professional who wants to work for universities in Washington, New York, or Boston can very quickly—for example, with just a few hours of Internet research—make an intelligent guestimate of how many positions are in *these three targets.* Since a target consists of a geographic area, field, and function, there are three targets here: Washington/universities/fund-raiser, New York/universities/fund-raiser, Boston/universities/fund-raiser. It's not hard to do the math. Are there 25, 50, or 100 positions in *each* of these targets? If the job hunter doesn't have 200, then the targets have to be expanded or supplemented. So how about adding Baltimore and Philadelphia? How about considering museums as well as universities? What will it take to get to 200?

To reinforce the necessity of working toward these large numbers, another mantra at the Five O'Clock Club is "always try to get 6 to 10 things in the works." With this idea in mind and pushing you forward, you'll have a much better chance of actually contacting all the people who represent those 200 positions. You *might* want to set yourself the goal of contacting 200 people, but that's not really the idea here, since one hiring manager could be the decision maker on several positions that would be of interest to you.

But we will always recommend *researching and searching* for more people to contact to achieve volume and momentum. It's very common for job hunters to focus on a few things they manage to get off the ground, because they earnestly hope that one of them will turn out to

be the pot at the end of the rainbow and bring an end to the job search agony. But in the real world, having *at least* 6 to 10 things in the works is vital because five of those precious opportunities will fall apart through no fault of your own. Anyone who has had three or four promising possibilities collapse knows what a blow it is to morale and momentum. If you earnestly and energetically work your 200-position written marketing plan—always pushing to get at least 6 to 10 things in the works—the knocks and blows of job search will feel more like speed bumps than roadblocks. In the pages that follow you will read about Five O'Clock Clubbers who took this message to heart and set the gold standard.

Strength from Numbers: Having 6 to 10 Things in the Works

Stuart discovered the Five O'Clock Club after he was well under way in his job search. After losing his job he decided to put most of his effort into networking. "I called a lot of my contacts and didn't have problems getting interviews." When he got into the small group at the Club, however, he learned the value of follow-up and volume. In fact the second time he attended the group was right after an interview, and the group helped him draft a strong follow-up letter. Listening to the group on interviewing in general, "I became a more confident interviewer, and I got much better at the follow-up." In fact the opportunity that turned out to be his next job came through a contact and required three interviews before the offer came. After each, Stuart strategized follow-up with the group.

But even while he was nurturing this situation to fruition, Stuart kept generating more interviews. When the offer finally came, he was able to negotiate from a position of strength. "I got the offer by phone and said 'I'll get back to you.' I was happy with the money—it was more than I had been earning before. But I had learned from my group that offers are negotiable, and there were some things about the package that I wasn't happy with." Because the company knew Stuart was considering other opportunities, it adjusted the package to bring him on board.

His group leader complimented him on the push to get more interviews to be a stronger candidate and for not losing momentum. "He came consistently. He never missed a session."

A New Job Soon After September 11th

Nigel lost his position in pension fund investing at a major corporation, but he wasn't convinced it was really a disaster: his boss hadn't been that great, he had a terrible commute, and he was sure he could get more money elsewhere.

Nigel arrived at the Five O'Clock Club ready to work the methodology. "I tried right from the get-go to have 6 to 10 things in the works, and I used all four techniques for getting interviews." This was especially critical since he had begun his job hunt in earnest in the weeks preceding September 11th, after which many opportunities were put on hold. "The beauty of having 6 to 10 things going is that you don't have all your focus on what appears to be the ideal job, because that can disappear."

Trying to get 6 to 10 things in the works meant that he talked to as many people as he could, which meant that a lot of people knew what he was looking for. And on the same day two people alerted him to an ad that had appeared in a small trade journal. The new chief investment officer at a major not-for-profit was looking for someone to focus on building up the private equity portfolio. "That started the ball rolling," Nigel recalls. He hit it off very well with the key decision makers at the not-for-profit, who asked him back to meet board members. In the wake of the September 11th attacks, it was difficult for members of the board to get to New York, so he was invited to interview on a train to Washington! An offer followed a few days later.

Nigel recommends being very well prepared for all the interviews you work so hard to get. "Of course you should anticipate all the questions you hope they don't ask, but much of the time they never even come up. It's very important to go in with a list of substantive questions. This can help initiate dialogue, and it separates you from the competition."

Nigel attended 11 sessions at the Club and achieved all of his objectives: he found nicer people to work with, eliminated the bad commute, and got the money he was hoping for.

More Effective Networking

Alice found the Club after almost six months of job search. She had been networking intensively—she estimates that she had made 300 to 400 contacts!—but something was missing: she wasn't making the best possible presentation, either on paper or in person. Through Five O'Clock Club coaching she was able to improve her résumé and put together a high-impact Two-Minute Pitch, which she recommends practicing "again, again, and again." Being more polished helped her finally get interviews in quantity and the value of having "6 to 10 things in the works" became clear as well. "Treat your job search as an assignment, with set deadlines and a clear outcome in mind," she recommends. Knowing that success depends on having 6 to 10 things in the works "helped me keep that focus." Alice landed a job as an executive at a retailing chain, but even in the final stages of the hire, she didn't let up trying to find those 6 to 10 things.

Given her impressive networking campaign, Alice obviously is no stranger to the phone and points out that voice mail can actually give you feedback. Always listen to the message you've left on voice mail if given the option. "And ask yourself, 'Would I hire this person or pass her on to someone else?'" By stressing the Two-Minute Pitch, the Five O'Clock Club helped Alice become more aware of how the world was seeing her. She recommends the complete Club methodology:

"Repeat your Five O'Clock Club mantras to yourself several times a day. They work."

Alice got her position after attending eight consecutive sessions.

Things in the Works and Like a Consultant

Hal combined private sessions with a Five O'Clock Club coach and eight sessions at the Club to move from day-to-day sales to client support at an interactive professional services company. He praises the Seven Stories for the first boost he got when he began with the Club. "It is a very powerful tool; it helped get me centered and find out what I was passionate about."

Because he was attempting a fundamental change in function, when Hal launched his campaign he put less emphasis on answering ads and using agencies. While the Club advises having 6 to 10 things going at all times, Hal applied himself to go beyond this. Through direct contact and networking, "I tried to keep 20 things going at all times." This level of activity naturally paid off, and when Hal got into companies for meetings, he didn't squander the opportunities. He took to heart the recommendation to adopt the consultant mentality and concentrate on listening and learning. He didn't focus on closing, but asked questions and did as much as he could to move the process to the next level.

When offers eventually fell into place, he still kept sending out letters until a deal was struck. When the time came for salary negotiations, he also relied on his coach and the books to come out well ahead of the game. Hal's small-group coach praised him for "really following the process and attending consistently."

Becoming an Insider

Barbara arrived at the Five O'Clock Club with a solid understanding of what she wanted and found that targeting and research provided a way to get there. With a strong finance background and a desire to move to warmer weather, she wanted to specialize in high-yield bond analysis and work in southern California.

"With this target in mind, I went to the library and researched in the *Nelson Book of Investment Managers.* I made a list of the key decision makers in southern California." She generated enough response to justify a trip to the West Coast for networking meetings. She got lots of feedback on her résumé by asking for it in her networking meetings and received a key piece of advice that reinforced the Five O'Clock Club methodology: "You want to present yourself as a member of the high-yield bond analysis world." Even though she had an MBA, she decided to strengthen her credentials by working on the CFA. Once she had finished the first level, she made another major attempt to find what she wanted. This time she uncovered a significant lead through the Bloomberg Website. "I responded with my résumé, and included a cover letter with several bullet points."

Barbara got a call to come to California for an interview. "But I wanted to get a feel for the situation before I made the trip. I asked to speak to the investment manager. I wanted to find out where they were in the hiring process. I wanted to know if he had any concerns about me. I also wanted to talk to someone who knew him. I wanted to find out what kind of a situation this really was."

"I did tons of research, not only about the company, but also about all the people I would be meeting with. I researched the backgrounds of everyone who worked in the high-yield bond department." It all paid off. Barbara got the offer she wanted after seven hours of interviewing. "I just tried to keep in mind what I'd heard at the Five O'Clock Club about interviewing, 'It's showtime!' They didn't want to know my life story, they wanted to hear about all the good things I brought to the table. Because I knew so much about all the people I met, I kept the process conversational and friendly—'I see you went to Kansas State.' But I also made sure to ask what I'd been taught at the Club: 'Where are you in the hiring process? Who are my competitors and how do I stack up?'"

Barbara attended eight sessions.

Keeping the Big Picture in Mind: Aiming for 200 Positions

Matthew's hard work at the Five O'Clock Club resulted in his landing a CFO position at a private investment company. He was able to report his success during his 15th session with his teleconference small group, one reserved for executives earning over $200K. Matthew credits the weekly sessions with keeping his search grounded in reality: "Hearing the issues people are dealing with and how they're structuring and pursuing their searches completely informs your own search. What are the other people doing well? What are they not doing so well? You have something against which to measure how you're doing."

As is the case with all people who join the Five O'Clock Club, Matthew was expected to do his Seven Stories and Forty-Year Vision. He had been through career coaching before, so knew the importance of assessment, but he found his Seven Stories a revelation: "There are lots of assessment tools that tell you what you're good at and what you like, but the Seven Stories Exercise tells you in your own words what you have loved to do over and over again. It's incredibly insightful. The Forty-Year Vision helps pull out your core values and what you hope to have in your life."

Being well connected in his community in the Mid-west, Matthew was ready to launch an intensive networking campaign. "I surely knew enough people to get a good job search off the ground." But his coach wanted a campaign based on more than a strong rolodex, so recommended that he take time to make his map of 200 positions that he was going for. Since he was aiming for CFO, this actually meant coming up

with 200 companies. "I was convinced that there were not 200 positions in my geographic area—I just wanted to start networking. But my coach said, 'No, construct your list of 200 companies first.' It took me a month to do it and required a lot of spadework. I went to the Websites of emerging companies, private investment companies, early stage companies, and local venture firms."

Constructing this list proved to be the key for Matthew's successful search, and he sums up its value in four categories:

- "It actually gets you excited about your search because you see all sorts of possibilities."
- "It increases your confidence that if something doesn't work out with one group of companies, you have lots of other options."
- "It reduces your attachment to any one situation."
- "It becomes an incredibly wonderful tool for networking meetings."

In fact, Matthew brought his networking meetings to the level of sophistication that the Five O'Clock Club has always recommended: "I sat down with people with my map of 200 and said, 'Let me tell you what I'm trying to do. I want you to tell me which of these companies you like, which ones you don't like and I shouldn't waste my time on, and which ones you might be able to refer me in to.' It was very effective. You're giving people a very tangible problem to help you with—as opposed to a general, 'This is what I'm trying to do. Who do you know?'"

Matthew's map of 200 was also instrumental in keeping 6 to 10 things in the works, which he recommends emphatically. "I met with two companies repeatedly for three months. The natural tendency is to assume, 'One of these is going to work out, so I'll just focus on these things.' But in one case they decided not to hire anyone after all, and, in the other case, they weren't able to create the position they'd hoped to. So find more things even if you're sure that something is going to come out right."

Matthew welcomed consulting assignments as part of his strategy. "If you're consulting while you're job hunting it helps to keep your confidence up and gives you something to talk about during interviews." Above all, however, he recommends using your map of 200 positions/companies during networking and pushing to get 6 to 10 things in the works—and keep working all elements of the Five O'Clock Club methodology. "The audiotapes are not only informative, they're inspiring. The books and audiotapes are fabulous. Anything you'd ever want to know about job-search you can find in either or both."

Consulting as a Technique for Career Change

"I started the job search on my own," Harriet admits, "which was a big mistake. I hadn't had to look for a job in more than 16 years." After 15 years at a major sports and entertainment marketing company, she had taken a year off to work on an executive MBA abroad. Ordinarily she would have been welcomed back by her employer, but the country was reeling from 9/11, a recession was in full swing, and a hiring freeze was in place at her former company. Many of her former colleagues had been laid off.

Harriet spotted the listing for the Five O'Clock Club in *Crain's* and decided to get help. Her group coach immediately recognized that she needed a crash course in networking, one of the primary ways for generating leads and meetings. "At my first session she forced me to go to an executive networking meeting. She told me that I had to network with at least five people or she wouldn't give me her free pass!" But, of course, the coach and the group put Harriet through the Club tutorial on how to network the right way. "I learned what it means to network properly. It's not the old-fashioned backslapping and hurried business card exchange. It has to be genuine. You have to listen, you have to figure out what your needs are, what the other person's

needs are, and try to make connections. And always, always, follow up."

Harriet has followed the strategy that many of our Club members find helpful: using consulting assignments to enhance the résumé and generate cash flow. She spotted a newspaper notice for a project manager at a major library that was looking for someone to coordinate a photo essay competition and exhibition for four months. As is common with short assignments, the hiring process was over in just a few days. "Part of the reason in this case was that my references were very current," Harriet points out. "The library was able to reach them immediately. As the Club recommends, always keep your references up to date on what you're doing. Send them cards, take them out for coffee."

Harriet gives credit to her small group for pushing her to do the right things. She showed the group a brochure for an association conference, but had excuses for not going ("I'm not an insider." "It's too expensive."). But under the group's urging she went and by the time the conference was over, she felt like an insider, had built her network further, and had more confidence that she was headed in the right direction. "I heard everyone at the conference talking about how much they love their work. That's really rewarding." Which also reminded her of one of the quotes included in *Targeting a Great Career:* "Find a job you love, and you'll never work another day in your life." (Confucius)

Remaining His Own Boss

Originally Dennis got a boost from the Five O'Clock Club during the dot.com boom a few years back. At that time, after attending his weekly group for a dozen sessions he landed in a fairly intense dot.com environment. "It lasted about 18 months. It was fun and it was interesting, but the workload was too much. I got laid off along with about 40 percent of the staff. Actually that was fine by me. I wasn't all that happy."

The post 9/11 environment wasn't conducive to finding on-payroll jobs, so Dennis welcomed consulting work—especially a role that allowed him to exploit his prior *shopping* experience. Not shopping as most of us think of it, nor even as the typical corporate buyer might have in mind. "You've all seen my work," Dennis told the Five O'Clock Club meeting in New York. "I worked for the Transit Authority. I bought railway cars, the new technology trains. I also bought the telephone and radio equipment for the system." Based on this experience, Dennis was hired by a firm as a consultant—a strategic sourcing consultant.

And he remembered his Five O'Clock Club training. He went back to our book on salary negotiation and followed all of the suggestions for launching and pricing a consulting business. After more than a year on his own—turning down payroll jobs to remain his own boss— Dennis generated about $150,000 cash flow. "I'm having fun, it's my company. I'm doing things that are in the book. I'm out there promoting, I'm interviewing while I'm working on my current four or five contracts, looking for the next assignments." Going by the book means connecting with industry associations and, for Dennis, that means attending meetings of the National Association of Purchasing Managers. "I got to know the president and I'm writing an article with him."

Dennis had originally reported at the Club when he landed the dot.com job in what now seems another era, but he asked to come back to report on his successful consulting practice to give encouragement to others. This is not surprising, according to his coach, who recalled that Dennis "really followed the methodology and was very helpful in the group."

A Career Shift—Based on 20 Years of Experience

"Don't go at it half-heartedly," Jason advises, admitting that he was depressed when he first arrived at the Five O'Clock Club. "I had been a copywriter in advertising for twenty years when I lost my job, and I plummeted. I didn't want to do anything." Given this frame of mind he didn't even do his Seven Stories well. "I didn't take the Seven Stories seriously and had to rewrite the exercise several months later—then it helped guide my search."

Jason was actually embarking on a career change or at least a career shift. After so many years in consumer advertising, he didn't relish remaining in an environment with such punishing hours. "I wanted a job again, of course, but I really didn't want to get a job that would keep me at the office until midnight." Jason had worked in public relations once upon a time, but didn't find doors opening in that direction. "I got some meetings, but no one wanted to hire me because salaries were so low and people were afraid I would bolt as soon as good copywriting jobs came along."

In developing his targets, Jason had included medical advertising as a possibility, but encountered resistance because he had done mostly consumer copywriting—even a medical portfolio developed on a freelancing assignment didn't carry enough weight. "I kept hearing, 'You're a consumer writer trying to write medical.'" But he decided to try another approach to gain entry into this field, inspired by a pep talk by one of the Five O'Clock Club coaches about the importance of joining associations. "I went to a lot of association meetings to hear presentations. During one I asked the speaker a lot of questions and afterwards went up to speak with her. She was the creative director at a medical advertising agency." Jason had found a sympathetic ear and someone who was willing to help. "She didn't have a job for me, but she became a mentor. She fed me a lot of names and became a major resource." Jason also joined a professional association made up mainly of ad agency executives who participated in a networking database, which brought him into contact with a lot of people.

Jason finally landed an interview that proved to be his entrée into medical copywriting. He honed his pitch on why he would be a good hire, and he finessed the money issue. "I had to do a lot of tap dancing. Salary was secondary and I told them so. I wanted to get into this new field, so I never mentioned a figure. I let them give me a range—and they brought me in at the top of the range because of my experience. I said, 'I haven't been on staff at a medical ad agency, so I would consider myself a junior, but look at what you're getting creatively'—and they agreed."

Several weeks settled into his new job, Jason was gratified that he had pushed hard to get 6 to 10 things in the works: he got calls to come in for interviews, the payoff for contacting many PR people. "But I like my new job a lot, and it positions me well for my new career." His extensive network is now in place, and he maintains his memberships in associations, positioning him well for another job hunt when the time comes.

A Career Change After Working 18 Years

Five years ago Eugenia, whose home is in southern California, was looking for a way to earn a living and stay at home with her baby. She and her husband decided to launch a housecleaning business; they incorporated, with Eugenia as president and manager. At one point they had a staff of six employees. "But the business climate isn't very favorable in this state for enterprises as small as ours," Eugenia pointed out. "And when you're self-employed, everyone else gets paid first—you get what's left over." Late in 2002 she began thinking about going back to work as a salaried employee with full benefits. Prior to being a business owner, she had worked for 13 years at a local publishing company, departing there as a printing manager.

Eugenia had been following the *Kate and Dale* column in her local Sunday paper for a long time. "Even though it's an advice column for job hunters, I liked to read it from the business-owner perspective." The Kate in this case, of course, is the founder of the Five O'Clock Club, and Eugenia visited the Club Website. She discovered that we offer small-group strategy sessions by teleconference and signed up for twenty.

She began listening to the recorded lectures assigned for the week and reading our first book on targeting. "I was really flopping around," Eugenia says—perhaps a little too hard on herself for someone who had stayed with one company for 13 years and then run a successful business for five. But consistency in her case, she admits, didn't amount to having a direction. "I'd pretty much lived my life going with what came up and not developing a plan. The assessment forced me to think about what I really wanted to do." The Seven Stories pointed Eugenia in the direction of a paralegal career, and she began networking with that in mind—and armed with Five O'Clock Club advice about approaching interviews as a consultant. "That was one of the most helpful things I learned—thinking of yourself as a consultant. It was very different from any other job-hunting advice I'd come across. It made a lot of sense to me."

A friend introduced Eugenia to a federal judge who was looking for a personal assistant, and Eugenia was hired. No legal background was required, and her new role positions her perfectly for the future. The judge will be training her, and she will be able to complete her associate's degree—a requirement for becoming a paralegal. If Eugenia had any doubt about making such a dramatic career change at age 42, the judge herself is already her role model: she got her JD at age 42.

In reviewing her successful transition, Eugenia credits that crucial often-neglected first step, assessment, and making use of the group. "It's easier, of course, not to do the Seven Stories and the Forty-Year Vision. It's hard to really think about what you want to do and set goals. And the weekly group meetings were especially helpful. They kept me accountable. I wanted to have something to report about at the next session!"

A Move from Publishing to Academia

"I was pleasantly surprised when I found out that my company had arranged for Five O'Clock Club outplacement," Kevin says. He was one of about 300 employees let go by a publishing giant in the summer of 2003. A graduate of New York University's Stern School of Business, he had heard Kate Wendleton speak a couple of years previously at an alumni event, and he had once spent an afternoon at Barnes & Noble reading one of the Five O'Clock Club books. "I ended up reading almost the whole thing in a couple of hours. It made so much sense I bought it a couple of days later."

When Kevin's two-year job at the publisher came to an end and he was assigned to work with a Five O'Clock Club coach and small group, he intensified a self-examine process that was already under way. "I did the Seven Stories, which confirmed what I had already suspected. That is, the track I had been on was surely not in line with my likes and talents. I had been in the private sector, in business and marketing, for over ten years. I had been asking myself if this was something I wanted to do long term. I didn't want to look back and claim to have generated tons of revenue and sold lots of products. I know I like kids and I like sports. I realized that I really wanted to have an impact on young people."

With this kind of career change in mind, Kevin realized that he needed to do extensive research on the not-for-profit world. "I was able to get a lot of meetings, and I wouldn't have been able to do it without applying the Five O'Clock Club concepts. I used all four ways to generate interviews, and I did the follow-up required. I am not an outgoing person—not the kind who loves making phone calls. It was difficult, but I learned how to do it effectively."

He also learned what many job hunters discover when they explore a tentative target: it's probably not a good idea after all. "I learned a lot about the not-for-profit world, and I realized that I wasn't cut out for working at a children's not-for-profit in general. But I did narrow it down and decided that a school was a place where I could be very happy."

Kevin happened upon the right contact while taking a class, where he met a school administrator. He was called in for interviews at a New York City independent school and was hired as an admissions officer.

Kevin feels that he is in full possession of career management techniques that will last a lifetime: "The Five O'Clock Club principles have become so engrained—they feel second nature to me now."

Turning Down Jobs to Stay on Course

With 15 years of corporate marketing behind her—10 in financial services and 5 in publishing and media—Roberta had all the right instincts for marketing herself. But she confesses that application of Five O'Clock Club methodology was the key to marketing herself successfully in a tough market and coming up with a job she didn't have to settle for. "It actually took me about a month to find a job, but 18 months to take one! I had a lot of job offers, but would have been unhappy if I'd taken them."

Roberta endorses without reservation the Club advice to target 200 positions, in order to get 6 to 10 things in the works and have choices. To achieve the 200, she networked relentlessly and used targeted mailings. "Call everyone you know, come up with your pitch, reengage people you haven't talked with in a long time—it will pay off. Even if you haven't been in touch with someone for six months or a year, send an article to that person if you think it would be of interest. True networking is 'adding value' to relationships that should be long-term. Don't be afraid to make that phone call." She estimates that she sent out almost 200 targeted mailings alone. "I always customized the résumé, by the way, even if it was a matter of changing only a word or two here and there. And in the cover letter I customized the bullets. I got in to see almost all the people I wrote to."

One of Roberta's favorite techniques, as Five O'Clock Club suggests, is to court the gatekeepers. "I really relied on the secretaries. You know it can take up to eight attempts to reach the people you've written to—which is painful. The secret is using the gatekeepers. I wrote thank-you notes to secretaries, which I've never heard of anyone else doing. Even if you don't ever get through, you will get information."

Roberta usually got rave reviews from interviewers about her knowledge of the companies and the industries. "People said to me, 'You're so prepared' but I cannot imagine not being prepared! If nothing else, go to the company Website, find out three things that they really care about and one good buzz-phrase. Just 15 minutes of this kind of research can make all the difference."

Roberta also believes in careful interview follow-up, as the Club recommends, but she applied our advice in her own way. "I always sent my letters after the interview by e-mail. Everyone sends letters, and interviewers expect them. But don't necessarily rush to write the thank-you note. Unless you know a decision is about to be made, wait a few days and write something really thoughtful. That's how to be sure your letter will be read. People read what's thoughtful."

Roberta began attending a Five O'Clock Club branch in Manhattan, then switched to one of the telephone groups. Her intensive efforts—and refusal to accept offers that would take her off strategy—paid off. In the home stretch she received three offers and landed a position as Senior Vice President chief sales and marketing officer for a major consumer survey service.

Thinking Outside the (Geographic) Box

After losing her job as an editor at a major publisher, Adelaide discovered one of the truths about using ads to find a job. "In three months I saw only one ad for full-time editorial work." But it was her professional network that proved to be helpful in moving her in a new direction, one that, as a self-proclaimed introvert, she had not entertained very seriously: freelancing.

An author with whom she had worked at her former job asked her to edit a manuscript, and it was a welcome assignment and not just for financial reasons. "I got such a charge out of talking about books and business again," she says. "It was a big boost." But it also made her realize that there might be other such projects, which lifted some of the gloom from her job search. "I did a targeted mailing to authors to introduce myself and got very positive response. People told me, 'We're always looking for editors.'"

When Adelaide had been focused on getting a full-time editorial job with a publishing company, her target was her home market, New York. But identifying freelance assignments from individual authors or packagers (who create book products to sell to publishers) meant that she was not limited by geography. "There are a lot more people I can contact. I can do freelance editing for authors anywhere, San Francisco or Minnesota." Adelaide reported at the Club after she had begun her push into freelancing: "I'm at the beginning, but I'm cautiously optimistic." Hence the important lesson from her experience that expanding her targets can be the key to a successful search: whenever a job hunter can be flexible about the third element of a *target* (as defined by the Club), namely, geography—there *will* be more opportunities to consider. Adding more freelance assignments to her résumé will strengthen her position with each passing month and increase her chances that she will find her way into a situation that will convert to full-time employment.

Of course doing a targeted mailing and making the requisite follow-up phone calls can be painful for someone who shies away from the self-promotion that freelancing requires. "Job searching for introverts, that's me," Adelaide confesses. "But once you dial the phone, for the most part I found people very willing to give."

Top Credentials in a Tight Market

When it comes to looking for work, not many people have been spared from the realities of a three-year bear market. But Martin was confident that, with degrees from Wharton and Columbia and experience with some of the most prestigious Fortune 500 firms as his former employers, he would have no trouble landing a new position. "After five or six months of unreturned phone calls, however, I realized it was going to be an uphill battle."

His first foray into the job market had been somewhat tentative. He had hoped to see results after working with one networking group. Actually, he had been pleased to have some time off, after being in a senior position that required 90 percent travel. With little to show from his tentative job search, he decided to get involved with other networking groups, and he joined the Five O'Clock Club.

One of the first course corrections he made was to recast his résumé, basing it more soundly on assessment. "To make my résumé work for me, I made it into a variation of the Seven Stories. You need to ask, 'How do I add value? What is my legacy?' You look back over your career, look at the things you've enjoyed—they usually go hand-in-hand with what you're successful at. You want to highlight them, communicate them more than anything else on your résumé. That was a good start in turning my job search around."

He also characterizes attending weekly Club sessions as a good start. "This is the one place that you can get feedback that you can trust. I needed to redetermine and redirect how I was doing things." Martin also realized that broader networking was essential, so he signed up for major industry conventions and launched targeted mail campaigns in his primary markets. He worked hard to get a lot of things in the works and was pleased to get an offer he *could turn down* because it required 50 percent travel, which held little appeal after being on the road 90 percent of the time. "But I was able to do what the Five

O'Clock Club suggests: I leveraged one offer to get another." He ended up in a job he's thrilled with, VP for Management Information Systems at a major fashion company. Martin also advises job hunters to have their Two-Minute Pitches ready at a moment's notice. He took the call inviting him to come in for the interview on his cell phone in the parking lot at a Home Depot.

Looking back on a job hunt that took far longer than he imagined, Martin sees value in the experience nonetheless. "If I could have taken short cuts to get a job faster, I don't think I would have done it. In the process, I've learned a lot about myself that will help me position myself as I go forward. And I know I'm a better manager because I've been through some tough things I could not have imagined myself going through."

Martin's group coach points out that "he was very driven, but he was also very caring. He reached out to others in the group, he offered help and always followed through with it." Martin advises others still in the process, "Do the work, solicit feedback, be creative, and feel good about yourself."

Applying Assessment and Targeting for the First Time

Alison admits that she was one of those people who knew how to get a job, although, after months of searching, it wasn't happening, and it had been 16 years since her last foray into the job market. "I thought I'd just answer ads and call headhunters and go on a few interviews." Being a senior information technology consultant in a market when hiring was not the trend, she needed a wakeup call that came in the form of a push from a friend who could see that she was out of touch. "She almost bribed me to come to the Five O'Clock Club. 'You've got to go and find out about the new skills needed for a job hunt.' I didn't know what she was talking about."

But she soon learned and devoted full energy to doing a job hunt the Five O'Clock Club way. "I did the whole process, including the Seven

Stories, and refashioned my résumé and cover letters. My advice: get all these mechanicals out of the way up front. That way you'll be in a position to respond to fresh leads. And she found that the weekly meetings provided valuable guidance. "Use the group—that's the best possible thing you can do. Work on your pitch with these people. Find out how you come across. Are you targeting the right people? That should come across in your pitch. And people in your group will usually have insights into your industry."

Alison also learned the value of being organized in a job hunt—in terms of strategy. "It's really *really* important to work from your target list so that you don't go off in a thousand directions. You may hit a few things by luck, but mostly you need to get organized and stick with the process."

Now armed with solid assessment and a refined pitch, Allison began getting interviews as her networking paid off. "All the ads that I answered produced nothing. Everything I achieved was by talking to people and always asking whom else I should talk to. Of course there will be a lot of rejection, but don't take it personally and don't stop contacting people. Keep calling!"

Alison landed a project management consulting position, and within a week after starting that, she got calls for two more interviews. Being in a depressed field, her search proved longer than most at the Five O'Clock Club: she attended 18 sessions, with a three-month break. But Alison gave back to the process as well as benefiting from it. Her group coach commented, "She was a terrific help to others in the group. She gave really great commonsense advice."

Even When a Friend Has a Job for You, Try to Get 6 to 10 Things in the Works

Esther is an advertising and sales executive and sees that the Five O'Clock Club methodology has wide application. "It not only helped me get a job, but helps me in my career. A lot of things I learned here I will be able to apply in the rest of the world out there." She sells advertising for a radio station.

Her position came from someone she had job-searched with at the Five O'Clock Club who, in his new capacity as sales manager at the radio station, recognized that Esther had exactly the skills and experience he needed to grow the sales department. Before the final offer came through, however, there was a lengthy delay while the budget for the position was approved. But Esther wasn't one to wait and hope for the best, counting on the promised job. She continued to conduct a full-scale campaign for a new job, attending the main Club branch in Manhattan for 13 sessions. During her "graduation speech" she suggested the top principles that were particularly helpful in her search for job hunters to follow:

- Read and study the books. "This is essential. Don't gloss over them. There's a lot of great information; some sections I read and reread. My hint especially: learn and master the telephone techniques. People are *not* going to call you back!"
- Get your basic tools in place: your résumé, your Two-Minute Pitch, and cover letters. You can't make an effective "sales presentation" until these things are ready.
- Get a job search buddy. Job search is a difficult and lonely process, and you need a buddy who knows the Five O'Clock Club way. Friends and family want to help but really aren't tuned in.
- Don't negotiate with yourself. Don't argue with yourself about going on a networking meeting or an appropriate job interview—even if the money isn't good enough. Go anyway!
- Follow up, follow up, follow up. Don't sit back and wait for things to happen.
- Keep your momentum going. If there's something you need to do, get it done! If necessary set up rewards for yourself.
- Do not rely solely on networking. Use direct contact. It does work and it can open doors.

- Keep interviewing until the deal you want is done. Never assume that anything is definite until it is.
- Job search is not a straight path. It is a circuitous route with twists and turns, highs and lows. But if you set a clear direction, stay focused, and fasten your seat belt, you'll come out okay.

Being Ready for the Right Opportunity

"I thought I knew everything about networking and looking for a job," Calvin admits, although he hadn't been in the job market for a long time. He had been caught in a downsizing after almost a decade with this company, primarily in a public relations role, and, upon the suggestion of a coworker, he asked for Five O'Clock Club outplacement. Since it was summertime and he wanted to spend time at his home at the shore, Calvin opted to attend weekly club meetings by teleconference—but not right away.

After a few weeks off, however, he was not so sure that taking it easy was the best strategy. "I kept hearing that the market was bad and that people were taking a year or more to find a job. I needed some structure. I needed some help. I needed to suspend disbelief and get with the program." Even so, he resisted his coach at first, but "once I found out that he was right on a couple of issues, I realized he knew what he was talking about and I should just put my faith in him."

Calvin tackled the Seven Stories Exercise and found that it provided a helpful foundation. "It was really great for me. It helped identify what I should be doing. I saw the threads in my life that brought satisfaction."

He attacked the job market by networking heavily, mainly because he had so many contacts in the public relations world, but also because writing targeted letters didn't appeal to him. "It was bad enough that I had to deal with unreturned phone calls from people I knew!"

And the lead that turned into his next job indeed came through somebody he knew, but he's thankful that this connection didn't come before he had learned important techniques about job search at the Club. "My résumé was a mess, I needed practice, I hadn't mastered my Two-Minute Pitch, I wasn't all that clear about my objectives. If I had talked to my new employer when I was just getting started, I wouldn't have been hired."

"The synthesis of all the elements was very helpful," Calvin points out. "The books, the CDs, the group, and the coach—it all worked. I just had to buy in, even if I had my doubts." All doubt was certainly removed at the end of the process when he was offered the job he wanted at a Public Relations firm. "I was prepared to take a step back on money, but my coach said 'no way!'—and he helped me negotiate salary. I had about ten things in the works, including another offer. It was an embarrassment of riches. So I didn't have to step back. I got 50 percent more money and a better title."

Calvin advises job hunters: "Don't get freaked out by the Club's advice to target 200 positions. You can get to that number pretty easily if you just open your mind and expand what you're willing to do. You can't be lazy. Commit to the method and talk to everyone. Whatever is working, just keep doing more of it." Calvin attended his telephone group for ten sessions. His coach was Bill Belknap.

A Targeted Letter to the President of Stores

Beatrice had been the manager of a major retail store when she got the news that she would be part of a major downsizing. It turned out not to be such bad news after all because she ended up having to move a couple of hundred miles away for personal reasons. Her company provided Five O'Clock Club outplacement, and she embraced the Club method enthusiastically. "The process is very important. I loved doing the Seven Stories and the Forty-Year Vision. The books are very helpful. I've got them all marked up and put tabs in them. And the CDs remind you of the essentials. If you don't listen to them over and over, you can get off track."

Since Beatrice was targeting positions far from home, she decided to rely less on networking and more on direct contact. Now when she tells how she landed her new job with one of the nation's major retailers, she gets startled reactions from coworkers. "I sent my résumé and cover letter to the president of stores. Everybody says, 'Are you kidding me?,' but it worked." The president passed her résumé along, and she was called in for an informational interview, which lead to a second meeting, a job interview. But her targeted mail campaign paid off across the board. "While I didn't get to 6 to 10 things in the works, I did have 4 to 5," and she was weighing two other offers when she got the one she wanted. In her new position she supervises five departments with annual sales of $23 million.

At the beginning of the process Beatrice confessed that she hadn't done a résumé in six years, but she worked with her private coach on hammering out résumés tailored to different positions. And she took part in the weekly phone group steadily for about two months. "The group was most helpful. When you hear other people making progress, you want your own successes, so you try harder. It's not about 'woe is me'—it's about what you need to do. You just have to make sure you stay focused."

Beatrice has already referred friends—and her mother—to the Club, but cautions that the process won't work without resolve. "There are days when the last thing you want to do is read the books or listen to the CDs, but do it—you've got to do it, because it works, it really does. Stay optimistic and upbeat."

Getting Her First Job in the United States

One of the first things Brenda had to concentrate on after arriving in the United States from England was her job search. Her husband's company had arranged a relocation package for them that included a Cultural Awareness Day, and one of the speakers recommended the Five O'Clock Club to help trailing spouses find new jobs.

Brenda called the Club and the following week attended her first telephone group, facilitated by coach Sylvan Von Burg. Being new to job search in the United States, she found the Five O'Clock Club methodology a crucial road map for navigating an unfamiliar job market. "I used the whole process. I don't think it would be a good idea to follow just bits of it," she advises. "At the beginning I was saying, 'What am I doing?' Then I could see how it all fit together, changing my whole way of thinking. The Forty-Year Vision was helpful to see where I wanted to go so I didn't just jump at any job." The books turned out to be her primary guide: "I'm very much a book person. I used them all the time for reference. I read them every day."

In England Brenda had been a bank auditor, and, not surprisingly, she got the cold shoulder from most agencies since her U.K. experience didn't seem to align well with audit openings here. And since she knew almost no one, networking presented a challenge. Thus, direct contact and responding to ads were the approaches she worked the most. It was six months into her search that Brenda spotted an ad in a local newspaper for a compliance position with a multinational audit company. She checked out the company's Website and found the listing there as well. Using the Five O'Clock Club template for the cover letter, Brenda submitted her résumé. The next day she was invited in for interviews—which turned into an offer. Because she had made the effort to get 6 to 10 things in the works, she had three other offers the same week, and several months into her new job she was still getting responses to her résumé. So now she has an American network and does not intend to let it die. "I send e-mails to everyone every few months."

Throughout her tough search, Brenda attended her weekly group by phone 18 times. "Being in the group I had the feeling that I wasn't on my own. When I got the very negative responses from agencies, it was useful to have the group and the coach tell me that this was okay. The Two-Minute Pitch is so useful. I practiced it in the group to get feedback before I went on interviews. There were a few people I saw all the way through their job searches. It was always very exciting when people landed jobs." "My coach was excellent," Brenda adds. "Sylvan was so helpful, so patient."

Keeping Up the Good Work

When Gerard came back to the weekly meeting to report on his successful job search, he had just accepted a part-time consulting assignment, so he shared suggestions for maintaining momentum in the market. His new consulting job had, in fact, resulted from a networking meeting he had gone to months earlier. He admits that he didn't keep in touch as faithfully as he should have, but even so he received an e-mail asking if he were still available. "I always push for the face-to-face meeting," Gerard points out, "so I called right away to arrange a time to go in. A week later I started on the job."

Gerard's job hunt fell during the summer months, and he learned the value of the Club's advice about not giving up because of the season. "Make sure you keep networking during the summer," he insists. "When September comes, the hammer will fall and everybody will be out there looking. So it's very, very important to try to get those 6 to 10 things in the works. For me, this was not only for practical reasons, but just to keep my sanity during the summer." This activity, in fact, led to interviews, and at the time he started the consulting assignment, he still had several other opportunities pending.

But there are dead-ends to avoid. As an IT specialist himself, Gerard had this warning: "My advice to IT people especially is to get off the job boards. Trying to fit yourself into those little niches is a waste of time. Use other methods for getting those 6 to 10 things going." In reviewing other Five O'Clock Club techniques that had proved useful, Gerard suggested: "Use the books and plagiarize the templates for the cover letters. Act like a consultant, which means anticipating the needs of the companies you're talking to. And you've got to keep *repeating* what you can do. You've got to remember what good trainers do: They say, 'This is what I'm going to tell you,' then they tell you and review what they've told you. That's what to do in your cover letters and follow-up letters."

Gerard attended 14 sessions at the Grand Central Branch and was in coach Jim Borland's group. Jim pointed out that Gerard had finished his college degree during his job search. "His energy was tremendous," Jim commented. "He worked very hard and was really a great help to other people in the group."

The Power of 6 to 10 Things in the Works

When Aaron signed up to attend the Five O'Clock Club in New York, he was a transplant from another state. He had been the trailing spouse when his wife got a job; his own company happened to have no presence in the New York area. But his company had wanted to help him nonetheless and purchased outplacement for him at one of the traditional firms. "It was the biggest waste of money," Aaron says. "I wish I hadn't put in any time there. I spent my own money to come to the Five O'Clock Club."

The weekly strategy group that the Club offers—in contrast to the widely available support and networking groups—appealed to Aaron greatly. "It was well worth the money. I liked the group, I liked the focus. We critiqued each other, we critiqued the résumés, even to the fine points of what portions to bold and underline. This was great help in keeping the résumé relevant, keeping it pointed." Aaron has a strong sales and marketing background, having worked at several Fortune 500 firms. So he knew his skills could be transferred, as long as the résumé positioned him correctly: "I probably had ten different versions of the résumé."

Being a marketing professional, Aaron realized the importance of the Club's mantra about having 6 to 10 things in the works. But being new to the region, this was a challenge. "I started with a network of zero," he admits. His small-group coach, Bert Marro, notes how much the group admired his determination: "He really did keep going at all times. When something fell apart, this gave him the power to say 'so this didn't work for me, there's more coming along.' He had the consistency of a machine—and I mean this is a favorable way."

Aaron combined direct contact and networking and was careful to make full use of every opportunity. "In one situation, I didn't get the job because they took an internal candidate, but I got the names of three new leads from the person who interviewed me." The achievement of 6 to 10 things in the works gave him the confidence to turn down offers that he might otherwise have jumped at; in one case he was able to say no "because it just didn't feel right." Having a lot going on helps with getting through the rough patches. "We all have our days, our ups

and downs. You have to say, 'okay, this has been an off day, but tomorrow is another day, I have to get back into it.' The more effort you put into it, the faster you'll get results."

Of course, achieving a high level of activity takes discipline and willingness to think creatively. Aaron devoted segments of each day to different activities, such as a couple of hours on the Internet for research, and looking off the beaten path. "Keep plugging away at it," Aaron advises. "Don't limit yourself. Look beyond the big names in your field. I ended up being hired by a midsized company that is looking to double its growth. Don't just look to the brand names, do the research to find out who is growing or wants to grow."

Aaron was pleased to return to a Club session to report on his success. "It's been exciting being here. I'm kind of sad to be leaving, but I'm going to make sure to keep in touch with the group members."

The Payoff from 6 to 10 Things in the Works

Jonathan had been a sales/marketing manager, but left his job to follow his wife to a new job; he was the trailing spouse. His wife had received a promotion that required them to relocate to New York from Canada. He had no contacts in the United States, and feared that his Canadian experience would be discounted in the U.S. market. But he knew instinctively that individual initiative and face-to-face contact were going to be the most effective ways to land a job.

He brainstormed with his small group how to expand his targets. Since he and his wife had just moved, there was little flexibility about geography. He had a passion for sales and marketing, so function was pretty well set. So he was prepared to investigate many industries.

Since his Canadian company had U.S. clients, this became the first source of networking meetings. As he began to learn more about various industries from his secondary and primary research, he also explored smaller second-tier companies through the D&B Million Dollar directory. The business library at a college near his new home had the directory on line, and he developed lists of companies based upon their location, SIC code (industry), and size (sales volume and number of employees). With the help of his coach and small group, he revamped his résumé, posted it on several job boards, and updated it regularly to keep it fresh.

He began to generate meetings through direct and targeted mail. He relied as well on leads from his small group. He kept current with professional and trade journals and attended trade association meetings; he turned into a "meeting machine." His philosophy was: Call until they say "No."

With all this activity he managed to consistently get six to ten things in the works. Whenever one fell through, he followed up with a thank-you note, indicating his continued interest, and went onto his next. When he read articles he thought might be of interest to others, he sent copies to targeted people in his growing network; he followed up with phone calls.

Jonathan was able to generate interviews and ended up with three offers. The first came from his third choice, but with that offer in hand he was able to get a matching offer from his number one choice. By virtue of his energetic application of Five O'Clock Club methodology, Jonathan had conquered the U.S. market.

A Case of Strategic Exiting

By Max Lorenz

At the time Sam approached me for career coaching, he was a 47-year-old CFO with a health-care company in the Midwest. He sensed that he could use some help making his next career move. He had been with the company for 14 years and his enthusiasm was waning. Sam was working for his third CEO in four years, and, although he was well respected by his direct reports and the corporate staff group of the parent company, he knew it was time to move on. Despite being an anchor on the executive team, he felt underutilized and unappreciated for his contributions. The stream of new CEOs was an irritation.

Over the years, Sam had provided key leadership roles for several professional associations that were in alignment with his company's business. He had thereby broadened his network of contacts and developed a very strong reputation across a segment of the health-care industry.

I assigned Sam to work through the Five O'Clock Club assessment exercises, including the Seven Stories and Forty-Year Vision. He found them very illuminating and continued with the other exercises, including the Ideal Scene. He found that the process provided career clarity and made a thoughtful decision to leave his present company with a "win-win" objective in mind.

Once launched on the Five O'Clock Club approach, Sam embraced the concepts of job targets, identifying Denver as one of the most desirable geographic areas—especially for lifestyle reasons: he and his wife enjoyed many outdoor activities, such as hiking and snow skiing. He targeted mid-to-large financial services consulting firms, seeing himself in the role of senior consultant. He crafted a marketing plan and identified 75 to 100 positions for his first pass in the Denver area. Obviously one of his major assets was his strong network of industry contacts.

Although he was excited about such new career opportunities, he also wanted to maintain his reputation with his present company. He set a 3-to-6-month timetable for his part-time job search, since he wanted to complete several key projects before he left. There was the possibility that his future consulting firm could be a service provider for his current company.

During the course of four months, Sam generated multiple interviews and ended up accepting a senior consulting role with a Denver firm. He traveled to the corporate parent company to communicate his resignation and offered to

assist them with the selection of his replacement, who turned out to be one of his key staff members. Sam left his company on the best of terms and moved on with considerable excitement to his new position. He credits the Five O'Clock Club methodology for his success in moving his career forward to meet both his career and lifestyle needs.

Not the Prettiest Race, but One of the Bravest

By Ruth Robbins

Rebecca is a bright, articulate, and enthusiastic political scientist and social policy professional. She joined the Five O'Clock Club and was assigned to my group as she was completing her doctorate at a college in New York. She had a strong academic background and wanted a career in a not-for-profit or government organization.

Rebecca was well prepared—as was her natural inclination: she had done her homework by reading the Five O'Clock Club books. She had a decent résumé and had already landed interviews with such agencies as Planned Parenthood and a few NGOs (Non-Government Organizations) involved in resettlement and economic development. Although she was interviewing fairly consistently and was buoyed up by the strong response her résumé was getting, her approach was too scattered.

She needed to apply the Five O'Clock Club concept of organized targets. We altered her basic résumé only slightly, since it was reaping good results, but created a strong targeted positioning statement. She worked on creating a new targeted campaign so that her efforts could be more focused.

Now she targeted positions such as policy analyst, program manager, and development/fund-raising specialist. She aimed for a variety of New York organizations, including women's reproductive rights agencies and foundations, children's services and NGOs focused on third-world economic development. Her energy was unflagging, and her bright confidence was a delight to the group. She cemented a good relationship with a job buddy in the group with a very different profile from hers—an engineer with an MBA—and it was fun to see how well they complimented and encouraged each other.

Rebecca found jobs posted on idealist.org and philanthropist.org. She networked intensively looking for information and leads. She attended professional and academic meetings, exchanged cards, and e-mailed people with whom she had met. She made direct contacts. Now she was being called in for second and third interviews, but for several months nothing came to fruition. Finally there was a payoff: in the summer of 2004 she got two job offers: one from a well-known refugee resettlement organization and one from a start-up social policy think tank. She decided to accept the former because it wasn't a start-up, and it offered more money. The organization liked Rebecca so much that one of the senior directors called from a cell phone to make the offer. Unfortunately the happy ending didn't last long. Within a week, due to internal snags, the offer was rescinded. Rebecca called the think tank, but they had already hired their backup candidate.

Somewhat angry and disappointed, but not devastated, Rebecca returned to the Club and to the structured personal marketing plan that we had worked on. She once again renewed old contacts, wrote more direct contact letters, answered numerous ads, and got more things going. She did not despair but moved on with renewed determination. Two months later she landed a good job with a major international policy organization. She is able to apply her astute political, analytical, and writing skills and does some occasional international travel.

Rebecca's resilience and confidence in the face of adversity recall a line from one of my favorite

movies, *Chariots of Fire.* When a coach sees the front-runner stumble and fall, but then pick himself up and, against all odds, come in first, he observes, "Not the prettiest race I've ever seen, but certainly one of the bravest." Rebecca's job search was more painful than most, but in light of her grace, confidence, and determination, it was certainly the bravest I'd seen.

The Down Side of Having 6 to 10 Things in the Works

By Terry Pile

Elliot had been a marketing director in brand management. After leaving a Fortune 100 company to try his hand at consulting, he decided to get back into a large corporate setting at the vice presidential level. He signed up for the telephone strategy sessions and was assigned to my small group. He methodically developed a marketing plan, identifying his industry and targets. With the Five O'Clock Club approach firmly in mind, Elliot's goal was to get 6 to 10 things in the works, so he expanded the geographic basis of his search.

Each week Elliot reported to the group on his progress, in terms of the positions he had targeted and the stages of the search that he had achieved. For example, he would say, "I have eight things going in stage one, four in stage two, and two in stage three."

One of the possibilities in Elliot's stage three, a position with a biotech firm, looked like "a sure thing." He'd been called in for four interviews altogether, and he could taste the offer coming; he was told that the next meeting would be with the

board of directors. But then he got word he'd been edged out by a competitor. He admitted that it took "almost two weeks to bounce back from the disappointment," but the best cure was to keep trying to hustle up interviews, so he didn't stop his search to lick his wounds.

Indeed, about a month later, Elliot was juggling three job offers and trying to buy time before committing to the job that positioned him best for the future. He found that one of the most painful parts of the process was turning down offers—having to break the news to hiring managers! After accepting an offer, he wrote a letter to the other participants in his Five O'Clock Club small group, sharing some insights about how he played the end game. It's clear that Elliot had positioned himself well enough for the company to see his value.

"The initial dollar offer was actually *above* the advertised salary range. With trepidation, I requested a higher salary, more vacation, and a more defined bonus structure. They came back the same day and granted me all three. Consider this: I had been without permanent employment for more than three years; I was hired by a S&P 500 company in a *different* industry at the *same* title level and at *greater* salary than I had before at a much smaller company. And the new job is in a desirable area of the country with half the cost of living of where I was before.

"Isn't it a little frightening? The Five O'Clock Club method is so effective it is scary, and hiring managers can get hurt! These job-hunting methods are lethal and must be used with extreme discretion. When job hunters have several offers, I think the Club needs to also teach them the art of letting hiring managers down gently."

CHAPTER SIX

The
Five
O'Clock
Club

Networking: The Right Way

So it's time to network to find a new job. When people bother to do much study of the job search process, they soon discover that they'd better gear up for networking. Although looking at the want ads is commonly what people do first, it's sadly the case that answering ads and registering with agencies don't have much impact. Combined, these two approaches result in only about 15 percent of the hiring in the United States.

Hence networking has a reputation for being the best approach—and, in fact, this is almost true. The championing of networking is somewhat misplaced because it can distract job hunters from using *direct contact*—more about that shortly—and because job hunters commonly network poorly and people have grown weary of hearing from so many folks who *don't get what it means* to network. Many job hunters assume that calling everybody on the whole rolodex, making clumsy inquiries about job openings, is networking.

When I give speeches on career topics to professional and alumni associations, it's fairly easy to make the point about networking properly. I like to walk up to someone in the front row and pose a few questions:

"Hi, what's your name?"

"Mark."

"Well, Mark, if I called you out of the blue tomorrow morning and said, 'Sandy Lane suggested I give you a call. I'm looking for work. Do you have a job for me?' what would you say . . . 99 percent of the time?"

"I would say 'No'."

"Of course you would, even if Sandy Lane is your best friend. But what would you say, if, instead, I said to you: 'Sandy tells me that you play a key role in your organization. She thought you might be able to give me your evaluation of the companies I've targeted in my job search. Would you be willing to spend a few minutes with me to talk about that?'"

"I would probably say 'yes'."

"You would probably say 'yes' because the pressure is off to find me a job and because you like talking about your profession. Naturally, you like being thought of as someone whose opinion is valued—and, of course, Sandy is your friend."

Networking is not about asking for jobs. Networking is about gathering information that can lead to your next job—but, even more importantly, it's about building lifelong relationships. If Sandy has referred you to Mark, chances are you and Mark can benefit from knowing each other for years to come. If you can build a network of several dozen—or even several hundred—people like Mark, your professional development will be enriched incredibly and job search in the future will be a lot easier.

Some of the basics to keep in mind when you set out to network:

- Treat each person as a respected colleague with whom you might share insights and information, not just a source of leads. It's really bad form to start out by saying, "Can you think of someone in your organization whom I can talk to about openings?"

- Have your Two-Minute Pitch ready. You're not calling to have a chat. This is business, and you will help the person you're calling *get the picture* if you can articulate your abilities, needs, and goals very clearly. Be prepared in terms of knowing yourself very well.

- But also learn as much as you can about the person you're calling. If Sandy has suggested that you call Mark, she might have told a little or a lot about Mark. But you will have a lot more confidence when you pick up the phone if you know as much as possible about Mark's background and accomplishments. If you have a lot of facts in front of you, it will be easier to spark conversation: "I see from the article you wrote two years ago for the association journal that you played a major role in the Acme merger." Do a Google search on the people you plan to call, or try www.zoominfo.com. You might be come up with some truly amazing facts to enrich your conversation.

Earlier I mentioned *direct contact,* which tends to get lost in all the noise about networking. The simple truth is that you *won't have time* to network into all those companies (representing 200 positions) listed in your marketing plan. Direct contact means writing

directly to companies for whom you *don't* have networking contacts. This usually involves writing well-targeted letters and making follow-up phone calls. As terrifying as this may sound to some people, our research has shown that Five O'Clock Clubbers get more than 30 percent of their meetings through direct contact.

But who knows how many people fail to get more meetings through simple networking because they *misunderstand* networking, do it ineptly, and thus squander leads and opportunities. In this chapter you will read about job hunters who mastered the art of networking.

It's Never Too Late to Follow Up

Maurice had been unemployed almost five months, having lost his position in Internet marketing with the collapse of the dot.com world. "At first, I was like a horse out of the stable—I sent my résumé to 300 people. I got a few meetings and interviews, but they all came to nothing." This intense effort had consumed his efforts in the spring, and he decided to 'take the summer off.' But by August he was getting worried and arrived at the Five O'Clock Club to try to turn things around. "I made friends in the group and related to the things they were going through. But I thank the group leader as well. He wasn't afraid to tell me what I should be doing to jump-start my job search again."

Networking, according to Five O'Clock Club methodology, is keeping in touch with people on an ongoing basis. So Maurice's task was to reconnect with people he had approached in the spring. In reviewing the e-mail he had sent, Maurice remembered a CEO he had heard months earlier at a breakfast panel. At the time they had chatted, and the CEO had asked for Maurice's résumé, but he had heard nothing more. "So I wrote him a new e-mail. I copied the old e-mail message and said, 'If anything has changed, let me know. I've been keeping up with your company and know I could do a great job for you.'"

Two days later Maurice received a call from human resources. "I had two very long rounds of interviews, meeting with 10 people. I wrote follow-up letters to each one of them. I told them everything I could possibly think of." He got the offer he wanted, but knows that he really didn't get the chance to work the full Five O'Clock Club methodology—in the sense of having 6 to 10 things in the works. He now stresses the value of personal networking and following up, even after many months, and, as an Internet marketing specialist, he cautions against putting very much stock in finding a job online. "The job boards are useless. I got nothing out of a couple of hundred postings. Pursue very targeted networking and be persistent."

And even after many months in the job market and only two sessions at the Five O'Clock Club, Maurice found great value in the Five O'Clock Club assessment exercises. "By all means do the Seven Stories and the Forty-Year Vision. They were really helpful. It was brilliant to do them."

Networking . . . and Surrounding the Decision Makers

Sonia was well under way in her career as an economist with a major Wall Street firm when her job was eliminated in a merger. She looked upon this turn of events, however, as an opportunity to try to break into the asset management world. She wanted a role that would give her more connection with people.

One of her contacts actually knew someone who worked at one of the firms at the top of her list, and she had little trouble landing a networking meeting. This new contact, Sonia reports, "was very gracious and led the meeting. He said, 'Since you are trying to make this

transition, here are some ideas to help you get into the asset management world.' And four days later, he even called me with the name of someone else in the company I should talk to."

When Sonia made this call, she found an even more promising situation. There was an actual opening, and she was told, "This would be a great fit for you." When she went for the meeting to discuss the "great fit," she found out that interviewing for the position hadn't even begun yet, and she resisted the temptation to jump right into the process. Recalling Five O'Clock Club strategies, she frankly admitted that she didn't want to be the first person interviewed. Since the company usually took weeks or months to make hiring decisions—and since several of the key decision makers were due to be out of the office traveling—there was no opposition to Sonia's suggestion.

In the meantime, she had "targeted broadly" and kept other opportunities moving along—to the point, in fact, that she was about to receive an important offer. By this time her favored company had, in fact, interviewed a few other people and welcomed having her come in to meet their management team. The interview was a resounding success—"we really clicked"—but she was told that the hiring decision was probably several weeks away. "At this point," Sonia admits, "I sent an e-mail a little on the aggressive side. I said, 'Your company is my top choice, but I have other offers.'" But she also recontacted all the people at the company along the way who had helped move her up the chain and who had been championing her cause. "I kept the ball rolling with everyone. And after one final interview in which I met with five people, I was told I would get a call on Friday with their decision. The call came after 3 o'clock and I accepted on the phone." Sonia proved that the hiring process can be accelerated by having a lot going and by surrounding the decision makers: "Keep networking and circling back." Sonia attended eight sessions at the Five O'Clock Club.

Took Over at a Very Senior Level

Looking for a job over 50 "is absolutely more difficult," according to Bill Kovacs, Director and Vice President, Senior Counsel and Chief Compliance Officer for a major financial institution. "It's harder, but it's do-able." He is enthusiastic about The Five O'Clock Club. "The fundamental product is very solid. It's much better, far more useful than my outplacement package. It went beyond keeping track of how many letters you sent. At my outplacement service, the attitude was to ignore the over-50 issue. But my Club coach said, "Yes, it's true, if you're over 50, you've got a problem. Now let's get on with it.'"

As an attorney who chooses words carefully, Bill is reluctant to use the word discrimination. The problem, he suggests, is prejudice, how people at age 40, 50, or 60 are perceived. "If you're over 50, people assume you're a health risk, have an ego, are set in your ways, and are probably not up to date."

So he suggests that facing these issues head-on is crucial. "If you get a phone call from a recruiter and don't address these fears, you don't get a second phone call."

Add competition to prejudice and the job search becomes especially difficult. "There are 50 qualified lawyers chasing after every good job." Being extremely proactive in the market, however, paid off. Bill admits that he had failed to cultivate an extensive network of contacts in his field, which probably made his job search more difficult. But he adopted networking intensively. Making full use of contact management software, "every three months I'd go through my list of more than 400 contacts. I'd make the phone calls or send the letters." This eventually paid off.

And his age worked in his favor. "A 63-year-old lawyer was retiring early. The company wanted a person with more than 20 years' experience. They wanted someone who could come in immediately and do this job with no training—just show up and take over at a very senior level."

For Bill, keeping up at his level means intensive reading—and amassing information. He admits that reading SEC rule releases is not especially fun, but he brings home many hours worth of reading per week. "I read with discipline, taking notes. I have a personal reference library, currently 36 file drawers of hard copy." He recently acquired a scanner to help store, manage, and access his growing library. To keep up in today's world, he advises, "you've got to be a computer junkie."

Despite the hours that he must spend on diligent reading, Bill loves what he does. "I enjoy working. Retirement doesn't appeal to me." But he would like to see more balance in the way the American workforce operates. "Today, if you're going to be highly compensated, you've got to work 60 to 90 hours per week, 49 to 50 weeks a year. I would love to be able to do two-thirds of the work I do and have one-third more time for myself—but not retire."

Bill attended the Chicago branch of the Club.

Making Connections at Professional Associations

"Whenever I got depressed during my job search," Vincent points out, "I picked up one of the Five O'Clock Club books and read something, or I picked up the phone to call somebody—that's what the methodology said I should be doing." Attempting to change direction with his career, he stuck with his telephone branch sessions for 16 weeks and had a couple of private coaching sessions as well.

Vincent had left a long career in banking to take a position in new business development for an energy company. He knew he faced an uphill battle to return to a financial institution, but decided to target project finance positions with major money center and foreign banks.

After reading the books he immediately adjusted his approach to the job market. He worked hard to redesign his résumé the Five

O'Clock Club way. "My initial résumé, which I'd done on my own, got zilch!"

Members of his strategy group urged him to join key professional associations, and this proved to be a major breakthrough in his search. At his fourth meeting at one of the associations, he met an executive from one of the banks on his target list. Having sent his résumé to several people at the bank—with no response—he asked her in a humorous tone, "How do I crack into your bank?" "May I take a look at your résumé?" was her response. Vincent wanted her input as much as anything. "Could you just review it and tell me what you think?"

A few days later Vincent received a call from one of the bank's senior vice presidents, asking him to come in for an interview. The first interview ended up being six hours long, and he was brought back three days later. An offer soon followed—for a position the bank had been trying to fill for six months! The face-to-face meeting at a professional association had proved to be the key.

Not long after starting the new job, Vincent saw further payoffs of the Five O'Clock Club method. During the weeks attending the telephone sessions, he'd worked hard to get 6 to 10 things in the works, and three job offers came in from companies in his secondary target. Happy to be in a position to turn down these offers, he gained more confidence about his worth in the market.

But he had also gained an appreciation for the value of networking. He had learned as well the importance of professional associations, and during his weeks working with his strategy group, he had contacted members outside the weekly sessions. He plans to keep up the relationships. "I know one thing: I don't want to lose the network."

Re-Networking to Keep Her Career on Track

Julie found that, although she was an HR recruiting professional, there were "no tricks of the trade" to get her through "the nightmare landscape I was in for a while." For many months she faced a bleak job market for recruiters and admits that she was "in pretty down spirits" when she arrived at the Five O'Clock Club. "I was on the board of an association of professional recruiters," she recalls, "and all six of us were either unemployed or had settled for positions outside our careers."

Julie found the Seven Stories and the Forty-Year Vision helpful because they "showed me that my career really fits me and that I wanted to stay in it. And I became determined to use the skills I learned at the Five O'Clock Club to figure out where the jobs were and to eliminate the competition when the time came. I told myself, 'I'm going to be prepared to be the candidate who gets the job.'"

Julie realized that she hadn't been networking properly. She really hadn't made it to Stage 1—keeping in touch with 6 to 10 networking contacts on an ongoing basis. "The lecture on re-networking really made sense. I went back and talked to people I hadn't been in touch with for three months or six months, and that's what led to getting the interviews that paid off"—at a major media company. One of the VPs who had to sign off on hiring a new senior recruiter told her, "I'm going to recommend that they hire you." "That told me I'd applied what I'd learned at the Five O'Clock Club. When I went into the interviews I addressed the problems I could help them solve. As a matter of fact, I got a lot of help from my small group. Some of them knew the company and helped me see the issues I should address."

Julie also decided to take Five O'Clock Club guidance on résumés—sometimes a difficult step for HR professionals. "My new résumé was very different from what I'd used in the past. But moving to a 'résumé of quantifiable achievements' worked. It even helped after I got the job. When my new boss sent out an e-mail announcing my arrival, he selected highlights from my résumé to help make the introduction."

Julie recommends taking nothing for granted when trying to get your name in front of people.

"If you know you're qualified for a job, send your résumé by e-mail, fax, and hardcopy. This increases the chances it will get noticed. Sometimes e-mailed résumés are deleted or get parked in a database. Contact all the people you know who may be supportive and e-mail them your target lists. You'll soon learn who wants to be helpful, and stick around those people!"

Julie's group coach points out that she attended nine sessions consecutively, and "she did everything religiously, applying all parts of the Five O'Clock Club methodology. She was a great contributor to the group—and when you enthusiastically help others in the group, it lifts your own spirits."

Finding Support at the End of the Long Haul

"I got my job through the *New York Times*," Ellen admits, echoing the popular ad campaign. The happy ending came after an agonizing year-and-a-half out of work and wasn't as easy as the slogan makes it sound. Almost the hardest part, she admits, was the reaction of friends as the months dragged on: "You're still out of work? How long has it been?"

But one friend suggested that she try the Five O'Clock Club. "So I joined the Club and bought the books—which are phenomenal. I felt knowledgeable about cover letters, interviewing, and networking, but the Five O'Clock Club gives you good reinforcement to stay focused. One of the things I loved most about the Club was having a coach. Mine called every Sunday night to check in, to see what was going on, and to urge me to come to the Club the next night. She is very compassionate, very supportive. You need to be surrounded by supportive people, especially in such a tough job market."

Ellen's market is public relations, an industry especially hard hit in the New York area in the last few years. Out of work long before 9/11, that disaster only made matters worse. Although the job she finally landed—a public relations/media

role in health care—came through a newspaper ad, Ellen points out that nothing came from the many other ads she answered. And nothing at all from registering with agencies and headhunters.

Hence she encourages job hunters to network intensively. "Join alumni and professional associations, meet people at church or synagogue. You have to get out and tell people who you are. The more people who know you the better." And being "connected" can count for something on interviews as well. "Ellen is, in fact, very active in her own industry association," her coach points out. "This was a very good selling point for the position she ultimately landed."

Having discovered the Five O'Clock Club methodology after job hunting for a long time, Ellen found that it provided an additional boost in confidence: "It's encouraging to know you're doing everything you possibly can. It will lead to the goal of getting a job." Ellen attended the Club for five sessions.

Making and Marketing the Smallest Thing in the World: An MIT Engineer as Entrepreneur

As thoroughly dependent as we now are on our diverse array of electronic tools, wouldn't it be nice if we never had to see the dreaded words "low battery" ever again? Well in the not-too-distant future, your laptop battery may last for hundreds of hours, and your cell phone could go for months without a recharge—thanks to the ingenuity and vision of Five O'Clock Clubber Len Dolhert. He knows the huge potential of the exceedingly small product that his company now promotes globally. Len's products are particles, very tiny pieces of matter that measure *no more than a 100 billionth of a meter*—or 100 nanometers.

Len is a unique talent: an MIT engineer with an MBA from Wharton who loves to promote new ideas and solutions. While employed for a large chemical company that specialized in chemicals for the construction and oil industries, he helped with three projects that evolved into businesses; these involved superconductivity, electronic components, and the creation of a chemical that destroys asbestos without removing it. These endeavors gave him a taste for being on the cutting edge—and becoming a pioneer.

Len discovered the Five O'Clock Club as his MBA work at Wharton was coming to an end, and he felt the need to get help planning his next career move. "The Club has a good reputation. I bought the books, listened to the CDs, and went through the process." And as is the case with most other job hunters, he found the Seven Stories helpful: "I like seeing the big picture. I saw that I like being in charge, or at least being among those who make the decisions that determine the direction of an organization. Creativity and variety ranked very highly."

Thus the launching of his own business was a natural move, especially since he was able to partner with another Five O'Clock Club member, Robert Dobbs, an engineer who was working in material science as well. Initially there was a period of technology setup to enable the creation of nanoparticles. "We have an extremely cost-effective technology that makes tiny particles. We can make more of them faster than anybody else." They incorporated as Primet Precision Materials, Inc. with Len as president. It is headquartered in Maryland, with a site for research, manufacturing, and demonstration in Ithaca, NY—handy to Cornell University and its world-renowned scientific talent.

Transforming lead into gold isn't one of Len's goals—but how about finding a substitute for platinum? For the millions of people who use batteries a lot, this might be just as welcome. One of the applications for Primet Precision Material's tiny particles is in the reinvention of fuel cells, whose technology now is based on platinum. Obviously expense is a factor when making *anything* out of platinum. But current research promises an alternative, as Len explains: "Methanol goes onto the surface of a particle and becomes oxidized. Through the oxidization

reaction there is an electron transfer. You design the fuel cell to capture that electron to produce electrical power. Micro fuel cells can replace batteries, but they would last much longer than what we're used to today."

The nanoparticle technology can be applied even more broadly in the realm of electronics, which thrives on miniaturization. "As electronics become smaller," Len points out, "components become smaller, and parts of components have to be made smaller. Some of the products are polymers filled with particles—the particles give the polymers certain electrical properties—and the particles have to get smaller. We enable the continual shrinking of products." Primet Precision Material's process is environmentally friendly and has many potential environmental applications. One of the most common chemicals that touches us in our daily lives in a huge variety of applications is titanium dioxide; it surrounds us, for example, in paper, plastics, paints, cosmetics, and sunscreen. Because Primet Precision Materials can make titanium dioxide particles at the nanometer level, it could have a major impact on the way many products are enhanced and produced. Titanium dioxide nanoparticles will also enable a host of revolutionary new products:

- Advanced photocells to convert sunlight into electricity
- Highway sound barriers that neutralize auto emissions
- Catalysts to remove pollutants from plants and industrial facilities
- Self-cleaning surfaces, and surfaces that use the sun to kill germs

That's just some of the applications for only one material. There are many other materials that can benefit from Primet Precision Material's process. For example, iron nanoparticles have been shown to neutralize pollutants in groundwater, and coal nanoparticles might be used to both allow sulfur removal and then produce new, clean-burning liquid or gas fuels to replace gasoline and natural gas.

Len and his colleagues are now at the commercialization phase in the development of their business. One of the aspects of the Five O'Clock Club methodology that appealed to Len at the outset is that it mirrors the process for selling any product. "You have to look at your market," he stresses, "and how big that market is—you have to aim at 200 positions. It's the same process for a business, and you have to have a marketing pitch."

The Club's emphasis on networking and tapping into associations has been a key element in the Primet Material campaign to reach out to the appropriate industry leaders. With headquarters in Maryland, Len and other members of his marketing team can easily attend important conferences. "We are very familiar with materials science and nano-technology associations," he notes. "There are many nanotechnology meetings in the Washington DC area." This enables his team to rub shoulders with presidents and heads of research and development from around the world.

Primet Precision Materials is looking for global penetration and has targeted companies that would be most likely to purchase their nanoparticles or hire them for codevelopment roles. Primet Precision Material's nanoparticles will enable other people's inventions to be commercialized. Theirs is the only process that can be scaled to the production quantities that will be necessary for wide-scale use of new inventions that require nanoparticles. Titanium dioxide manufacturers are among the types of companies that Primet Precision Materials is targeting. "Titanium dioxide alone is an $8 billion industry, mostly large companies with over $500 million sales, but also several specialty niche producers," according to Len. The semiconductor and electronics manufacturing industry is another target. A third target is the fuel cell industry, which will grow phenomenally if we can get the platinum out. GM, Exxon, and many, many other companies are working on fuel cells, but they need nanoparticles. That's where we come in." The nano-revolution is ready to roll because Primet Precision Materials has figured out how to make these materials cost-effectively and in large quantities, both of which are necessary to supply new materials to the world's leading companies.

Len has also made use of MIT and Wharton alumni, looking for people who might work at important targeted companies. He points out that it would be a mistake to overlook the retired alumni: "You can assume that many of them still have good contacts at the companies they used to work for." Len reflects his attachment to Five O'Clock Club lexicon when he says, "We have many more than six to ten things in the works. Now we're focusing on the major six to ten."

Len attended the telephone Insider branch of the Five O'Clock Club for a fall season and found that learning came through the CDs, books, and group. "I listened to the CDs in the car; they were great. But also through the books and the group I got a pretty good idea of how to approach job search and career planning." Having the group to connect with every week added an extra dimension: "You can learn all the techniques that work, but doing a job search is an emotional thing too. It's inevitable that you'll hit low points or need advice on how to handle a question, a company, or a person—or how you're feeling at the time. Hearing words of advice and encouragement from peers and a coach is a very good thing. It makes for a complete package— from the intellectual approach to the emotional support.

Len Dolhert, Robert Dobbs, and their colleagues may be reached through their Website, www.primetprecision.com

Getting 6 to 10 Things in the Works Can = Having Your Own Business

Just as an editor at *Forbes* magazine once came to the Five O'Clock Club for help writing his résumé ("I can't write about myself very well"), marketing and public relations executive Idris Mignott decided to turn to the experts when it was a matter of marketing himself. This was in 1999, and he was with Sesame Workshop as senior promotions producer. A friend had told him about the Five O'Clock Club; he looked at our Website, ordered the books, and worked the method without actually attending the Club. He landed a six-month assignment with God's Love We Deliver, a regional nonprofit, as senior consultant for strategic partnerships, which turned into a year-and-a-half assignment. He then moved on to the Leverage Group, a consulting firm, to help launch the inaugural year of the Tribeca Film Festival.

By 2002 Idris was looking to give his career another boost, and this time he decided to attend the Club in person. He worked first with one of our coaches, then began attending the Grand Central Club in Manhattan.

Although he had done the Seven Stories Exercise in 1999, his coach urged him to work through it again, and he now views this as a key to moving his career in the right direction. "It gives you an opportunity to see important threads in your life in print. Right there on paper are the things you're best at and what you have to offer. The exercise revealed my gift for "production and showmanship," as my coach put it. This time the Seven Stories really showed me as an entrepreneur. Prior to that I'd never thought of myself that way—not at all."

And now actually attending the Club for the first time, Idris was able to draw on the power of the weekly group. "The group was great. It helps keep you focused and on-point. It's great to get specific tasks and assignments, then have feedback from different perspectives. That's invaluable."

Idris also took to heart the Five O'Clock Club recommendation about targeting 200 positions, which can also mean trying to reach 200 people to tell them who you are and what you do. He says that about one-third of his effort was put into direct contact, which means writing and

calling people whom you don't know. "That's the most challenging, and you've got to put in the hours." But he also pursued the networking relentlessly. "Even if you have only two contacts, they can lead you to four, and they will lead you to eight."

And, Idris cautions, don't start networking without thorough Five O'Clock Club preparation: "Approach each meeting as a consultant. I really believe the Club's doctrine about not going in and asking for a job. Your position has to be, 'I'm a person who can offer services and solutions.' Have your Two-Minute Pitch ready. And never leave a meeting without the name of at least one more contact."

But, naturally, Idris began networking with his friends, one of whom owned a clothing boutique on the Lower East Side, one of Manhattan's hottest and up-and-coming neighborhoods. She said she'd love to hire him to promote her store—and so would other merchants in the area—but they couldn't afford to do so. "I saw an opportunity to help the entire shopping district," Idris said. He told her he was willing to put together a program to promote her store that would involve other young designers in the area. Within a few days, Idris came up with a major expansion of one of her initial ideas, which would include a neighborhood-wide marketing initiative to promote the area's cutting-edge fashion.

Putting all of his creative and promotional energies into developing the project, he turned it into a spectacular outdoor fashion show that became known as Stores-a-Go-Go, held on September 22, 2002. It was planned to coincide with New York Fashion Week, and he billed it as the "downtown alternative to Fashion Week." He attracted corporate sponsors, including a division of Estée Lauder cosmetics, as well as having it partially underwritten by the Lower East Side Business Improvement District, which operates under the auspices of the City of New York. It was a tremendous boost for local businesses and became part of the economic revitalization of a community still reeling from 9/11. There was "tons of press about it," as Idris puts it, and *Paper Magazine* described the event as follows:

> Far away from the Bryant Park tents, a groovy consortium of Lower East Side artists and designers initiated an outdoor street runway. Sponsored by Hot Head hair products and Jane cosmetics, this Stores-a-Go-Go event advocated democracy, fun and fashion for all and aimed to kick some sense into the lazy Lower East Side economy. Unpretentious yet daring and exciting, this alternative Fashion Week set up shop on the legendary Orchard Street block that is famous for its discounted leather goods and trendy boutiques. The event showcased local designers freshest wear on the last day of Fashion Week. Looks from MShop Anastasia Holland, Johnson, Shop, Vo, Forward, Skella, Vlada, Sena, and Scott Nylund strutted down the runway to a DI set, and the designers delighted the crowds with their New York attitude.

And Idris's strategy of initially offering his services pro bono paid off. The City wanted Stores-a-Go-Go as an annual event, and he was tapped as the executive producer for the following year. Even more important, he garnered six consulting offers because of his work on the project. This launched an entrepreneurial career and company, and his advice for other Five O'Clock Clubbers—whether looking for payroll jobs or consulting positions: meet with as many people as you can, don't be afraid to do volunteer work to build your résumé (no one needs to know whether you were paid or not), and stick with the message, "I can provide solutions!"

Mastering Résumé Follow-Up

Darren is not one to believe that all things come to him who waits. And he decided to follow the Five O'Clock Club's suggestions about getting in

the door for interviews when an opening has been posted—and he landed his new job as a result.

"I belong to an online networking group for financial executives and receive its free daily newsletter. There are daily tips and job postings. I saw a job posted and went to the company's own Website and found it there as well. I submitted my résumé through the company Website."

Then the real work of outclassing the competition began. Most people who submit résumés wait for the phone to ring, but Darren began the kind of proactive campaign to get interviews that the Club recommends. "I searched the database of the networking group and found a former and current employee of the company. I reached both by phone and the current employee happened to be the treasurer, so I made a point of keeping in touch with him." But through his research Darren also discovered that the CFO of the company was a fellow alumnus of his college. He wrote him a letter and managed to reach him twice on the phone, which resulted in being referred to the company controller. "The controller's secretary wanted me to talk to him by phone, but I insisted on a face-to-face meeting. We ended up meeting one morning for coffee for 45 minutes." Darren was called in for two rounds of interviews and got further insights on the situation as a result of other networking. A contact that he had known for over 10 years was working for the company in a consulting role. "She gave me insights on the influencers and helped me strategize my approach." He got the position of senior finance manager for a New Jersey-based technology company.

At the same time that Darren put full energy into getting to meet the right people, he also paid attention to enhancing his marketability. "I went after consulting jobs while I was searching. I contacted a former boss who hired me for a project, and one of the members of my Five O'Clock Club small group had a consulting job for me after he landed a new position. These contacts are so important when you go on interviews. They show you've been busy, and they give you something substantial to talk about."

Darren's small-group coach was Cynthia Strite. "Cynthia kept telling me, 'Don't settle for something you don't want. It won't be interesting. Keep pushing for what you want.'" And Darren set the standard for surrounding the decision makers when he found out about an opening through an advertised position. He will tell you that the ball is always in your court.

A Role Model for Networking: Talking to 200 People . . . Really

"My biggest fear when I was laid off," Malcolm claims, "is that I was going to spend my days watching television and being depressed." Given his approach to finding a new job, however, he can be accused of underestimating himself. The layoff came because business at his firm, which was reducing its presence in the United States, had slowed considerably. "I was unhappy," Malcolm admits, "because I didn't have enough to do." He typed "career coaching" into the Google search field and was soon on the Five O'Clock Club Website. At his request, his company paid for Five O'Clock Club outplacement.

An investment banker with a highly specialized function, Malcolm knew that finding exactly what he wanted to keep his career on track would be an uphill battle—maybe worse than searching for the needle in the haystack. And he knew that watching daytime television was not going to make it happen. "I realized that I needed to be extremely disciplined. I got up every morning at 6:00 to read two newspapers, the *Wall Street Journal* and the *Financial Times.* By 8:00, I was at my desk, ready to make calls."

Reaching out to as many people as possible—to deepen his understanding of the market and unearth the rare opportunity that would fit his goals—appeared to be the best approach. Malcolm turned to two primary

sources: his college alumni database and a listing of the major players in his market niche. "I ended up talking to 200 people. I first sent e-mails, then followed up with phone calls. My coach, Bill Belknap, helped me write the e-mails, which were aimed to get conversations going: 'I'm looking to speak to you for advice. Even if you feel that your area of expertise is pretty far removed from mine, I'd like to hear your views on the market. I know you don't have a position for me, but I want to hear your opinion.' That was the real hook. People would talk to me for hours." Almost all the people he wrote to agreed to speak with him, either in person or by phone.

The extensive network that Malcolm built over the months proved to be a crucial factor in landing his new position. On a major Internet job board he spotted an ad for a job—*exactly* what he had been hunting for—but didn't trust the process of submitting his résumé through this route, especially since he didn't have exactly the educational background that the ad stipulated. His networking, however, had already resulted in tentative relationships with two officers at the company that had advertised the position. He approached them, was put in touch with the hiring manager, and was called in for the interview. An HR officer later acknowledged that the company had not even *looked* at the résumés that had come through the Internet listing, perhaps because there were too many. Hundreds of people scan such ads and simply hit the "send" button.

The interview process was a rigorous one, and Malcolm's extensive network of new contacts paid off here as well. He was asked to study a massive document and within a few days give a presentation on the document to a committee of company officers. "I was really panicked about this. But I created my presentation and went back to some of my new contacts and said, 'May I show this to you?' They were willing to let me practice on them." It was also a great advantage during the interview process to have already talked to dozens of industry specialists. "I was so well informed. It really paid off."

But Malcolm warns that such an aggressive networking campaign can be unmanageable if it's not done right. "Don't e-mail 100 people within just a few days and expect to be able to follow up in a timely fashion. Do it in waves of 20 or 30. I also set up a system of binders: one for my alumni association contacts, one for the industry leaders, and a third for the new people whom I was referred to by both these sources."

As is the case with all Five O'Clock Club outplacement packages, Malcom's included a full year with his small group, which proved to be very helpful for his protracted search for a rare position. "I attended regularly for 10 months, and I listened to the recorded lectures faithfully each week before the conference call. These were extremely useful. I learned a lot of things I'd never even thought about. You actually get to the point of saying, 'Boy, I really don't know how I got a job before I knew all these techniques.' And the coach, Bill Belknap, was one of the best things. He's such a champion of the methodology." Malcolm was careful to build a proper foundation before attempting to contact 200 people. "I did the Seven Stories, which is a great confidence booster, and I rehearsed the Two-Minute Pitch in the group quite a bit."

Working 12-hour days in his new position, Malcolm is determined to maintain the network of contacts he so painstakingly built over the months. "I'm whittling away at those 200, getting out handwritten letters to everyone with my new business card enclosed. And I'll do holiday cards as well. I'll try to stay in touch with all these people at least twice a year."

Moving Ahead in e-Commerce—with The Five O'Clock Club in Reserve

"The Five O'Clock Club system really works," Jeff acknowledges. "You've got to keep at the system. If you don't do your Seven Stories and Forty-Year Vision, your résumé and your pitch won't come out real well." Initially positioning himself as management consultant, managing director, or international marketing director, Jeff's search for an Internet position had been at a standstill. After extensive work with his Five O'Clock Club small group and coach, he changed the heading on his résumé to read E-Commerce Executive. "Within two weeks, the phone began to ring."

Jeff used the Internet for most of his research and marketing efforts. "I did my research on two or three industries and contacted executives by e-mail. I got a lot of response. In November and December—right during the holidays—I got about 30 interviews and follow-up interviews." With four offers, Jeff reviewed his Forty-Year Vision and asked his small group for guidance. "They helped me sort out the list of offers."

Jeff accepted a position as vice president of international marketing, responsible for developing marketing strategies and overseas portals. He sees a critical need for people with marketing expertise in the e-commerce world. "The technology people don't know how to develop markets. Many Internet companies are falling apart because they are too heavy in the technical area but don't know how to make money." Jeff realizes, however, that an e-commerce career can be risky: "You never know what's going to happen to dot.com companies. I'm pretty sure I did my homework right, but I'm going to keep my ties to the Five O'Clock Club."

He attended six sessions before landing his position.

Getting Help from a Colleague— from 10 Years Ago

Rudy admits that he is shy. After 26 years on the job at one bank as an audit officer, he was not happy at the idea that he would have to network to find a new employer. But he did rise to the challenge, and he used the methodology and resources of the Club to achieve his goals. "You must read the books," he counsels. "I'm over 50 and I had to read them about three times before I really began to pay attention and do some of the exercises. The Seven Stories Exercise actually works. It helped me get back to my core needs, desires, and attributes. I've read a lot of career books—they all have good ideas. But the four Five O'Clock Club books really put it all together."

And, despite his shyness, he worked at networking and direct contact. "We all know people have hit the lottery on Monster.com, but they are few and far between. When you use networking, you'll find a much warmer reception when you approach people. But it is a two-way street. You've got to be willing to offer help as well as ask for help." Rudy also learned the value of casting the net as widely as possible in search of people who might play a role in connecting him with new opportunities. He contacted a former colleague—whom he had not seen in 10 years—and arranged to have lunch. Rudy's new résumé reinforced the former colleague's positive impression of him, and he offered to pass the résumé on to someone he knew at another major bank. This led to the payoff interview.

Having read the books—perhaps for the third time!—Rudy knew that follow-up was the key; a thank-you note would not separate him from the competition. "That night after the interview," he reports, "I drafted an e-mail explaining in detail why I was suitable for the job. The next day I got the message: 'We're very impressed with how you handled yourself.'"

The small-group experience at the Club was especially helpful for Rudy, since it provided access to job search buddies. To a shy person, for whom the requisite networking is anathema, feelings of loneliness and isolation can be a major hindrance. The group enables forced introductions to others who may be in the same boat, and Rudy bonded well with three others in his small group. They kept in touch by phone and met every two weeks for lunch. While this peer support was welcome, Rudy also advises tapping the expertise of the coach. "I arranged for a couple of one-on-one sessions with the coach who led the group, Jim Borland. These sessions were invaluable. Jim helped the lessons of the book to come alive. I needed help in seeing how to apply what the books said about the day-to-day search."

One of the inspirational quotes that helped Rudy through the process came from (perhaps) an unlikely source. When Gracie Allen was dying, she told George Burns: "Never put a period where God intended a comma." On the evening that Rudy described his successful job search at the Club, he reported, "All along I have kept a journal of my search. The only time I put in a period is when I took this new job. This is just a way of saying that, no matter how long you may have to work at it, don't give up hope."

Don't Assume Anything

By Bill Belknap

Sometimes dream clients have blind spots. Maxine, a seasoned Wall Street executive and one of the participants in the weekly telephone group that I lead, followed the Five O'Clock Club methodology religiously. She joined the call every week and was a consistent contributor; she worked at least 40 hours a week on her job search.

She took networking very seriously and did it very well. However, there was one important networking resource that I had great difficulty convincing her to use. She balked at calling her alumni office. This, by the way, is a common failing of many executives. Some surveys show as many as 70 percent don't bother to contact their alumni offices.

What was Maxine's excuse—or, more kindly put—her rationale? She had graduated from Wesleyan, and she assured me that "most Wesleyan grads go into the arts." I reminded her that *she* had made the transition to the world of finance! Surely she was not the only one. To nudge her along, I decided we would discuss the alumni office approach on the next telephone strategy meeting; everyone agreed she needed to network with alumni. That's one of the great things about our weekly groups: peer pressure!

She finally agreed that it wouldn't hurt to call. Guess what? The alumni office gave her the names of 125 grads who worked in New York City in financial services. She was thrilled and went on a campaign to contact every person on the list. And, yes, through one of her alumni contacts, she landed a terrific six-figure job at a major investment bank.

CHAPTER SEVEN

The Five O'Clock Club

How to Ace the Job Interview

What stands between you and your next job? If you have even a passing familiarity with the Five O'Clock Club methodology, you know that getting the *right* job requires a lot of hard work: forging a well-positioned résumé based on assessment—not just adding a few lines about your most recent job—spending many hours researching your targeted areas, and writing and telephoning the people who represent the 200 positions outlined on your personal marketing plan. Since there's no 9-to-5 structure to a job search, people who are truly committed to the process find that it takes over their evenings and weekends. No wonder we don't like to job hunt! Many of the Five O'Clock Clubbers have said, "I had to work harder than I did on my last job."

But perhaps the most dreaded portion of this ordeal is *the interview:* the moment when you go on display. In fact, the interview is the culmination of all your hard work (well, *not really*—but more about that shortly). You've done the research and the outreach, you've worked hard to get people to agree to meet with you—and then you have to go through with it! As we say at the Five O'Clock Club, "It's showtime!"

You're on display, and there are certain expectations about what's supposed to happen. The classical, traditional approach to interviewing almost guarantees that it will be a stressful experience. "You're there to get the job! Be sure to sell like crazy, and convince them how good you are and how much you want the job." As you leave for the interview, your best friend or spouse wishes you well: "I hope you get the job."

What can you do to take the pressure off? How can you manage expectations? How can you increase the odds that you will *eventually* get an offer? I'll just mention a few things here, as a preface to these wonderful accounts from Five O'Clock Clubbers about how they aced the interview. Of course, be sure to study our book, *Mastering the Job Interview and Winning the Money Game* to get the full scope of the Club's methodology for doing well on interviews.

We have a caricature of job hunters who take the wrong approach. We often speak of "the grubby little job hunters" who show up for interviews to plead to be hired. As if with hat-in-hand, they expect to win favor by being well dressed, sincere, and eager. We tell well-prepared Five O'Clock Clubbers to get 6 to 10 things in the works, because "five will fall apart through no fault of your own." For the grubby little job hunters, sadly, five usually fall apart because it *is* their own fault. They show up for interviews hoping to get offers, with little understanding of what it means to *interview well*. The Five O'Clock Club offers research-based recommendations for interviewing well.

Be Prepared: Know the Company and the People

One Five O'Clock Clubber in recent memory asked that an interview be postponed so she would have time to do proper research. When she received a call from an agency urging her to go on an interview the next day, she suggested moving it off for a few days. It turned out not to be a problem; the overeager agency just wanted to get her in as soon as possible. But it's no good going on an interview without doing the proper homework. Via the Internet especially, it's possible to learn so much about the companies and, in some cases, the people you'll be meeting with. The company website is the most obvious place to start, but there are many other sources for gathering information. *You want to be an expert on the organization before you walk in the door.* In the interview, you will be dialoguing with hiring managers and department heads about the company, its problems and needs. You will look weak and unprepared if, to put it bluntly, you ask dumb questions. Especially when it is so easy to be informed, those in a position to hire are not impressed when candidates betray a shallow understanding of a company and its competitors.

Be Prepared: Know What You Have to Offer—to *That* Company

Five O'Clock Clubbers rehearse their Two-Minute Pitches in their small groups to get ready for *showtime*. Whenever you have a new

company in your sights, figure out how you should position yourself *to that company.* A well-developed generic pitch is essential and should be honed and polished, but make the adjustments appropriate for each company. One Club member reported that he had been trying for many months to get an interview with a major company in his industry. When he finally got the telephone call following up on his résumé, he was holding his baby, and his two other kids were running around the living room. The television was on, and his wife was getting dinner ready. But his Two-Minute Pitch was so well rehearsed and imbedded in his mind that he was able to "flip the on-switch" and make his case to the company executive—despite all the distractions.

The perfected Two-Minute Pitch is the key to being triumphant when job hunters face the moment they dread the most: the interviewer looks across the desk and says, "So tell me about yourself." Of course the dread is erased to the degree that you're *prepared.* Job hunters may have a jumble of information about themselves in their heads—much of it irrelevant to the current situation—and, chances are, it will come out jumbled and irrelevant if a lot of work hasn't been done to get it right. That's why we have the Seven Stories Exercise, the Two-Minute Pitch, the 3×5 cards, *and* the drill of rehearsing the pitch in the small group. Rehearsing in the small group, in fact, is a form of interview practice. All these are designed to make it much easier to make your case to hiring managers.

Act Like a Consultant

"So tell me about yourself" is just one of the questions that causes panic for job hunters. Some of the other dreaded questions include: "What are your weak points and strong points?" and "Where do you see yourself in five years?" In countless job search books there is plenty of advice on how to handle these questions, hence many job hunters assume they're *prepared* when they are armed with clever responses. But it's relatively easy to deflect such superficial questions. If this is what you're worried about as you get ready for interviews, you're worried about the wrong thing! Being clever or smooth when you face these little traps won't win important points during the long course of interviewing.

The primary key to success in interviewing is adopting a mind-set that shifts the focus *from you to them.* Let's put it this way: instead of going in with the wish, *I hope I get the job,* you should be saying, *I need to find out what the need is.* Why do they need to hire someone? A consultant tries to analyze and grasp the situation and make suggestions about solutions. Getting and giving information is the primary purpose of the interview—and discussing potential solutions. For the grubby little job hunter, the interview is an adversarial situation: "It's me against them. They have something I want—a job—and I've got to persuade them to give it to me." The consultant assumes that everybody is on the same side: we're all trying to find solutions and satisfy needs.

Leaving the Interview "Dumb and Happy": What You *Don't* Know Can Hurt You

Job hunters have been shocked to find out, after a series of wonderful interviews, that they came in *second.* "But how can that be? They liked me—they *really* liked me!" That may be true, but, unfortunately, it's not the whole story. We say that people leave interviews "dumb and happy" because they neglected to ask crucial questions *about the hiring process.* It's all well and good—it's absolutely vital—to get a full understanding of the job you're interviewing for. But you're rarely interviewing in isolation. What about the competition? And do you really think that hiring managers are 100 percent sold on you—with no reservations at all?

Maybe they did like you—*really* liked you—but was there anything about you that they *didn't* like? Obviously, it would be helpful to find out! And who else is in the running? Were you the first person they interviewed? The third? The last? If you've not sized up the situation from these perspectives, you've not interviewed as well as you thought you did. You've not interviewed *smartly.* So it's important to ask, usually as the interview is coming to a close: "Where are you in the hiring process? What are you looking for, that you've not yet found, in the candidates you've seen so far? Is there anything in my background that would make you hesitate to hire me?" They may like you, but do you have weaknesses or flaws—or so they imagine—that will damage your chances of getting to the finish line? If you don't know what they're imagining, you may be out of the running, even as you're celebrating how much they liked you! Probe for their reservations. Probe for insights and information that will help you strategize next steps and make your case later in the game. Read more about these techniques in *Mastering the Job Interview,* and use your small group at the Five O'Clock Club to brainstorm follow-up based on information about the hiring process.

The Interview Is Just the Beginning

As I mentioned earlier, the interview is commonly viewed as the culmination of so much hard work. But many job hunters don't get offers because when they walk out the door after the interview, they say, "Whew, that's done!" As far as they're concerned, the movie is over—"The End." Of course, some (but, by no means all) follow the recommended protocol about sending a "thank-you" note—and then wait and wait for the phone to ring. Chances are, this is going to be one of the five things that fall apart—and it may very well be the fault of the job hunter. He may or may not be surprised when the rejection letter arrives in the mail.

But the interview is not the culmination—*if* you want the job. Turning the interview into an offer requires more hard work that your small group at the Five O'Clock Club can help with. Even if you don't want the job, having an offer might come in handy to give you more power and leverage for getting the offers you *really* want. So it's helpful to look at interviews as the culmination of *some* of your hard work. Interviews are the beginning of a different kind of work. In the next chapter you will read about Five O'Clock Clubbers who poured on the steam *after* their interviews. During their meetings with hiring managers and department heads, they gave and got information; then, making full use of this knowledge, they worked hard to move the process forward and outclass the competition.

Networking as a Consultant

Vincent discovered that he really hadn't been networking at all, after calling almost 30 of his closest contacts to ask for a job. "I might as well have said, 'Are you now, or have you ever been, a member of the Communist party?' People get funny; they get nervous when you ask them if they have a job." Vincent had lost his job as legal counsel for a Fortune 500 entertainment company. It had been his dream job, and he had assumed he would be there forever. But when the company hit a slump and cut 500 jobs, his position was eliminated.

Having been in his field for 20 years, he had assumed that his contacts would be his salvation—and they were, once he realized the mistakes he'd been making. After starting with the Five O'Clock Club, he learned that networking means staying in touch with important contacts on an ongoing basis and approaching them as a consultant. Following the advice of his small group, he decided to recontact the people who had said, "No, I don't have a job," and changed his script completely. Vincent summed up his new approach: "Instead of begging, you're trying to make the point: I have

something to offer. I'm not asking for a favor. I want to give you something, form an alliance with you, and build a friendship. Hence your question has to be: 'Do you know of someone who would like to talk to someone with my skills? I have a lot of experience in music, videos, movies, and the Internet.'"

In his new networking campaign, Vincent suggested getting together for lunch with one of his contacts and approached the meeting as one consultant talking to another. "I went into the lunch upbeat and positive and described some of the clients I'd been working with. He was impressed and wanted to help me." Within a couple of weeks the contact helped set up a meeting for Vincent, although there was no opening. "But it turns out there was a need. They liked me, I did well on the interview, and my friend had recommended me. They created a job for me."

Vincent had been out of work for almost six months when he arrived at the Five O'Clock Club. He landed his new job after only three sessions. His group leader recalls how he changed course with his networking: "He grasped what he was doing wrong. It's the kiss of death to ask for a job and he learned that you have to keep in touch with people. Networking is not giving it just one shot with everyone."

Assisted Serendipity

Margot had a successful career as owner of a retail business, selling a high-end luxury product. It gave her flexibility while she was raising her family, but "it had become rote. It was not stimulating in terms of using my intellectual capacities." She went back to school and got a master's degree in human resources management, which boosted her into a new career.

She relocated out of state to accept a position as director of human resources in a corporate environment, but regretted being a long distance from her family. Three years later, in January

2002, when the position was eliminated, Margot was stunned. But she had already been sending out résumés—in fact, she had been testing the market since the spring of 2001.

Having known about the Five O'Clock Club for a long time, she decided to sign up for our weekly sessions via teleconference, known as the Insider Group, and plunged into study of the methodology. "The CDs are wonderful. They repeat what's in the books, but it's another way of learning; they reinforce each other. Then attending the group was another reinforcement. The discussion brings the methodology into play."

Margot had hardly begun her sessions when she got a call from a major not-for-profit to whom she had sent her résumé nine months earlier, asking her to come in for an interview. She recalled that the job posting she had responded to was "perfect," so was delighted by this "bolt out of the blue." It was a long drive to get to the interview, "so in the car on the way I listened to the CD about turning job interviews into offers. I had my 3 × 5 card and I had my pitch down. I was really working hard at doing it right." It turned out to be a marathon interview, with the director of human resources and the department heads who were the key decision makers. At the end, she was left alone with the human resources director, who offered her the job. "I was stunned. The Five O'Clock Club message is that the purpose of the first interview is not to get an offer, but to get a second interview—and here I had the offer!"

Margot was relieved that money was not mentioned. She was promised an offer letter after reference checks had been completed. "I went home and read the books and listened to the tapes on salary negotiation. It turns out that they had pretty rigid salary ranges, but I was able to get the top of the range, instead of "near the top," and I was able to negotiate on non-salary issues."

Although the interview in Margot's case had come almost as a gift, she credits a key element of the Five O'Clock Club methodology in doing

so well on the interview. "The most useful thing I learned was that I was a consultant. That really took the weight off. It made me the person to get information, rather than someone who just had to provide a lot of information about myself. I was not passive. I was not being acted upon. And I had to chuckle after the interview. I found myself using the actual words I'd heard on the tapes—and they work: 'What wakes you up at two o'clock in the morning? How can I help you? What are the biggest issues you're facing right now?' "

Margot attended three teleconference sessions.

Think Like a Consultant

"I had never taken the approach of the consultant," Hector confesses. But the Five O'Clock Club approach to interviewing seems to have worked especially well in his job search in academia. Now in his new job as a dean at a New Jersey college, Hector recalls his interview by the departmental committee: "I cannot underline how important it was to act like a consultant." The committee had never been asked by a candidate, "Where do you want to be in six months?" "What's your biggest worry?" As any good consultant would, Hector took notes and, in his follow-up letter, was able to address their concerns in detail. Since there were 12 people on the committee, he addressed his letter to the committee chair and enclosed enough copies—individually signed—for everyone.

Hector also surprised the committee with another question inspired by the Five O'Clock Club methodology; sensing that some committee members were not entirely sold on him, he asked, "What do you think is the weakest part of my candidacy?" By simply asking the question, he was outshining the competition, and his major weakness—a missing piece of experience—was no longer seen as an issue.

Hector found that his job search turned around when he discovered the Five O'Clock

Club. His counselor and group coached him on tailoring his cover letters to specific higher education want ads—something he had not done before—and he ended up with three interviews for three highly desirable positions. As the Club warns, however, two fell away through no fault of his own. But by acting like a consultant he proved that Five O'Clock Club interviewing techniques work as well in academia as in the corporate world.

Hector attended six sessions.

Getting a Career Back on Track

Pierre had been away from his chosen field of urban planning for almost a decade, and he knew he was fighting an uphill battle. He found that the Five O'Clock Club approach to correct positioning and research played a major role in helping him overcome objections and get back in. He decided to respond to three jobs posted on a Website; working with his Five O'Clock Club small group and counselor, he crafted cover letters to show that his experience was a match for the stated requirements, relying heavily on the language of the ad itself to describe his background.

But once the letter and résumés were on the way, he went into high gear to outclass the competition; since it was an Internet ad, he knew there would be plenty of competition, and he could assume that most of the other candidates would have current experience. He networked heavily to find out as much as he could about the company and the key players. He was able to reach people who knew the hiring manager, and he called the president of an industry association to get suggestions and insights about the company. By the time he went on the interview, it was hard for the hiring manager to see him as unconnected or out of touch—and he landed the job. Pierre combined high-impact positioning with in-depth research; the combination of the two made for a successful job search. He attended the Manhattan Central Branch for two months.

Learning the Price of Networking Without Positioning

Natalie is one of the leaders in her field, but is the first to admit that her job search skills left something to be desired. Her position was eliminated in a corporate merger, and she found herself in the job market for the first time in 13 years. "I have a stellar résumé," she said. "I had this completely unrealistic expectation that when I told people I would be available, they would be clamoring to have me." She set out to network on a massive scale and, because of her position and reputation, many doors were opened. A year later, she confesses, "I had an incredible collection of business cards."

But she still didn't have a job, although a few teaching and writing assignments had come her way. Her networking had put her on the trail of the Five O'Clock Club, and she began attending sessions. She credits the 5OCC, especially the books, with giving her crucial insights about strategy and positioning. She learned that people wouldn't be "clamoring" to have her until she helped them grasp what she could do for them. "The Five O'Clock Club gave me a different way of approaching interviews: trying to identify company needs and positioning myself in terms of their needs." She credits the Club with giving her "heightened awareness" that turned the situation around, and she acknowledges the role of her coach in inspiring her to listen more carefully. On the interviews, she says, "I could hear his voice in the back of my head!"

Natalie credits the weekly sessions with "keeping me motivated. The Five O'Clock Club gave me strategy. I'm just sorry that I didn't find the Club sooner." She attended Club meetings for almost two months.

Competitive in the Interview

"On interviews, I always carried with me some evidence of being physically active," Ed Mills remarked. Sometimes it was his tennis equipment. He plays in the state championships for seniors. On the interview for his current job, when the conversation came to "outside interests," he pulled from his briefcase a picture of himself hiking at 14,000 feet on California's Mt. Whitney.

Ed acknowledges, however, that no matter how much he has been able to make the point that he is a high-energy person, age discrimination was probably a factor in his job searches.

"Some opportunities went away, and I didn't quite know why." But he also is confident that being over 50 actually worked in his favor in landing the position with 13/WNET because of the amount and breadth of experience he had to offer: "Fifteen years ago I would not have been as attractive a candidate."

The key, Ed admits, was correct positioning, one of the fundamentals of Five O'Clock Club methodology, especially since he was attempting to move from the not-for-profit world. With the help of his counselor and small group, Ed built a résumé that drew attention to his accomplishments and to his strengths on the technical side of direct marketing. With a high-impact, well-positioned résumé, the age factor didn't get as much attention as it might have. And he attended sessions at the Club to maintain momentum.

Ed was happy to land at 13/WNET, which, although a non-for-profit, "is a big station and it's a business in competition with for-profit companies. My position uses the full range of my abilities; it's challenging and it's hard work and it's good."

In the months preceding his new position with 13/WNET, Ed was busy with several consulting assignments that helped him hone his computer skills—a vital factor in remaining competitive with younger workers.

Ed's formula for keeping up to date also includes being active in professional associations, where he is often invited to be a guest speaker; last year he served as treasurer for his 40th-year college class reunion.

If retirement is taken to mean slowing down or cutting back, that doesn't seem to be part of Ed's agenda. "I suppose that looking 15 years out, I might not work full-time. I might do some consulting, I might travel and play some national level competition in tennis."

Using E-mail List Serves to Keep Up

"Do you have children in college?" was the interview question that made Jack Feldesman suspect that age might be an issue. He is sure, however, that salary was the larger concern in his case. "Of all the interviews I had, at least 90 to 95 percent were for positions that paid less than I had been earning." Jack knew that being in a job for over 20 years—and advancing steadily—had put him in this position.

Jack ended up in a job very similar to the one he left, so adopting the Five O'Clock Club's "consultant mentality" during the interview process was appropriate. He knew the issues and problems he would be facing and was able to position himself effectively. "The match couldn't have been closer."

One of the concerns about a candidate who has been at a job for 20 years may be adaptability more than age. Is the person simply too set in his ways or even out of touch? Jack makes full use of Internet resources to make sure that he is not growing stale. "I'm a member of a number of professional societies, including the American Society of Association Executives. They have a computerized list serve in a number of functional areas of the nonprofit world. I belong to their finance and administration list serves. You get online and see e-mails from hundreds of other people with similar interests, with questions on how to do this or that. It's incredible the amount of knowledge and information you can pick up. Your e-mail inquiry goes out on the list serve to over 1000 people, and you get responses in a matter of minutes. This is a great form of continuing education."

Jack feels that getting the right kind of help in job search is important. Attending Club meetings gave him a boost: "This kept the juices flowing. You meet with people weekly, you're told what to do, what not to do. Job hunting can be very lonely. There were fresh ideas. I went through an outplacement service that, frankly, did not help. If they had done as much as the Five O'Clock Club did, I would have landed sooner."

At the mention of retirement, Jack speaks of keeping busy. "I'd like to be doing something interesting 10 or 15 years from now. I'm going to be working for a long time. I haven't had a career peak yet."

Jack attended the Maryland branch of the Club.

Learning the Five O'Clock Club Method on the Road

"I listened to the whole set of tapes four times." With a 40-minute commute each way, Bernard decided to put time in the car to good use. Feeling unchallenged after 15 years with an insurance company, he knew that finding a new path would require hard work and concentration. "On my way to work, instead of listening to the radio, I put in a tape. This got me thinking about what I needed to do that day, who I needed to call. And on my way home, I would listen for ideas, so that after helping get the kids to bed, I would know what I needed to do to keep the search moving."

By his own estimate Bernard devoted about 20 hours to the first Five O'Clock Club book, especially the assessment exercises. "The long-term vision was the most helpful concept. So many people are focused on 'What am I going to do now for a job?' versus 'What do I really want to do down the road? Where do I see myself in 15 or 20 years?' So many career books tell you how to get the next job, rather than help you reach your career objectives."

But Bernard wanted human interaction to supplement the books and tapes. Since he is on the West Coast, he signed up for 10 teleconference sessions and connected with a coach by phone for several private sessions as well.

He settled on four initial targets, but serious drawbacks in three of them soon became apparent. He decided to launch a major campaign in the fourth: executive recruiting firms. "I did my research, identified A, B, and C lists, and mailed résumés and cover letters to 88 companies. I got calls from 15—most on the B and C list. But I was glad to start my meetings with them. I went on 10 to 12 interviews, just so I could master the terminology. By the time I got into the high end firms, they almost looked at me as if they were recruiting someone from another firm."

Bernard got into the high-end firms by making the requisite phone calls to the remaining 70+ companies on his lists. This produced 25 interviews, which resulted in several offers. Having more than 6 to 10 things in the works helped Bernard negotiate from a position of strength. "One of the firms told me they were giving me the best offer they ever made any candidate. They said, 'What's your next step?' I said, 'I've got to evaluate your offer in comparison to all the others I've received.' They kept pursuing me." It was around the time of his ninth teleconference group session that he landed his new job.

In his new role Bernard recruits and places executive level candidates in a niche market. And he sees firsthand the need for career assessment that helped him so much. "As a recruiter, I see people change jobs as fast as they change pants. A lot of them really don't have any idea what they want to do, and these are very senior people."

Using the Club on an Ongoing Basis

With a strong background in marketing, consumer products, and brand management,

Lucille has followed the strategy of building her résumé by taking long-term assignments with major companies. "I get to put premium companies on my résumé, and I leverage that as I move forward." She came back to report at the Club between assignments and talked about applying Five O'Clock Club techniques and using the support that the Club provides.

Networking the right way, for example, is a matter of building lifelong relationships, and Lucille decided that this idea should apply to recruiters as much as to anyone else. "The major assignment that I just completed came through a recruiter. We hit it off, and I made a practice of keeping in touch with her; we built a nice rapport. I think I was the first one she called when she got the job order for the position."

Lucille points out that the consultant mentality is naturally a good idea when interviewing for a consulting job. "I did a lot of research, I examined the products I'd be working with, and I studied the products' primary competitors. I tried to think as I would if I had already landed the job, and that really helped." All this preparation before the interview proved useful on at least two levels: "It eased a lot of my nervousness, and it showed the people I was interviewing with that I was thinking about their business." Lucille also asked key Five O'Clock Club questions that prepared the way for doing effective follow-up: "If you have any reservations about me, what would they be?" and "What would you like to be able to say six months from now about the person you hire?" She also points out the importance of attitude: "I tried to match their need with a descriptions of my accomplishments, but if I didn't have the accomplishments, I tried to match it with enthusiasm."

Even while on long-term assignments, Lucille always thinks of herself as job hunting, hence her desire to stay connected with the Club; she has attended more than 20 sessions. "I find it helpful to talk to other Five O'Clock Clubbers while I am on assignments," she points out. "She

is excellent at pulling networks together, her small-group coach says, "and at buddying with others. She leaves nothing unturned."

The day after she reported at the Club, Lucille was heading off on a new temp position, "and I want to come back and report on that."

Making It Easy for the Hiring Manager

"When I got into my group at the Club," Jasper admits, "I realized that I really wasn't focused like the others. I had been unemployed for many months, mainly responding to the want ads and searching through job boards." And he saw that he had been squandering interview opportunities. "I could talk about my skills, but I never took that extra step to show how I could bring value and benefit to a company. I left it up to them to figure it out. Basically, I was saying to people, 'Here are my skills, just hire me.' That didn't work."

Jasper tackled the Seven Stories with the help of his group coach and found that his interviewing improved immediately. The Seven Stories Exercise, of course, is designed to help people discover what to do with their lives, but it can give a boost to interviewing skills. "When I was asked questions, I answered with some of my stories."

Within three weeks of starting with the Five O'Clock Club, Jasper ended up with a consulting assignment—not exactly what he was looking for, but he viewed it as a stepping-stone. The person who had hired him for the assignment "remembered my stories and suggested me to someone else, who called me in. I had three interviews and just kept telling more stories. I also listened carefully and answered questions so that people could see that I could do what the company needed."

But Jasper's success can be attributed as well to his conversion from a reactive posture (looking at ads and scanning job boards) to a proactive one. He took seriously the Club's stress on trying to get six to ten things in the works and began networking relentlessly. He attended five sessions at the main branch in Manhattan.

Seven Months . . . and Seven Weeks

"The Club helped me organize my thoughts properly," says Aaron. "Being in the group helped boost my morale and restored my confidence in myself." He had discovered the Club after a bruising seven-month job search. "I had a couple of early leads that seemed promising, but then went nowhere. My search had gone stale."

Aaron had a sense that his résumé might be part of the problem, and, working with the coach, the résumé went through "about five iterations." "Be sure to keep careful track of where you sent which résumé," he advises, "so that when you go in for an interview you'll know which one they're looking at." Aaron also realized that his hatred of interviewing undoubtedly had been working against him—probably because he never followed the practice of being totally prepared. "The Club's recommendations about knowing who you're going to be talking to and what the company is all about are extraordinarily helpful."

Ironically—in view of his fruitless seven-month search—he found out about his new job from a man who had been a colleague several years earlier and now worked with Aaron's new employer. "I had help from my friend finding out the kinds of things that the Club recommends. I called him up to learn what a person was like, what their role was, and what part they played in the process. So I wasn't going up against the unknown."

Joining the Club meant that Aaron was now prepared for the opportunities that came his way. After seven weeks working with his small group, he landed his new position as a project manager at a major financial institution. "The company has 10 trading systems and 23 accounting

packages. My role is to integrate them into one system." Aaron's group leader, Cynthia Strite, says, "He was a little beaten down when he arrived. The group helped him turn things around. He attended seven sessions diligently."

Mastering Interview Techniques . . . "and I'll Be Back for More"

"I'm one of the few who found a job from a job-posting Website," Brittany points out, and she found full value from the Five O'Clock Club methodology, even though she came into the program when she was well along in her search. By the time she started working with her group, she was at the interview stage. "The number one thing I learned here was to act like a consultant. It is so important, and it is so different from what I had ever done before. This totally changed the way I acted on interviews. When people asked me, 'Do you have any questions?' I was one of those who said, 'No, I think you've covered it all.' After coming to the Club, I always went in with backup questions, just in case." Brittany also learned the consultant techniques of uncovering objections and crafting thoughtful follow-up letters. "When I was called in to get the offer for the job I have now, I was complimented on my letters. That was really a nice thing to hear. They had read and appreciated them."

Brittany decided to ask for a private session with her group coach, Renée Lee Rosenberg, as she was getting ready for the final interview when salary would be discussed. "People are really afraid of salary negotiations—and I was no exception—but I was thoroughly prepared after my session with Renée."

Brittany also learned a lesson about applying for jobs that you know aren't right for you. The lesson is: don't assume anything. "I knew I was overqualified for the job I applied for, and I was pretty sure through much of the interview process. I didn't know what was going to happen. But by acting like a consultant, I negotiated the job during the interviews. So be sure to put full effort into every single interview, even if you're uncertain whether it's going to be something you want." Brittany ended up with a position as manager of customer acquisition marketing. "She was extremely committed to our interviewing strategies," Renée reports.

But this happy ending has made her eager to learn the entire Five O'Clock Club methodology. "I have yet to do my Seven Stories and Forty-Year Vision. I never did direct mail, which is something I'd like to learn. So I'll be coming back to use all of my sessions and learn more."

Even When Getting the Next Job Looked Easy

It's always tempting to say, "Well, that was easy. You were lucky," when we hear how some people got their jobs. In Laura's case, her teacher in a summer class invited her in for an interview, and she was hired. But her job search activity in the weeks prior to this opportunity, including her participation in the small group at the Five O'Clock Club, played a substantial role in being able to make the crucial interview a success.

Laura had been laid off from her job at a major university—a job that she loved and was highly committed to. "I was heartbroken. The last thing I wanted to do was start networking. I was very cranky about the whole thing. But I decided to push myself. I came to the Five O'Clock Club and heard people in my small group who were not giving up." So Laura summoned the energy to network and began reaching out. "I e-mailed everyone I knew, everyone I'd ever worked with, everyone on the faculty. I discovered that the more I reached out, the more I got back." She was especially interested in getting work as a freelance writer. "It didn't look very promising," she admits, "because magazines are crashing left and right." But she targeted about a half dozen friends in corporate contexts who might know of

opportunities for freelance writers, and this approach paid off. "I consistently got writing assignments."

Her coach Renée points out, "Laura followed the principle of not being afraid to network with anyone, even with people she hadn't been in touch with for years." Laura says, "Telling everyone, getting out there, was very helpful," which means she had a lot of practice describing her skills and telling her story when the "easy" interview came her way.

Making Luck Happen

Chandler can recommend the Five O'Clock Club advice about keeping in touch with people on an *ongoing basis.* An IT professional who had to persevere through a long job search, he decided last December to write "gratitude e-mails" to all the people whom he had contacted or met with during the preceding months. "Always acknowledge the people who have helped you— the Club keeps drilling this into you—whether it seems to have gone anywhere or not. You just never know." One of the recipients of the gratitude e-mails remembered that Chandler's résumé was still on his desk; he had not forwarded it to a major cultural institution as he had been planning to do. This unintended delay might actually have worked to Chandler's advantage, since the résumé arrived just as the institution was looking to hire an IT manager. Seemingly out of the blue, he received a call to come in for an interview.

Chandler knew that he had competition; in fact, he knew that he was the first person to be interviewed. "So I followed Five O'Clock Club advice and adopted the consultant mentality. So, in a sense, I took advantage of being the first one in. After the interview, I sent a consultant's report to the CIO with my recommendations. I got pulled in for the next round." It turned out that the next meeting was a conference with all the people he would be managing if he got the job.

"I just kept up with the consultant approach," Chandler points out. "I said to the group, 'What can I do for you, to help you do your jobs better?' That touched off a conversation that lasted for two hours. The boss had to come in to break up the meeting. After I was hired, I found out that the other finalist for the job had looked at the group and said, 'Nice to meet you. I'm interviewing for the position.' There was no chemistry at all. Basically, I knocked out the competition."

Since Chandler's résumé had been submitted by a friend, he praises the value of networking. "I'd never had to look for a job in my life. I hated the idea of networking. It terrified me, especially since we were in the midst of a recession." And he grants the value of ongoing support. "I had been out of work for a year, and obviously my spirits rose and fell. I had the support of my Five O'Clock Club group to keep me going." His small-group coach was Jim Borland, who points out that Chandler is an example of staying focused and determined. "He never lost sight of what he wanted to do, he never lost faith, and he kept coming back. We're very proud of what he accomplished."

Being Ready for Luck

We know from our work with thousands of job hunters that a few searches require months of blood, sweat, and tears, while others appear to be a cakewalk. But even an easy stroll to a new job can demonstrate the truth that *luck favors the prepared.* And Heather knows that she probably landed her new job easily because she had been well grounded in the Five O'Clock Club methodology. Unemployed as a result of a downsizing, she had been attending her group faithfully, but, due to family distractions, had not been pursuing her search aggressively.

Part of being prepared for the rigors of job search, of course, is attitude, and Heather's coach, Bill Belknap, helped her get to the right place emotionally. "You're never prepared psychologically for a job search, and I might have wanted to indulge myself with self-doubts. Bill didn't ignore these; he addressed them as normal feelings, and I was able to move on, which was extremely helpful. Bill was very focused, knowledgeable, and reliable. He gave excellent advice."

The group played its role too in her being ready when the right opportunity presented itself. "The group was motivational because the information that people provided was very useful. Hearing what others had to say, what they were doing, the things they were encountering—all this was very specific and helpful. This was what got me going for the week."

Heather's luck took the form of a chance encounter with a former colleague while shopping, which resulted in an invitation to send her résumé, which then resulted in three interviews and a job offer. But was it all so easy as it might appear at first glance? Heather points out that the situation developed in her favor because of principles stressed by the Five O'Clock Club. "It was most helpful," she points out, "to know that you can *negotiate* the job. I would have walked away from a number of opportunities, including the one I ultimately got, because they started talking about jobs I really wasn't all that interested in." To overcome this, she points out, "I played the role of the consultant, as opposed to focusing on my needs. I stayed focused on the company's goals and they ended up being really impressed—but you have to work at that. And, by the way, you can't respond immediately when they try to start talking about salary." The extra effort that helped her get the offer was to do a short-term research project for her prospective boss. "This reminded her of the quality of my work," Heather says, "and her colleagues got to see me in action."

She recalls that, after dropping off her résumé initially, she was even hesitant to make the follow-up phone call. "It doesn't feel good to make those calls, even in a case like this where she had asked for my résumé. But Bill kept saying to me, 'Make the call, make the call!' So I strongly recommend that job hunters do that. And when you get in for the meetings, keep in mind what the company needs. Think *broadly* about how you can be of service to them. Make them realize that you're valuable."

Landing on Her Feet— With an Ocean View

"I read the Five O'Clock Club books over and over during my three-hour commute—and they're fabulous," says Joanne Jenkins, a senior human resources executive. But after 18 years of the daily back-and-forth between Manhattan and New Jersey, she was not in love with spending so much time on the bus. She was ready for a change, and, in her case, change was precipitated when she was downsized as the result of a merger.

Joanne had actually attended the Five O'Clock Club before this happened and arranged for outplacement with the Club because all of our packages include one year of career coaching: "I didn't think that the typical three-month program offered by other outplacement firms was enough."

Wanting to eliminate the long commute, Joanne initially focused her search on central New Jersey. "I did a lot of networking," she says. "I did everything by the book. I listened to the CDs at the gym. They made the time on the treadmill go quickly. I listened to them again and again. They gave me ideas, and I'd go home and follow through."

When her 15-year-old son moved to Florida with his father, Joanne and her fiancé decided that her search could be expanded geographically. "We wanted to get away from the crowded Northeast," she says, "and one of the areas worth exploring was the Carolina coast region. I looked at a Myrtle Beach online newspaper and saw an ad for an human resources manager. It asked for résumés by snail mail, so I sent a personalized cover letter too, explaining that I was planning to move to the area. At the time I'd already sold my house." The letter brought a response from the CFO of Coastal Development and Realty, and a series of telephone interviews and conversations ensued.

It turned out that the company—a 300-employee firm—was looking for a seasoned human resources executive who could launch the HR function, especially as a new hiring phase was about to begin. Joanne was told later by the CEO that she was always his favorite candidate— although there had been three finalists—and her success can no doubt be traced to adopting the consultant mentality and thorough follow-up. "I went after it with a vengeance, using all the techniques from the books and the CDs. I treated it as a consulting assignment. Every response to him was thought through—other things that the company could do or how I might approach a problem." During each phone meeting, Joanne always had new proposals and suggestions. A face-to-face meeting was arranged when Joanne said she was planning a trip to the area. In preparation for this meeting, she put together a four-page outline of what she would do during her first 60 days on the job. "That really knocked his socks off," Joanne says, and the CFO, who had considered hiring her as a consultant, offered her a permanent job instead.

Joanne was assigned to Mary Anne Walsh for the one-on-one coaching included in her outplacement package, mainly because they already knew each other, but she attended the weekly teleconference group led by Phil Ronniger. She took part in 11 sessions. "There were good people in the group who were very helpful," she notes, "and Phil came up with ideas and suggestions I'd never have thought of. It was his constant prodding that pulled me and the others out of the normal approaches. It was great to have both Phil and Mary Anne on *my* side."

While Joanne praises the consultant mentality and thorough follow-up, she also points out that mastering the Two-Minute Pitch is vital. The first call that she received from the CFO in response to her résumé came as she was visiting someone in the hospital. "My mind was lots of other places at that moment," she says, "but the Two-Minute Pitch was so engrained in my mind I was able to pull it right out."

And there was another aspect of the Five O'Clock Club methodology that resonated especially with Joanne. "The Forty-Year Vision truly helped me sort out where I want to be five or ten years from now—and how I might get there. I'm not going to live forty more years. I'm 56, so we shortened it a bit, but I still saw things I could be doing to prepare myself for where I might be heading. The Five O'Clock Club opened my eyes to lots of other worlds and different approaches, and I needed that."

Joanne's new office is in Holden Beach, North Carolina, and, in fact, is located on an island on the beach. As it happens, she was relaxing on the Jersey beach when the call came on her cell phone, offering her the new job. "I've always landed on my feet," she points out, "but this time it looks like there's going to be sand under them!"

Answering an Ad Meant Outclassing the Competition

Perhaps because he's an engineer, Rigo Martinez was a natural for the highly structured job search methodology of the Five O'Clock Club. A resident of Jacksonville, Florida, he had been following the "Kate & Dale" column in his Sunday newspaper. The Kate in this case is the founder of the Club, so he visited our Website and signed up.

Not one to cut corners, Rigo began the process by working hard at the Seven Stories. "This exercise was most helpful. It forced me to dig into my past and revisit the things that I enjoyed. I realized that teaching should be a part of what I do." So while he was unemployed, he went back to the school where he got his MBA and got certified as an instructor.

He also appreciated that he needed to master two other Five O'Clock Club tools: the Two-Minute Pitch and the 3×5 index cards. "I actually developed several Two-Minute Pitches to use for different targets. I used the Two-Minute Pitch in telephone interviews and when I was in front of hiring managers. The 3×5 cards helped keep me focused on what I wanted to tell people."

Although Rigo did listen to the CDs when he was in the car or even out for a walk, he relied more heavily on the books. "These are fantastic. They have so many examples of what people have done in searches. They put me in the mode of being back in school and gave me things to do every day. And for résumé preparation they are invaluable." Rigo also arranged for a couple of private sessions with his Five O'Clock Club coach, Phyllis Rosen, to help with his resume. "Phyllis fine-tuned the résumé that I presented to my new employer. Obviously it got me in the door."

As a Five O'Clock Club coach, Phyllis also wouldn't let her clients fall for the fallacy that job hunting can be suspended during the holidays. "One of the things that she suggested I could do during the holidays was research professional associations." And this effort put Rigo in touch with his new employer. "I went to the Website of the local chapter of one of the professional associations I was investigating. The ad for the opening was there, and I sent my résumé."

For the first interview Rigo was called in to meet with the CEO. "It's a small company, so I went right to the top." Later he was called in to meet with two other officers of the company. Well-tutored in how to do things the Five O'Clock Club way, he asked about his competition and found out that he was the tenth person interviewed. Rigo wrote carefully crafted follow-up letters to each person he'd met. "I covered the topics that had been gone over in the meetings, and I offered suggestions on how to do some of the things we'd talked about." But his interview preparation had provided the basis for his success. "There were my 3×5 cards, but I also had a separate sheet with the names and titles of all the people I was scheduled to meet with, and I had the questions I wanted to ask each one. When I left the last interview I was pretty sure I had the job." The written offer came a couple of weeks later. Phyllis was helpful at this point too. "The offer happened to be on the low end. Phyllis suggested a strategy to convince the employer that what I brought to the table had more value than what was offered. I called the CEO and followed her recommendations to the letter. The salary negotiation strategy was a success!"

Rigo's new employer manufactures machines, especially in the paper-converting industry. But the company also plans to expand its products and services. Rigo was hired for engineering division projects. Rigo recalls Phyllis Rosen's role as the teacher in leading his weekly small group by telephone. "She was really great during the group. She came up with new ideas on how to do additional networking and approach companies. She took careful notes during each session, and at the end of the hour she always had a list of things for us to do. That was invaluable. I had homework—something I needed to do that week. It would be embarrassing to get onto the conference call the next week and make excuses. That kept the momentum going."

Getting a Job Through E-mail

Scott admits that he took a job two years ago "for all the wrong reasons," and returned to the Five O'Clock Club to get it right this time. He admits that he hates job searching perhaps more than others. "I find it incredibly painful, incredibly anxiety provoking, not fun at all. But what *was* fun was having three or four companies chasing me with offers."

Applying Club methodology, he found himself in that fortunate position, and he credits the Seven Stories and Forty-Year Vision with keeping him on course. When he finally took the time to write his vision down on paper, it was clear that he considered small companies the ideal. Since he was being wooed by a Fortune 500 company that would have doubled his salary, he realized he was about to repeat the same mistake he'd made two years ago. He plunged back into the job market.

The contact that paid off came from a Website link. His new position is with a dot.com financial services company that was linked to the Website of the funding company. He came across their earliest press releases, and, even though the company was headquartered out of state, he dashed off an e-mail with his résumé attached. Three days later he got a call from the head of business development and a few days later was interviewed by phone by the president.

Scott had no desire to relocate out of state, but the opportunity was too interesting to jeopardize. He doesn't believe "no" is a good answer in such situations. "Whenever anyone says 'Are you interested?' always say 'yes,' no matter what it is—even if you're not interested. There may be something else down the road." It proved to be the right strategy; within a few days the company invited him to open their national sales office in New York.

Scott was pleased that no one talked about money until an offer was on the table. "I'm going to be hired at market rates," was his approach during the negotiations, and he came close to matching the Fortune 500 offer. But Scott puts most of the credit for his success on assessment: "The Seven Stories and the Forty-Year Vision were the most important things for me. They kept me focused on where I wanted to go." In his Forty-Year Vision he had seen himself in a firm with 15 to 40 people. The head count at his new company stands at about 20.

The Power of Positive Consulting: Conquering Interview Fear

By Mary Anne Walsh

I was recently asked which Five O'Clock Club job search technique is the most *power*ful. Power, after all, is about control, and having control during an interview can be a major advantage. Without a doubt, assuming *the role of a consultant* is the single most important factor in achieving power and control. When this happens, the hiring manager is more likely to make an offer. Consultants are usually called in because they have the power to make changes for the better.

I am reminded of one of my favorite clients, Joe, who was a member of my Insider telephone group. The first night that he joined, it was clear that he considered himself (as most job hunters do at the outset, I might add) a lowly job hunter. He was prepared to beg for a job. A key task of the coach is to change that thinking. This psychological barrier was diminished to the degree that Joe learned to think and act *like a consultant.* He had a few tricks that worked best for him. Actually writing "I am a consultant to Company X" helped him feel and act like one. Another trick he told us about was to wear a cap that had the word "consultant" on it. I'm not prepared to recommend that to *everyone*—it might make someone else just feel silly. Whatever works for you.

But Joe said the key thing: that *thinking like a consultant* reminded him of the skills that made

him successful in his previous jobs. It removed the intimidation factor and gave him confidence to focus on the problems critical to each organization. Proceeding with this problem-solving mind-set, he was able to set himself apart from his competition and got four job offers!

There have been other Five O'Clock Club clients who have been coached to act like a consultant and have reaped the benefits. One client, Phil, really struggled with interview phobia, even to the point of developing a nervous tick. We focused on removing these barriers by helping him develop a problem-solving mind-set. After doing extensive research about a particular company, he was fired up to go on the interview in a brainstorming mode. He got passed up the chain of command, and with each meeting he gained confidence and forgot about being nervous. With this self-assurance, he landed the offer.

Another client was paralyzed by fear of interviews. We worked together to replace the fear with a problem-solving mind-set. She *loved* to solve problems and was brilliant at it. When she got the job of her dreams, her new boss told her he'd hired her because of her ability to think on her feet during the interview. He then knew how she would perform on the job.

The consultant mind-set showcases your authentic skills and abilities. Freedom from fear allows you to be yourself and engage in a dynamic interview process. For "lowly job hunters," on the other hand, interviews can be stiff, contrived situations in which you wait for the next question and hope you have the answer stored in your memory bank.

The Insider teleconference groups offer Five O'Clock Club clients a unique opportunity to brainstorm every week with others who are working hard to master the consultant approach to interviewing. What better way to get ready to outclass the competition?

CHAPTER EIGHT

The
Five
O'Clock
Club

Going Beyond the Thank-You Note to Turn Job Interviews into Offers

At the back of all of our books you will find a page entitled, "The Lexicon Used at Five O'Clock Club." This is a handy tool to keep yourself fresh on the methodology: we want you to drill, drill, drill on the crucial elements of the job search process. You will notice that we have precise terminology to help you execute every important step. For example, we say that there are four ways to get interviews: networking, direct contact, answering ads, and registering with agencies. We have chosen the word carefully here: these are four ways to get *interviews—not* jobs. Does it sound like we're splitting hairs?

We make the distinction because *interviews are not offers!* You may be able to generate a lot of interviews, only a few of which will result in offers. It takes one kind of hard labor to get the interviews, but quite another kind of hard labor to influence decision makers after the interviews. Job hunters commonly think that when interviews are over they've done all they can do. Maybe say a prayer—a really sincere prayer if they want the job badly enough—send a thank-you note, and wait for the call from human resources. This is a *passive* approach that gives competitors the edge. It's like dropping out of a

race when there are several laps yet to go. "The ball is always in your court" is one of the mantras repeated at the Five O'Clock Club. Our members learn the *active* approach to interview follow-up.

One of the early Five O'Clock Club books (1992) was *Through the Brick Wall: How to Job Hunt in a Tight Market.* This title reflected an active post-interview mentality. Do you really want the job? Are you willing to go through a brick wall to get it? Are you *not* content to sit back and wait for people to make up their minds? *Que sera, sera* may apply in some circumstances, but *not here, not now.*

Post-interview activism, however, is a foreign concept for those who are accustomed to the conventional methods of job search. "What more can I do? Oh yes, send the thank-you note, but then—isn't it out of my hands?" Thousands of Five O'Clock Clubbers have learned that the ball *still is in your court* after the interview.

Consider this fact: if you have acted like a consultant and treated the interview as if it were a business meeting, there should be some foundation of rapport with the people you met—enough to justify further communication. This is the basis for a substantial follow-up letter at the very least. We call this the "influencing letter" because you're not *really* interested in just saying "thank you"—you want to have an impact on thinking, on the decision-making process. If you've taken careful notes during the interview, which may have included meeting with several people, you should have a lot of material for creating a substantial influencing letter. But what else can be done?

If you've found out on the interview that the department head hopes the new hire can fix a major problem, spend a few hours writing a proposal on how to get the job done. Put your ideas on paper, and let the decision makers have something to study besides your résumé. One woman, who was being considered for a position that had never existed before, wrote an outline of what she could accomplish in her first three months on the job. No one asked her to do this; she took the initiative and submitted the outline. Of course she was offered the job.

We say that this post-interview phase can be the brainiest part of the job search process: you're in the final hard labor phase, so this is when we recommend that you rely heavily on your Five O'Clock Club small group. The others in your group have gotten to know your search, they've heard your Two-Minute Pitch, and coached you to get ready to meet people. They're the ones to ask, "So what should I do now?" Having the five or six brains generating ideas and plotting your next moves can be invaluable. Every interview is different, every challenge is different, so get help in coming up with ideas for influencing decision makers.

Of course, there may be some interviews that leave you cold. Perhaps you generated a few meetings at companies on your B or C list. These meetings are meant to give you practice and help you learn more about the industry. You knew from the outset that you really wouldn't want to work at Glob Industries. So you really don't want the job. But it can be part of your strategy *to get the offer.* Your morale and self-confidence are pumped up; you tend to have a different attitude

and bearing *when you have offers*—even if some of them aren't so brilliant. You're moving forward from a position of strength; you'll have more leverage when you get the offers you do want. With several offers in hand, you're more likely to get the offer you prize the most.

In the pages that follow, you'll find inspiration from job hunters who learned that the hard labor *following* interviews turned out to be the most thrilling part of the chase.

Advanced Interviewing and Salary Negotiation Skills

Arturo was happy with his career in the not-for-profit world, but wanted to find a smaller organization with broader responsibilities. He answered an Internet ad that seemed to match his background perfectly. In fact, he didn't even have to make a follow-up phone call; the organization called him right away to ask him to come in for an interview. Arturo has been attending the Five O'Clock Club regularly and had already been absorbing the techniques for interviewing and salary negotiation. "I used a number of things I'd learned here. I met with the president, and, after we'd talked a while, he brought in several members of his staff. I asked each one in turn, 'What would you like to be able to say about the person in this position a year from now?' As each one told me, I took notes. Later, I wrote e-mails to each of them. The president also had a major concern about an upcoming computer upgrade. I called my own tech support person for some advice and sent a brief proposal about the problem to the president."

Arturo knew that things were going well, but he also wanted to negotiate the best salary. At the end of another lengthy conversation, the president finally asked about money. "But I said I didn't want to talk about money. I said, 'I think we should both have time to think about all we've discussed and meet again next week.' And

I wasn't going to leave without an appointment. I don't know where I got my guts from! The president couldn't believe I was refusing to talk about money."

Before the next meeting Arturo did more research on not-for-profit salaries and on the organization and its sources of funding. When they met again they found that, initially, they were about $20,000 apart. Arturo finally suggested a compromise figure, provided there was a raise within a few months—and they had a deal. Arturo attended four sessions of the Five O'Clock Club.

Learning that Follow-Up Matters

"I had done a lot of job searching on my own," Nancy declared. "I was always getting interviews, but I wasn't getting anywhere. I frequently got to the last interview, but I never got the offer. I was frustrated when I came to the Five O'Clock Club. I needed something new."

After reading the books, Nancy realized that her follow-up skills were weak. "I was not following up as I should have." And she discovered that she had to work on her interview techniques as well. By follow-up we usually mean devising strategies for influencing decision makers soon after an interview. But it can also mean revisiting situations that may seem hopeless.

Nancy decided to write to a company that had turned her down six months earlier and was rewarded with an invitation to come back. The human resources officer remembered her and a few minutes into the interview said, "You've been reading a book on interviewing, haven't you?" "I just smiled and kept the interview on course." And in an effort to outclass the competition, Nancy left a portfolio of materials that strengthened her case—she decided not to wait to send them as a follow-up. Two weeks later she got the offer.

Nancy's coach comments, "In her small group we got her Two-Minute Pitch perfected,

and we developed a whole series of ways for her to follow up and create additional reasons for her to get back in touch with people."

Nancy attended four sessions.

A Doctorate at Age 56

"I went back to graduate school at age 48 and got my doctorate in adult education at 56." If Barbara Plasker was intimidated by the thought of age discrimination, she didn't let it stop her. She strategized how to get into a new field and devoted a lot of thought to the issue of positioning. "The challenge for me is to find the right fit and get potential employers to see what I can do, to see my potential. I don't see age as a factor—I may be in denial, but I tend not to look at it in that way, although that does creep into my fears as I go through the process." Barbara found the Five O'Clock Club assessment exercises especially helpful in defining her goals and positioning herself to get into training and development.

Even before finding the Five O'Clock Club, Barbara knew that getting experience that she lacked would help her to move ahead. While in a counseling role at a university, she volunteered for staff development and faculty training projects. "These efforts were outside the purview of my job, but gave me experience toward my long-range goal."

Barbara feels that it also helps to position herself as a person with energy; age discrimination, after all, may be largely a fear about people over 50 keeping up. When applying for a job that would require her to learn educational software and work with a different population, "I told the president of the company that I had the energy and ambition of a 27-year-old." She positioned herself so well in fact—and with such enthusiasm—that she was offered $12,000 more than the job was advertised for. "The Five O'Clock Club methodology helped me negotiate the job first and then the salary."

Barbara says that she can't recall a time when she actually felt that age discrimination has held her back, but she notes that it can be hard to read. Is it there or not? She recalls one interview in which she might have been at a disadvantage simply because of the youth of the interviewer, who was a recent MBA grad. "He was a delightful young man, but I don't think he knew what he was doing. He asked me lots of questions, but I don't know that he heard the answers."

Barbara is not necessarily focused on retirement. "I love what I do. I want to continue doing it. I'm the breadwinner in my family. I'd like to work without the pressure of having to do it. In 10 or 15 years, I'd like to feel like I'm making a contribution to the world by using my gifts and talents, and I'm looking forward to enjoying my children and grandchildren."

Barbara attended the Manhattan Central branch.

Listening to the Salary Negotiation CD—Over and Over

"The process is great, the materials are great, the whole program is really terrific—it's the best thing I've found." So says Wayne, a Los Angeles real estate executive and veteran of 10 sessions of the Five O'Clock Club Insider meetings.

Wayne signed up for the Five O'Clock Club job search seminars after registering with FutureStep.com. Since he was attempting to leave his role as director of a not-for-profit, he knew that his old résumé was inadequate. He arranged first for private counseling to help with résumé building. "The Club approach to résumés is really different, and having the one-on-one input from a counselor on résumé building was a huge benefit."

Wayne had targeted commercial real estate companies, and he was about halfway through his Insider Branch sessions when he reached the salary negotiation phase with the firm that eventually hired him. "The tactical salary negotiation methods taught by the Club were

tremendously helpful. I listened to some of the CD more than once—I listened to the salary negotiation CD many times. What I learned was really central to pulling it off well. It's something I'd never done well in the past." He did it well enough to secure the position he wanted with a real estate investment portfolio.

The group had input on salary negotiations as well, and he found that it boosted his confidence to help others in the group who were just getting launched on the process. "You're telling them to hang in there. This helps you to hang in there."

"You're a Fair Person, I'm a Fair Person": Negotiating a 60 Percent Increase

"The last two years I took all my vacation time to do volunteer work." Spencer had decided to follow the advice of the Five O'Clock Club: if you don't have experience, get it. A marketing executive for a Fortune 100 company, he was well under way in a career that many people would have envied. But he realized that this wasn't what he really wanted to do. And his Seven Stories pointed him in the direction of his passion: he wanted to run something in the not-for-profit or political advocacy world, ideally involving fund-raising.

With two years of volunteer work under his belt, Spencer felt it was time to begin testing the waters: "I started my job search with some velocity near the end of 2001." He designed a three-page functional résumé, presenting all of his volunteer and fund-raising experience on the first two pages. "It was experience—it didn't matter that I wasn't paid." He relegated the Fortune 100 job to page three. And he launched an intensive networking campaign, using all the contacts he'd developed during his two years of volunteer work. The organization that turned out to be his new employer was, in fact, one that he had twice done pro bono work for; he found out about the job through networking, and the interview process went fairly quickly because the quality of his work was known.

But Spencer had mastered the Five O'Clock Club approach to interviewing and advises against taking anything for granted. "There were two situations where I really wanted to get the offers. And there were several second-tier opportunities that I wanted to keep moving along. I worked to get six to eight things in the works and actually had to put the brakes on to slow things down. It was pretty exciting."

Spencer also kept another Five O'Clock Club mantra in mind: the ball is always in your court. "At the end of the interview, always ask, 'What's the next step?' Maybe you even suggest the next step: 'I'll put together a proposal, and let's have another conversation in two or three weeks.' I tried to manage it along." But he cautions against trying to close too soon: "If they rush you, you may not be the right person, and it might not be the right organization—so it really makes sense to do the due diligence, to make sure it's the right fit."

Spencer was especially grateful to have the benefit of the Five O'Clock Club counsel on salary negotiations. "Before I came to the Club, I assumed that an offer on the table was 'take it or leave it,' but that's not the case at all." Having put himself on course to leave a Fortune 100 company, he was concerned about "remaining whole" on money. He did his homework on salary levels and knew what the market would bear—and he evaded questions about money during interviews. "As the Club suggests, I kept saying, 'You're a fair person, I'm a fair person.' I almost felt silly saying that, but it worked." When the crucial offer finally came, it was well below what he had been hoping. "Let's talk about the job," was his response. Spencer made a counterproposal, and the negotiations went "back and forth." "It was so beneficial when we reached an agreement—it was a win-win situation."

Certainly from his perspective! By negotiating the job, the final package, which included a housing allowance and guaranteed salary

renegotiation in 90 days, was 60 percent higher than what had originally been put on the table!

Consulting Leads to a New Job in a Roundabout Way

At the end of her nine-month job search, Jody could tell that it had been a much different experience this time around. Downsized from her position with a major telecommunications firm shortly before 9/11, she found interviews were much harder to generate in the following months. "I had to do much, much more networking, but I worked on my Two-Minute Pitch and practiced it on anyone who would listen. I went to conferences, association meetings, chamber of commerce meetings, lunches, parties—you name it, I was there. It felt very aggressive, but I got comfortable with it."

Jody also decided to try consulting as a "way in," although the assignment she accepted was not one that could work out long term, since it was a two-hour commute from her home. But the assignment led to a new job nonetheless, because she was so highly regarded by her temporary employers that they forwarded her résumé to a recruiter. "I'd been meaning to register with him," Jody admits, "but hadn't gotten around to it." The recruiter got her an interview at a major money center bank— actually four interviews in one day. "They said they were in a hurry," and she was hired to do statistical and competitive analysis in one of the small business divisions. Not without some follow-up, however, despite the company being "in a hurry." "About a week and a half later I was on the corporate Website and discovered some errors. I called the hiring manager and told him. Anything you can do that is proactive can give you the edge. Everyone else is sitting back waiting—so don't sit back waiting."

"This was my second search with the Five O'Clock Club," Jody points out. "The Club gives you lots of insights and good results." She attended the Club for 14 sessions.

Reaching Out to Other Busy People and Staying in Touch

Claudio had been a vice president at a major brokerage firm for more than 15 years, so it's no surprise that his network of contacts eventually paid off in his job search—but it took a while for him to reach the point of seeing the possibilities. He admits that, initially, he spent too much time and money playing instead of working at getting a new position. When the desire to get a job finally kicked in, he turned, as most people do, to the Internet, which actually netted him a job offer . . . that fell through.

"What really worked for me," Claudio observed at the end of his quest, "was rethinking all of the people I had met in 16 years. I made lots and lots of phone calls." He eventually ended up in conversation with a man who said, echoing the terminology of the Five O'Clock Club, "I'd really like to have someone like you on board, however . . ." The snag was the budget, but Claudio was persistent. "I followed the advice in the books. I said to the guy, 'Why don't we have lunch and talk?' So we went to lunch and we talked." It turns out that the budget problem was the need to hire three executives— one for systems development, one for change management, and another for process redesign.

After the lunch, Claudio followed Five O'Clock Club suggestions for follow-up. He wrote an "influencing letter" proposing a solution to the major budget hurdle that was blocking his way. "Basically I argued that he didn't need to hire three people. I was the generalist who could do all three roles. I said, 'You need to save money,' and I sold myself as the person who represented the solution. I got all of this, by the way, from the Five O'Clock Club books." The letter resulted in a second interview, during which Claudio was able to point to his résumé and say "Here it is" as the interviewer described the various skills needed to carry out all three roles. As a result, Claudio was invited to a third interview to meet four people, and he had an offer two days later.

Claudio advises job hunters not to give in to excuses for not doing follow up. It's easy to imagine that people don't call you back because they're not interested, but Claudio doesn't buy it. "This guy never had ten minutes to himself so he never called me back. I always had to keep calling him—he was so busy."

And Claudio relied heavily on the many resources offered by the Five O'Clock Club. "Steal shamelessly from the books," he recommends. "Steal the letter formats and other templates. Steal anything you can. Use them, they really work."

Outclassing the Competition at Age 58

When Bernard's job was eliminated in a merger, he was allowed to pick his own outplacement firm. A little Internet snooping brought him to the Five O'Clock Club Website—and he liked what he saw. Although he was in Texas, the company purchased the Club's outplacement package for him, and he was soon enrolled with a private coach and a full year of group sessions in the Insider Program. Bernard had been head of operations for a law firm, responsible for all nonlegal areas, which included finance, human resources, facilities, information systems, marketing, and strategic planning. He knew that the market in his city for this specialty was limited; there weren't all that many large law firms. While his skills could be transferred to another field, he wanted to continue his career in the law-firm arena.

Although Bernard had been using a functional two-page résumé to make his age less obvious, on the advice of his Five O'Clock Club coach, Bill Belknap, he switched to a chronological résumé. He had misgivings since this meant having a four-page résumé to bring out the richness and depth of his background, but he admits that "rethinking the résumé made a big difference." Recognizing the tight market that his own city presented, Bernard followed

Club advice about expanding his targets geographically and launched a multistate campaign; for several months he was traveling to other states for interviews.

By the grapevine, however, Bernard had heard of an anticipated opening at a local law firm, even though it was many months away. He submitted his résumé and did occasional follow-up—even as he pursued his campaigns in other cities. Of course the local grapevine had alerted many other candidates as well, so Bernard was among the 14 people who were called in when the firm began interviewing for the position. And he turned out to be one of three finalists. "But I bet the other candidates didn't know about the Two-Minute Pitch and how to write the right kind of follow-up letters," Bernard says. Working with Bill, he strategized the letters to send after the final interview, during which he had met with 13 people. He wrote the same letter to the six people who would be on his staff, but individualized letters to seven attorneys. Bernard also asked his small group for advice on follow-up and was urged to send a book to one of the attorneys. During the final interview he had described this book on firm management. "Someone in the group said, 'Send the book,' so I ordered it overnight and sent it on. When the partner called to offer me the job, he mentioned the book." Bernard had obviously outclassed the competition by demonstrating that age was not a factor.

In looking back on his progress through the job search, Bernard recalled several highlights. "The Seven Stories Exercise helps capture the things you like to do. Putting the words on paper livens up what you say. And knowing the Two-Minute Pitch was so important. Obviously a lot of people will ask about your background, and, unless you're prepared, you will wander too much." He recommends faithfully reviewing the CDs and the books. He was drawn especially to the motivational quotes found throughout the books: "They help you focus on the long term rather than on the ups and downs of the day-to-day struggle." Since Bernard's outplacement

package entitled him to call into his weekly group for a year, he made a point of faithful attendance. "It's a good process, you know you're not in this alone. Getting the Five O'Clock Club package was the right thing to do."

Everybody Heard Her Two-Minute Pitch

Juliana had been in her job for 11 years managing a call center when her job was eliminated. She was offered Five O'Clock Club outplacement and believes in making full use of the right tools for getting a task done—especially when the tools are provided free of charge. "The books are phenomenal," she reports. "I read them all cover to cover, especially the résumé book. I never would have had my résumé look the way it does without that. It really stands out." Juliana also relied on the CDs. "These were very handy, especially when I had an hour-long car ride on the way to an interview. They help get you in the right frame of mind."

Juliana realized that a polished Two-Minute Pitch would be crucial for her search, and once it had been perfected, "I told everybody. When I went to the beach, I told the people I used to sail with, I told cashiers at the grocery store and people I met when I went for a walk. All my best friends heard it—I didn't assume that they knew what I was looking for."

And she took seriously the goal of identifying 200 positions and having 6 to 10 things in the works, which meant using all four ways of getting meetings. "I networked like crazy. I talked to people I hadn't been in touch with for years. I used targeted mail for direct contact. I spent a lot of time on the phone getting the right names, and I got in to see people. I went to open houses, not to apply for the positions advertised but just to be able to hand my résumé to someone in person." Now several months into her new position, she reports that she's still getting calls from companies wanting her to come in for interviews.

Juliana was put on the trail of her new job when she saw a tiny ad in the newspaper. She was not surprised when she arrived at the interview to see the two-inch stack of résumés that the ad had pulled in. She suspects, however, that she was the only finalist because her résumé made her accomplishments and experience stand out. She was hired to be assistant reservations manager for a prestigious tour company, partly on the strength of her knowledge of call center systems. Her follow-up probably clinched the deal. "I listened to the CD about follow-up letters—how they have to stand out just like your résumé." During the final interview she met with three people. "I wrote three totally different letters, explaining what I could do and how I could solve their problems. Actually about a third of my time in the job search process was spent on follow-up."

Juliana relied on her phone group as well, attending 12 sessions during the course of her search. "This was very beneficial. Hearing what the others were doing motivated you to have something to report as well. Our coach had a lot of good input I never would have thought of."

A Scientist Lands a Job in a Tough Market

In 1998, just a couple of months after Kent got his degree in biology, he was hired by a pharmaceutical company. "Looking back I see how lucky I was to get a job that was related to my major," Kent says. He received management training at his new company and ended up working on the manufacture of vaccines. But 2003 was not one of the best of years for biopharmaceuticals; in the fall, over 100,000 people in the industry lost their jobs, and Kent was laid off in a restructuring.

He found the Five O'Clock Club through Internet research and joined the Maryland branch run by Harvey Kaplan and James Dittbrenner. As might be expected of someone steeped in the scientific method, he applied himself rigorously to the system described in our books. "I purchased the four books, read them all, and used three color highlighters to mark the most important things. The Seven Stories Exercise confirmed my desire to be a manager in biotechnology. I enjoy making a product that is going to make life easier for people and protect them from fatal diseases."

After the assessment Kent devoted major attention to the improvement of his résumé. "My résumé was abysmal, and the résumé book was indispensable in helping me recast it. The positioning statement brought out my experience and leadership style. From what people have told me, that was the attention-grabbing part of the document. You want people to give your résumé more than a ten-second scan. On one of my interviews, a supervisor asked if he could keep my résumé—his mother was looking for a job, and he wanted to show it to her!"

Given the tough times in the biotech industry in the Washington DC area, Kent followed Five O'Clock Club counsel about expanding targets geographically. He decided to open his search to the eastern seaboard as far north as Boston and began getting interviews. He also posted his résumé on a major Website servicing his field, www.MedZilla.com, and there it caught the attention of a recruiter who secured an interview for him. This turned out to be the lead that resulted in his new job.

Kent was fortunate to find himself in the hands of a very competent recruiter who briefed him thoroughly about the company, and he was also conscientious in using Five O'Clock Club techniques to get ready for his meetings. "I practiced all the interviewing questions, and a lot of questions that came up during the meetings were in the book. I had my wife and others ask me hard questions, so when I went in I was as prepared as I could be."

It turned out to be a big day. He had interviews with eight people and a group lunch with the people who would be his direct reports.

Kent had taken notes throughout the day, and "on the flight home, I had enough time to outline five of the follow-up letters I wanted to send. It made the flight go very quickly." He also sent a letter to the people in human resources, "who had put in a lot of effort coordinating the whole day." Kent got his offer letter about a week later. He was hired as a department supervisor.

Throughout his search, Kent took part in his Five O'Clock Club group sessions. "The group kept me on track. It was a constant source of reinforcement and encouragement. It helped me remember that I wasn't the only person going through a rough time. It was nice to hear the success stories. I could see the system working. I saw other people not just getting jobs—they found jobs they were happy with."

Being Age 55: Part of a Winning Combination

Shirley had enjoyed a varied career before being hired, in her early 50s, by a major children's magazine; she had worked in health care for a decade and had owned her own business. In her new job at the magazine, she was involved in promoting a program that encouraged reading, and she trained more than a dozen customer service managers in offices around the United States. She was disappointed after three years when the job was eliminated as part of a much larger downsizing. She was offered outplacement through the Five O'Clock Club.

She discovered that *assessment* was the first requirement of the Club's program, and she was energized by the Seven Stories Exercise and the Forty-Year Vision. "They helped me to formulate my goals. It was very useful to get them down in writing. Now, looking back, I'm amazed at the things I wrote in imagining my future. I thought there was no way they could come to fruition, but they did."

Located away from any large urban area, Shirley appreciated the weekly connection with her small group; in her case, she participated by telephone in one of the small groups facilitated by coach Sylvan Von Burg. "The group is a really good concept," she says. "I got good suggestions and lots of support. It's important to be an active participant on a weekly basis. Stay positive and be patient. And utilize as many options as you can, such as networking, scanning the newspapers, and using the Internet."

Although the odds *against* getting a job through an Internet posting are high, Shirley believes her use of Five O'Clock Club techniques helped her beat the odds—and the competition. She visited the job board of a local newspaper and found an opening that looked right for her. "I did what the Club suggests about answering ads. I created the table showing exactly how my skills and accomplishments matched the items listed in the advertisement. The vice president who interviewed me said that she was very eager to meet me after reading my cover letter. She told me it was the best one she'd ever seen."

Shirley got the offer for her new job about six weeks after the first interview. But the first response after that interview was an e-mail telling her that they had a few more candidates to see—in a couple of weeks! "I was really bummed out, but Sylvan told me to write a strong follow-up letter offering suggestions about how I could help with some of the problems discussed during the interview." Eventually Shirley was called in to meet with three key players at the organization and was offered the job. One sticking point might have been salary, but Shirley was in a position of strength as she had a couple of other opportunities in the works. She arranged a one-on-one session with Sylvan to help her think through the negotiations.

She was pleased that the organization stretched to meet her salary requirements; in this case, she simply remained at the level of her previous job. But her new commute is much shorter. And her age worked in her *favor*. The vice president told me, "You were always my number one candidate. I was able to get the organization to meet your salary needs because of your age and experience."

Shirley's new position is a coordinator's role with an organization that promotes social and emotional intelligence programs for schools, teachers, and parents.

She urges job hunters to "do the assessment exercises, however mundane they may seem. This does help with goal setting. It's amazing, once you get it. The Five O'Clock Club was very beneficial to me, and I hope people will take its message to heart."

Getting in Through an Ad: Outclassing the Competition to Get the Job

"You want to attack the roots of the problem. You want to effect change. Actually, you want to put yourself out of business." These were Roselle's comments after a few months on her new job with a major organization for the poor in a large mid-western city. Her role encompasses both development and advocacy, so she is becoming involved in the battles for affordable housing, decent wages, and better schools for poor neighborhoods. She is remaining on her preferred career track, since her previous position had been with an organization focused on the family problems of the poor. When that job was eliminated due to budget cuts, Roselle turned to the Five O'Clock Club for help.

During a previous job hunt she had worked with a career coach, unaffiliated with the Club, who used the Five O'Clock Club approach to résumés. This time she decided to join the Club. "When I found out my group was going to meet by telephone, I wasn't sure it was going to work. I had envisioned a place to go. But after the first couple of sessions I really got to know the other five or six people, and I really enjoyed the group." The group coach, Mary Anne Walsh, "was on

target. She made me think of situations in a way I might not have. I truly appreciated that." Mary Anne also made sure that Roselle was linked up with a job search buddy from the group. "We ended up talking four or five times a week. Having someone else to talk to who knows the Five O'Clock Club process is a great practical and emotional support."

Roselle tackled the basics, including the Seven Stories, even though she had completed the exercise during the previous job hunt. "I loved the books and the CDs. The process speaks very much to me as an individual—it's all very logical and methodical. There's a reason you're doing everything. Whenever I was stuck, I would go to the books. It was very challenging for me to do the follow-up phone calls, for example. So it was helpful to turn to the books and read the rationale for this technique."

Roselle didn't have much confidence in agencies, so she devoted her time and energy to networking, doing targeted mailings, and answering ads in the newspapers and online. On one of the major Websites for people in helping professions (www.idealist.org), she spotted an ad for the job that turned out to be hers. But she knew that such ads draw lots of résumés, so she needed to outclass the competition. "You need your pitch, how you're going to talk about yourself, how you're going to answer the standard questions. But you also need the consultant mentality. Find out what the issues are, and find out why they might not hire you. As the Club says, it's not good to leave the interview dumb and happy—which is what 99 percent of all job hunters do."

Roselle understood as well that outclassing the competition meant influencing the decision makers after the interview. "You've got to walk away from an interview saying, 'How am I going to pursue this intelligently and in a way that shows what I am capable of doing?' After the first interview it was clear that the job included a focus on advocacy. I needed to show how I would approach creating a campaign." She described her ideas in a follow-up letter. After the second interview, Roselle was sure most of her competition had been eliminated "it was probably down to only one or two others." She got the offer and had obviously proved her worth. The money was a little more than her previous salary. "I'm very proud of achieving that during the down economy."

It's worth noting, by the way, that Roselle's job search spanned the year-end holidays; her job offer came in January. "I really worked at keeping powered up during the holidays. It's true what the Club says, that people are more relaxed and willing to agree to meetings then. And I didn't want to lose momentum." Roselle cautions all job hunters to manage their expectations. "The job hunt is more complex than you imagine. To be effective, you've got to refine your pitch and analyze what you're learning from the process. Above all, understand that negative meetings can actually move you forward because of what you're learning. It's a cliché to say it, but many job searches are marathons, not sprints. Sometimes there may be marathons within the marathon!"

The Ad Was a Mistake, But It Worked

Jackie can testify that burnout can be a major motivator for making a career shift. After 20 years in a human resources role with a company in Manhattan, life was sending her a message. Several factors came together that contributed to her burnout: more than an hour's commute each way to work, a death in the family, completing her college degree at night—and being only a few blocks away from ground zero on September 11th.

Her company was happy to help her try to restructure her life and offered outplacement help. Being a human resources professional, Jackie was familiar with several outplacement firms. She chose the Five O'Clock Club, because "I knew the history of the Club, and it was able to connect me with a coach close to home."

Of course, the first step in the Five O'Clock Club approach to job hunt is the Seven Stories Exercise. "I had never done anything like that before. It helped to get me focused on what I wanted to do and how to do it. The exercise really made me take a look at myself. Obviously, I hadn't looked for a job in 20 years. It was very important to read the books and listen to the lectures on the CDs."

Jackie favored networking, but the job that turned out to be hers came from answering an ad in a local newspaper. However, the ad didn't make sense; it was for a human resources generalist at a hospital and included a checklist of required skills, but at the end were the words "entry level." Although this was a puzzle, Jackie was a human resources generalist, and the hospital was only a 15-minute drive from home. She faxed her resume and was called in for the interview. As soon as the pleasantries were over, she asked about the curiosity of "entry level" in the ad. This had been a mistake—two ads were to have run in the newspaper, not one. But the one ad had brought an avalanche of 200 résumés, even from Maine.

With her impressive experience, Jackie advanced through the interview process, and she addressed head-on one issue that was sure to be seen as a negative: she had never worked with union employees. "I told them I would be glad to take seminars on the topic. And I wrote careful follow-up letters to everyone. I made my case, including pointing out that I live nearby." The offer of employment came in an unorthodox fashion. "When I got home one day, there was a message on my answering machine: 'We just wanted to get back to you. Give us a call and let us know when you want to start.'"

Jackie's outplacement package included eight hours of one-on-one counseling, in her case with coach Sharon Kassakian. "An organization like the Five O'Clock Club is so wonderful. I felt like I could call my coach even if I was just having a bad day. It's so key to have a private coach. She made me do my homework. She was tough in a good way."

A Trade Show Reunion

Many people who lose their jobs receive Five O'Clock Club job search help because they ask for it as part of their separation agreement; that is, their *companies* agree to pay for our outplacement services. Pete Healy took this approach; he knew he wanted to work with the Club because, during his 14-year tenure with Moody's, he'd become acquainted with one of our senior career coaches, Chip Conlin, a Moody's human resources officer at the time. "I wanted to have him as my coach," Pete says, "because I knew how skilled he is."

Pete's last position was with Mergent's Inc., a former division of Moody's. He has enjoyed a successful 20-year career in financial information services, so the Seven Stories Exercise confirmed what he already knew about himself. "Still, I got more focus after doing this exercise," and points out that this kind of assessment would have been handy at an earlier age: "The Seven Stories and Forty-Year Vision were certainly helpful, but they would have been perfect when I was 22!" Pete relied heavily on the books to get a grasp of the Five O'Clock Club methodology. "The books are excellent! On a scale of one to five, they're a five. Chip is a five also."

With so many years in his field, Pete decided to use his network of contacts to get meetings, and it turned out that a trade show encounter with people he already knew proved crucial in landing his new position. He chatted with a couple of representatives of Edgar Online at the Securities Industry Association trade show. "I told them I was exploring the financial information services market, and one of them suggested that he call her in a few days because she knew of an opening at the company." Pete's interest was high; he considered Edgar Online a good fit because it is in the business of selling Securities and Exchange Commission documents and fundamental data, both of which he had worked with extensively in his career.

Pete was called in for an interview with the man who ended up being his manager. The day after the interview, Pete sent an e-mail thanking him for the meeting and indicating that he would follow up further in a letter by regular mail. For the letter he followed Five O'Clock Club advice about doing more than expressing thanks for the meeting. "The influencing letter is a great idea," Pete acknowledges. "I put a lot of thought into it. I summarized the meeting and my strengths and pointed out what I could do for the organization. My new boss said to me, 'Thank you for pursuing us.' He took the formal letter as a very good sign that I was interested and that I could do things for them." The process took a couple more interviews and a few more weeks, but Pete landed the job. He became assistant vice president of corporate sales, working with sales reps to bring in new datafeed business and also managing existing accounts.

While Pete played the end game well, he credits the role of interview preparation. "Following the format of the books was very helpful, as was the Two-Minute Pitch. I'd not done something like that in my previous job searches. The group was helpful for practicing the pitch." He attended the Penn Station Branch of the Club for two months, participating in Chip Conlin's small group. He saw Chip for five private sessions as well. To other job hunters, Pete advises, "Keep at it, keep at the networking," and, speaking as one whose career focus has been financial data, he notes the value of research: "Use the Web to keep up to date on companies in the industries you're looking at. Use Google to keep a watch on the people and companies you're interested in.

Making an Internet Lead Work: A Smart Cover Letter . . . and Follow-Up

For a lot of people, an Internet job search means surfing and clicking; that is, they scan job postings and mindlessly click to submit their résumés to dozens or even hundreds of companies. Frustrated human resources officers check their full in-boxes and wonder, "Did these people even bother to *read* the ad?" Perhaps because she is a human resources professional, Jasmine knew better when the time came for *her* to look for a job. She found an Internet posting at a not-for-profit organization that looked perfect for her, so she followed Five O'Clock Club advice on cover letters. When she clicked "send," she included a letter that drew attention to the exact match between the job requirements and her accomplishments. And she followed up immediately by telephone, since she was scheduled to leave town just two days later. She wanted to confirm that her documents had been received, and she let the human resources officer know that she was going to be unavailable for a week.

"I got back on a Tuesday," Jasmine reports, "and the next day I got a call to come in for an interview on Thursday. I met for an hour with the woman who turned out to be my boss. The chemistry was great! We really hit it off." As soon as she got home she wrote a letter detailing how she could help and sent it along with an article covering one of the topics discussed during the meeting. Jasmine feels this follow-up helped advance the process:

"I was called for the second interview, and the following Tuesday I met with two more people. As soon as I got home I e-mailed my comments and thanks, and by the end of the day I got a call offering me the job."

Jasmine attended the Club for 13 sessions, hardly missing a meeting. She was in coach George Hahn's small group. "Jasmine attended every week," George recalls, "and from the very first, it was all about the fundamentals. She worked on her résumé, her marketing action plan, and Two-Minute Pitch. She generated interviews and learned how to use the consultant approach. She did a wonderful job of applying the methodology."

It is important to note that Jasmine's search took place during the summer. "Don't give up during the summer," she urges. "It's not a time to get discouraged. I enjoyed the support from the group and George. It really helped me."

Finding Out Their Objections

At the time Loretta accepted her new job, she had ten possibilities in the works and two other offers. "This method really works," she commented, "but the most important three words I can say to you are 'persistence, persistence, persistence!'" One of her three offers, for example, had resulted from an interview that took place six months earlier! "But I kept in touch with the hiring manager every month." This is what the Club means by being in Stage 2: *keeping in touch* with people who have liked you—and can hire you— on *an ongoing basis.*

Persistence must, of course, be accompanied by substance, and Loretta left nothing to chance. When she landed the interview that put her on the path to her new job—through a former colleague—she knew she had a weakness, as well as the obvious strength that she was coming in on a favorable recommendation. Loretta's specialty is fund-raising for hospitals, but this new opportunity encompassed handling public affairs as well. "That was not something I was so confident about," Loretta admits, so she knew she had to do some research. She called a friend whose specialty is public affairs and said, "I need five key talking points about public affairs to help get me ready for this interview." Armed with new information and insights, she went for the meeting, and "I knew I'd made a hit." So much so that she was called back for a second interview with four people.

After the meeting, she followed up by telephone with the person who had arranged the interview, pointing out that she would soon have to make decisions: "I'm getting close to some other things, but I'm really excited about this." The answer she got sounded very much like a rejection: "Loretta, I'm not sure what's going on here, but you shouldn't turn anything else down." Loretta wanted this job enough to do exactly what the Club recommends: find out what the problem is! She called her original contact to help get feedback and shortly got the information she needed: some of the people on the second interview wanted to hire her on the spot, but others felt she had talked too much!

Loretta called back and asked for another meeting: "You know, my last interview was very rushed, and I was so excited at the time. There are more questions I have about the job." She was given the benefit of the doubt and invited back, and she made sure she didn't dominate the conversation. In other words, she overcame the talked-too-much objection, and she got the offer.

"It's not enough to interview," Loretta advises. "You've got to *probe*. You have to be *so* proactive and do whatever it takes to keep up your confidence." And as her group coach pointed out, nothing builds confidence more than having ten possibilities in the works as you go in for closing interviews.

IT Specialist and Landscape Painter

When Steve Markus lost his job with a major publisher due to a downsizing, the company offered Five O'Clock Club outplacement, and he made a start on reading the books and listening to the CDs. "The materials were very good, but I got lucky," he confesses. He landed a new job at a health-care firm within a couple of weeks. An IT professional, he was pleased to get the break, although he knew the new situation was not as stable as he would have liked. "I took a gamble with that job. They told me during the interview that there was a chance the company would be sold." Within a few months this came to pass. Eleven months after taking the new position, he was unemployed again.

"But I'd kept the e-mail address of my Five O'Clock Club coach, Mary Anne Walsh," Steve says, and he contacted her for help as he faced job hunting again. Because the Club's outplacement packages cover job hunters for a full year, he was welcomed back, and his time was even extended. For his renewed job search he targeted publishing, new media, and medicine, and pursued a search mainly by responding to ads in local newspapers and

answering online job ads. "None of the online ads ever really came to anything," he points out, but posting his résumé on Monster worked like a charm! He got a call from an executive at Moran Towing who had noticed his résumé there, and he invited him in for an interview. "Someone actually e-mailing you because of a posted résumé? It's rare that something like that happens," Steve cautions. Moran Towing, a marine towing company with about 900 employees, turned out to be his new home.

"My boss told me later that he had a whole stack of résumés to send rejection letters to," Steve says, so he knows that the effort that he put into effective follow-up played a role in outclassing the competition. The same afternoon of his first interview, he received an e-mail from the company asking for more information, and the next week he was invited back for a luncheon meeting with several people, and "I thought I mixed in pretty well." He wrote strong letters after this meeting. "Mary Anne provided good suggestions to help my follow-up letters have more punch. I reinforced what I would bring to the table." The next meeting was with the IT director, and Steve sent a letter to him as well. There was a final interview with the vice president of IT and the president of the company, and by the end of that day he received an offer.

Steve thinks that his new résumé helped make a difference. "I worked with Mary Anne on the opening section. We stressed my creative side more and that was a good thing. I think it was a big help." His creative side includes his artistic eye, since he possesses considerable talent as a painter of landscapes. He thinks this skill even contributed to his landing the new position. "Eventually this job at Moran may be 50 percent Website related, and my predecessor had pretty much been a pure programmer. But they'll be looking for help with Website design."

While Steve recognizes that he had success with the Internet in connecting with his new position—one totally outside any target he was considering—he notes that the success rate through job sites is "pretty small. There are so many now—it's overwhelming." He advises casting the net as widely as possible. "Don't be afraid to say to people that you're looking for work. Explore as many possibilities as you can. I play ice hockey, for example, but saying you're job hunting works with any kind of group or activity you're involved in. Tell everyone what you're up to.

To see Steve's gallery of paintings, go to www.stevesbrushwithnature.com.

Remembering the Five O'Clock Club—Ten Years Later

"If you know how to run projects and know engineering fundamentals and mathematics, all the rest is just details." So says Derek, a chemical engineer with a varied background working for Fortune 500 companies. For the last five years he has enjoyed a variety of consulting roles, which allowed for flexibility and versatility. But in early 2004, he opted to look for a permanent position, and he decided to get help in tackling his job search. "No matter how deep your professional expertise," Derek admits, "the job-hunting side—that is so difficult."

When he was out of work in 1993, ending an eight-year run with a major consumer products company, he came across the best-selling 1992 Five O'Clock Club book, *Through the Brick Wall.* "I remembered this one. It stuck with me. I had read other career books, such as the 'parachute' book, but these didn't have much substance. When I went to Barnes and Noble I discovered that *Through the Brick Wall* was out of print, but the other Five O'Clock Club books were there. I got them and read them all. They're so good."

A resident of a mid-western state, Derek wanted to join the Club this time around. "I guess I was somewhat skeptical about the telephone group. I tried to visualize how it would work. I had a very foggy, tentative idea about that. But I signed up for 10 sessions." As it turned out, Derek bought another set of five to see him through his entire search. He also teamed up

with job search buddies. "That was nice. We talked outside the group meetings and shared information." His group coach was Mary Anne Walsh, and he also arranged for a few one-on-one sessions with her. "She's really good. She's very experienced and has a good sense of things."

Derek discovered that neither the coach nor the group would allow anyone to skip the Seven Stories Exercise. He'd not bothered with this during his 1993 job search, and "going into it, I didn't know at all if it was going to be very helpful. But coming out of it—it really taught me things about myself that I hadn't considered. When you really work it, it's going to be self-revealing. Even if you're not looking for a job, it's a good way for people to learn about themselves in general."

Having signed up for Insider sessions by telephone, Derek received the CDs of Five O'Clock Club lectures. "I listened to them all. I played them in the car as I was driving. The really good ones I went back to, on The Two-Minute Pitch, the Seven Stories and the Four-Step Salary Negotiation Method." The latter he found especially helpful. "If you've not looked for a job in a while, you don't know the rules and norms. Without that CD, you're just deathly afraid you could do something outside the protocols."

Derek's two most promising job offers came through a headhunter and answering an Internet ad. In the interviews he worked to uncover any objections: "How do you feel about me? How do you think I'll fit in?" And he did careful follow-up, relying on Mary Anne to help with his influencing letters. With one of the offers especially, "I was pretty convinced when I left their office that they wanted me, but I think the letter helped nail it down. It also put me in a better position during salary negotiations. The letter distanced me a little bit further from the other candidates, which gave me more negotiating power."

As he reflects on his professional life during the last decade, one of the things that Derek regrets most is the failure to reach out to people.

"Maintain your contacts and sources, even after you have your job." He now advises, "Always maintain a low-level job search, refreshing your contacts on a continual basis. It's much easier to start an in-earnest job hunt if you have warm contacts out there and everything is in place. If you forget that for five years and try to jump-start the process cold, you're out of sorts for three months."

Getting Back to the Store

"I tend to stay at places for a while. I end up being passionate about the work," commented Marjorie about her 23-year career in retail, with only three employers. Her most recent run had been for nine years with a publisher, her last position being branch manager of a local distribution facility. Her company provided her with Five O'Clock Club outplacement. Marjorie lives in Virginia, so she participated in the small group by telephone, and her private coach was Jill Silverman in Florida.

"I had never had to do much job hunting before," Marjorie points out. "Even when I got my job nine years ago, it was the only place I had applied." She admits being intimidated by the prospect—"sometimes I felt like just digging a hole and crawling into it"—but Marjorie also describes herself as a "big reader," and studied the Five O'Clock Club books enthusiastically: "I read them and marked them up. They've got pages turned down and lots of Post-It flags. I really paid attention to the interviewing book, since this was where I had so little experience." And while many people tell us that they listen to the CDs in their cars or at the gym, Marjorie took another approach. "I loved the lectures. The

CDs are very motivational. I made quiet time to sit down in my living room and really focused on them. I had a legal pad and made notes."

Marjorie explored the retail market in Virginia and used networking and direct contact to get most of her interviews: "When I wrote targeted letters, I got a great response." But Marjorie spotted a blind newspaper ad that proved to be the winning lead. "I'd never answered a blind ad, but I liked the job as it was described." She followed the Five O'Clock Club method for answering ads, calling attention to how her background matched the needs. She was called into the interview at a family-owned retail clothing business, with stores only in Virginia. "Before the meeting I visited a couple of the stores so that I already had some ideas to talk about. The interviewers told me that they'd received tons of résumés, but that I was on the short list, probably because I'd stayed on my previous jobs for a long time. They normally promoted from within, so they are used to having people remain for long periods."

Marjorie's interview had been with two people, so she wrote different follow-up letters to each. She visited more of the stores and "submitted something of a proposal, based on what I knew they needed help with. I wanted to play on my strengths." She was called back in to interview with the president. This meeting was on a Friday and lasted two and a half hours. "Call me on Monday" was his parting comment, "Let's both think about this over the weekend." On Monday morning, "I was ready once again," Marjorie says. "I told him why I wanted to work for the company and why he should hire me." He offered her the job—to start the following Monday, as regional supervisor over 14 stores.

Because Marjorie's search had been focused on a limited geographic area, which made it hard to expand her targets, the job search took longer than most. But her outplacement package provided weekly participation in her small group for a year. She attended regularly for eight months. "I didn't miss many sessions. The really key thing was that I wasn't by myself. I developed two or three buddies in the group. We e-mailed each other a lot."

And, as is usually the case, her coach facilitated engaging her in the methodology. "If Jill hadn't been there, I don't know what I would have done. She kept me going. She forced me to be open to new ideas and helped to keep me focused." When the dust had settled, Jill reflected on Marjorie's success: "She had no problem diving in and following all of the Club's steps. She did her research and homework every step of the way. She called into the group religiously. Marjorie also gave a lot of support to others."

Negotiating the Job: Everybody Wins

Nigel had a very diverse background: film production (he had done one movie) packaged goods, and food were the leading three areas of his experience. He had recently returned to New York from a job in Finland, marketing Finnish food products to the U.S. market.

Although he enjoyed marketing packaged goods, particularly gourmet foods, he was promoting his independent film that was showing in the Chelsea film festival. He was in a small group at the Club, which tried to get him to focus and *prioritize* his targets for a job search. But this was something he seemed unwilling or unable to do.

A member of his small group was in the music business and introduced Nigel to some of her contacts in the entertainment industry, basically challenging him to follow up on his interest in the highly competitive film industry. It was clear that the glamour and excitement of film were attractive, but there was a low probability of breaking into the industry.

His small group was able to help him see a creative way to use his interest in film through his interest in food. He began to promote his film, which was in Swedish, to importers of Swedish food products, during several receptions in New York. Through contacts he made, and banking on his success in developing the U.S. market for Finnish food products, Nigel was able to get an offer for a product marketing position with a Swedish exporter.

Salary was the sticking point. The CEO actually made Nigel the offer at one of the receptions, and this informality allowed Nigel to buy time. He explained how thrilled he was with the offer, but asked to meet later, after the reception, when they could talk privately. He called his group coach immediately and they developed a negotiating strategy. Then Nigel met with the CEO and focused on acting as a consultant and negotiating the job. He drew out the CEO on his ideas and goals for bringing products to the U.S. market. Nigel countered with several ideas he had, which his Finnish company had used successfully to penetrate the U.S. market. In other words, Nigel showed that he could bring more to the table. This resulted in a 15 percent increase in the cash offer and the inclusion of an incentive compensation plan. Both Nigel and the CEO felt that a win-win agreement had been achieved.

Negotiating the Offer When You've Outclassed the Competition

By Anita Attridge

After completing her Seven Stories and Forty-Year Vision, Sally decided she wanted to use her research, analytical, marketing, and telecommunications skills as a consultant. She decided that her best bet would be small-to-midsized research consulting companies in New Jersey or New York. Of course, *testing the market* is one reason for interviewing, and, as Sally interviewed with such companies, it became clear that she was not a strong candidate for consultant positions; because of her lack of experience in this market, she would probably be outclassed by the competition.

As she accepted this reality, we began to brainstorm other areas that would provide her with the same type of work. Sally had continued to increase her market research skills by going back to school, so she networked with colleagues and alumni about the types of positions that would allow her to use her research, analytical, marketing, and telecommunications skills. As a result of these discussions, Sally targeted small-to-medium IT research firms. Through networking, she learned of a position with a small, well-regarded technical research firm. She got the interview and ended up with a verbal offer. Until Sally received the offer in writing, she continued to maintain her networking contacts and even had an interview with another company.

When Sally received the written offer, she was disappointed by the money, and there was no mention of working from home two days a week as had been discussed during the interviews. I huddled with Sally to help her prepare for the conference with the hiring manager. She wanted to get more money, and working from home was important because of the long commute. When Sally called the manager, she told him how excited she was about the offer and how much she wanted to work with the company. She then discussed her concerns about the money and the commute.

When the manager called Sally later he told her he would increase her salary by $5,000, however, he wanted her to work in the city for the first three months. The company would pay to have her stay in a hotel for one evening a week, and at the end of three months she would be able to work from home one or two days. Sally received a revised offer letter, stipulating the $5,000 increase and *two* evenings at a hotel paid by the company for three months.

Sally had followed the basic Five O'Clock Club "you're a fair person, I'm a fair person" approach, which works well once you've outclassed the competition. Both she and the hiring manager were on the same side: they both wanted her on the payroll. Sally was very clear about what she wanted and the priority of what she wanted, and she also explained why her requests were important to her. As a result, she was able to negotiate effectively to meet her needs as well as the needs of the company.

Salary Negotiation Based on Research

By Terry Pile

Vanessa had been laid off from a sales position in the publishing industry in Florida. Her company provided Five O'Clock Club outplacement services, and she was assigned to my small group that met every week by teleconference. Making good use of the Club methodology, she soon had a job offer taking her in a welcome new direction: the travel industry. Although the job was a good fit for her, the salary offered was a disappointment. It was about $10,000 less than what she'd been earning. Vanessa felt that the money represented a big step backward, however attractive the job itself was.

In the small group we encouraged her to do research and find out what other sales representatives with similar jobs were making in Florida. We also discussed other perks that might sweeten the offer. Taking the group's advice, Vanessa did salary research, using Websites such as www.salary.com and www.salaryexpert.com. Then she mustered the courage to *negotiate up*. Things are stacked in your favor, by the way, if you've outclassed the competition and the company doesn't want to lose you.

When the human resources manager asked Vanessa how she felt about the offer, she expressed her concern that it was lower than the market and referred the human resources manager to some of the salary resources she had used. A few days later, she was offered a $5,000 signing bonus *and* an increase in the base, bringing Vanessa back to her former salary level. In a tight economy, she was thrilled with the success of her negotiation strategy and thankful for the encouragement she received from her small group.

CHAPTER NINE

The Five O'Clock Club

Job Hunters Who Pulled Off Dramatic Career Change

"Plastics." This is one of the most famous pieces of career advice ever given—at least in the movies. It was offered to Dustin Hoffman's character in *The Graduate* by one of his father's pals who wanted to guide the young man to a lucrative career. By many standards this might be considered sound advice: choose a career to make the most money—or at least with an eye to always having a job. And we are frequently asked at the Five O'Clock Club, "What are the *hot areas* in the job market?" In other words, what markets are booming, what industries are doing a lot of hiring? People seem to feel that this is relevant to them. But is it?

Of course, it's not hard to come up with this information; anybody can consult bulletins from the Bureau of Labor Statistics and read the financial press in general. And it is good to know the areas that are hot—in case you're interested. Of course, it's also helpful to know the industries that are retrenching; even if you're keenly interested in a sector that's suffering, you'll be setting yourself up for a lot of angst if it's your only focus. So, by all means, *do* read up on what's hot. But being guided *too much* by such information is a good way to actually *back into the wrong career*—and countless people have done just that. If I were to tell you that hiring is booming in health care, construction, and airport security, does that mean that *you* should start hunting for a job in those areas and guide *your* career in these directions? Of course not—any more than you would buy a French impressionist painting for your living room if someone assured you it was all the rage. You might *hate* French impressionist painting. And no matter how many millions of products are made out of plastic, "plastics" is not a good career *if you're not interested.*

Yet so many people get into careers that they're *not* interested in! And it's not really a mystery. It's very rare for schools to offer courses on career planning. Maybe fresh out of college, under pressure from mom and dad to get a job, facing mountains of college loans, dazzled by promises from college recruiters, swayed by well-meaning advice ("plastics"), graduates commonly stumble into their first real jobs. They settle for jobs that sound like "real jobs"—with real paychecks—even if they don't have a solid understanding of what they're getting into. Five, ten or fifteen years later, having developed expertise in their "chosen fields," people come to the realization that the choice was not well made. It's from these employees we hear, "I'm not supposed to like it—that's why it's called *work*."

We see a lot of these folks at the Five O'Clock Club. They've reached their mid-30s, 40s, or even 50s and find themselves saying, "What *am* I doing? Do I *really* want to do this for another 15 or 20 years?" Especially as people are living longer with the prospect of remaining healthy well into their 70s or even 80s, there is a certain urgency about getting into a career that is satisfying. Why not find a job that allows you to say, "I'm looking forward to getting up tomorrow morning and going to work"?

The desire for personal satisfaction is one factor driving career change; the realities of the modern global economy are another. There is far more turmoil on the employment scene today than there was just a few decades ago. Staying with one employer for decades is now an almost impossible dream, although, in so many cases, being locked in for a lifetime at one place was a nightmare. But now we remind people that the average job in the United States lasts just four and a half years. We've come to take the churn for granted. But it also represents opportunity.

Being forced to job hunt every four or five years means that people now take stock more frequently than they did before. At least, the more frequent excursions into the job market *can* prompt job hunters to ask, "Is there something else I could be doing? Does it really make sense to stay in the same groove? Is there another way?—to avoid getting beat up every few years." When people arrive at the Five O'Clock Club wondering if career change is an option, we urge them to work hard on the Seven Stories and the Forty-Year Vision. Of course, we recommend this to all job hunters, but it is especially important for those who are struggling to figure out a major course correction. And, of course, we have to manage expectations. Career *change* takes longer and requires far more research and study than staying with the same career. It won't work to

approach hiring managers in a new and different field with the message, "I'm enthusiastic, a fast learner—so you won't regret hiring me to do something I've not done before." The message of the Five O'Clock Club is that you've got to sound like an insider. You've got to get some experience that applies to your targeted new career. "Trust me, trust me" will sound hollow if you stumble through an interview with elementary questions and betray a superficial understanding of the new field you hope to penetrate.

In the stories that follow you will see how career change can be achieved through discipline, determination, and hard work.

From Shop Owner to Web Designer

Warren's advice to anyone seeking career change is straightforward and simple: get *focused,* get *experience,* and get *help.*

He had been in business for years running a record store. It was no secret that the store was in decline partly because of the Internet. Not only can people order CDs online, they can also simply download their selections. This obviously being a sign of what was to come, Warren began thinking of an Internet career. "Who knows where it could take me?"

Warren found out about the Five O'Clock Club through a friend who had heard Club coach Phil Gittings speak at the Rotary Club. Warren attended more than ten group sessions and saw Phil for private sessions as well. Warren admits that this process was crucial for helping him to achieve the necessary focus. "Focus is really the key," he advises. "Throwing out darts anywhere and hoping they'll land somewhere—that's not a good way to do it. In his time as a coach, Phil has seen a lot. He knows the mistakes people have made. He knows what works."

Warren went to school for Webmaster certification, joined a local association of Web developers, and registered with agencies. Although the agencies couldn't send him out on jobs requiring heavy experience, he was able to land a few freelance assignments, and these proved to be the key in adding relevant experience to his résumé. As the months passed, he was no longer sounding like an outsider trying to get in, and his commitment and enthusiasm were obvious. He achieved the necessary momentum and landed a job with a Web development company after going on eight interviews in two weeks.

Reflecting on the whole experience, Warren said, "I've read in the Five O'Clock Club books that people who work with a coach and a group get jobs faster. I would tend to believe that. That's the advice I would give anyone trying to change careers. Get help. Get focused as quickly as you can."

From Law to Public Relations

Catherine spent more than 10 years as a journalist in the legal field, writing for *American Lawyer Magazine* and *The New York Law Journal,* and coauthoring a book. To enhance her skills in this area, she took a year off in the early 1990s and earned a master's degree at a law school in a program for journalists.

The infusion of new ideas and experiences during graduate work and subsequent freelancing assignments prompted Catherine to think seriously about other career options. She recommends keeping an open mind as a way of discovering opportunities that may be within reach. "Don't be afraid to start exploring what else is out there. Once you start talking to people—they love to share their own experiences—you learn more about yourself, you get a sense of how valuable you are in the marketplace. It opens a lot of new doors."

Catherine is also glad that she discovered the Five O'Clock Club. "It came into my life at a really good time. I was ripe for exploring new paths. The Five O'Clock Club *gave me structure;* it helped me evaluate my experiences and skills, gave me more ideas on how to go about doing research, how to organize my job search, how to

network and make contacts. It applied a discipline to the job search process that was very useful because I was freelancing at the time."

In Catherine's case, networking intensively paid off. One of her target markets was public relations, and networking brought her to the attention of her new employer. Because of her depth of experience and academic credentials, she was brought in as a senior account executive, and she saw her role change as the company grew; she ended up heading a new group, making full use of her skills as editor and trainer. This has provided an ideal environment for her own professional development: "I want to grow, learn, change, and have new opportunities and challenges all the time."

And she recommends *keeping an eye on the future:* "If you haven't been planning your career, you should be. I learned from the Five O'Clock Club that you don't just do that for your immediate job. It's something you want to do for the rest of your life."

From Sugar Beet Engineer in Holland to Mechanical Engineer in Philadelphia

Dirck took on the task of changing continents as well as careers. The family decided to move to America to be near family in the Philadelphia area, and Dirck was faced with the challenge of offering his experience to the U.S. market. He had done well as an engineer in the sugar beet industry—yes, Holland is famous for the tulips, but actually devotes more acreage to sugar beets! On this side of the Atlantic, sugar beets are grown primarily in Ohio, and sugar refineries are scattered in New England, New York, and Maryland. It was clear that other opportunities should be explored.

Dirck met Phil Gittings at a job fair and welcomed participation in the Five O'Clock Club. "I felt I needed coaching because I started the wrong way, depending on the newspapers. And I had difficulty networking due to my cultural background—networking is only done at very high levels in Europe." He had also been shocked by the huge fees charged by some of the retail job search firms. The Club proved to be the appropriate sounding board as he made his way through the American job search process. "The Five O'Clock Club sessions matched my progress." Dirck attended five or six meetings of the Club and got help evaluating a couple of job offers. He had pursued the sugar refineries, and these efforts resulted in an offer.

But he had been scrupulous about following all leads. While attending a concert at a local college, he'd seen a job posting on a bulletin board for manager of mechanical operating systems; the college itself was looking for an engineer for its physical plant. He applied, was interviewed, and offered the job, "probably because I matched their budget and because of my engineering experience."

While Dirck is reluctant to talk about having a Forty-Year Vision, Five O'Clock Club principles seem to have played a role in his decision to move into a different field. Although the refinery job paid more money, did it make sense from a long-term perspective? "If I had chosen the refinery, coming out of sugar, going back into sugar, I don't think I would have been able to leave sugar in the future. It was my strategy to choose this way. I have opened more fields for myself as a manager."

From Executive Assistant and Office Manager to Conference Producer

Can a hobby or volunteer work play a role in making a career change? Wanda proved that it can happen. After eight years as an executive assistant and office manager, she realized she wasn't building the career she wanted. "I was comfortable, too comfortable. It was routine. I wasn't learning and growing. I needed to change that."

Wanda had done volunteer event planning for nonprofits to put herself through school and

felt that she could build on her skills in this realm. But she knew that wishing wouldn't make it so. She was referred to the Five O'Clock Club and worked the methodology faithfully. The Seven Stories were "really, really helpful" and meeting with a coach "definitely got me more focused on the steps I needed to take. It got me centered." She acquired the very practical skills needed for making a job or career change: "The Five O'Clock Club teaches you how to network and how to go on informational interviews. I got to speak with people who did what I wanted to do. And the volunteer work really helped me. It didn't matter that I wasn't paid to do it."

Wanda sent out 75 résumés in an attempt to get six to ten things in the works, but admits that serendipity played a role in her case. "The first job I interviewed for, I was hired. I had the Two-Minute Pitch well rehearsed. I was assertive in a good way. I was quick with answers because I was prepared." Hired as a conference planner, Wanda advises career changers to "keep motivated, positive, and focused on what you want, not on what you *don't* have." And don't neglect key Five O'Clock Club principles after the job search is over. Of the Forty-Year Vision she says, "I'll do it over and over again, because it keeps me focused on direction and goals."

From Magazine Ad Sales to Internet Marketing Relations Manager

Brandon had spent over 10 years in ad sales, working for trade publications and consumer magazines, then moving into Internet ad sales. He sensed that the Internet offered a promising future, but ad sales was limiting in terms of learning and challenge. "It gave me only one aspect of the business. I felt there was so much more to know. I wanted to work 'underneath the hood.'"

Brandon also sensed that making a meaningful career shift, deeper into the Internet world, would not necessarily be easy, and he welcomed the guidance offered by the Five

O'Clock Club. "I used the Five O'Clock Club to keep focused and keep on a regular schedule." He credits his success to starting his search on the right foot: "I found the Seven Stories very helpful. I urge everyone to spend a lot of time on assessment and contemplating the environment you want to be in." He saw his coach for private sessions because the résumé required major work: "I had to get people's attention away from ad sales; we had to think strategically toward e-commerce and e-business." He also attended Club meetings faithfully. "It's helpful to pay attention to all of the topics in the lectures and work with the good people at the Club, the coaches and fellow group members. Staying on target is easier when you get lots of good feedback."

Brandon networked even more enthusiastically than the Club suggests, which resulted in a six-month consulting assignment at an interactive agency working on a Website relaunch. That gave him a boost into his permanent position as marketing relations manager at an Internet marketing firm. He feels that his Internet career is well under way, and he sees a promising future: "I've been asked to expand on this role."

Brandon's advice to career changers: "Use the Five O'Clock Club method. It works really well for lots of people. Spend time with a coach and find your individual course within the process."

Building a Career Change on Intensive Research

Greg had prepared for a career in academia, but as it turned out, there were few jobs in his discipline. Faced with having to make a career change, he selected a target that seemed to mesh with his interests and personality—but about which he knew virtually nothing: market research. He read the Five O'Clock Club books and applied the methodology in earnest. He joined a professional association and volunteered to be on committees. He learned the issues and

the terminology; he got to meet the players in the industry and attended dozens of workshops. In time Greg did a huge targeted mailing to 120 companies, writing cover letters based upon intensive study of trade journals. He got results because he was positioning himself, not as a career changer but as someone already knowledgeable in the industry.

When a hiring manager told him on an interview that he didn't have enough experience writing strategic briefs or making client presentations, he spent the next day writing a brief and faxed it to the company; he also put together a sales presentation, including overhead projections, and sent that to the company. Greg had become a known quantity through correct positioning and research. He added the follow-up suggested by the Club and got the job.

Greg attended the Five O'Clock Club for six sessions, and his advice to any career changer is, "Do your research, do your research, do your research, volunteer, and network."

Relying on the Two-Minute Pitch

Tanya also credits the Five O'Clock Club with helping her engineer a major career change. She had been a manager at a not-for-profit organization, and just a year later she managed to land where she wanted: as an in-house corporate trainer. As one of the first steps, she followed her counselor's suggestion to join the American Society for Training and Development and soon after accepted a committee assignment and began the process of meeting the right people.

But she forged ahead on other fronts as well. She spent a lot of time on self-assessment, especially the Seven Stories, and took classes to learn the Internet, Excel, and PowerPoint. Having been in the not-for-profit environment only, she wanted to experience the corporate world before going on interviews in her new chosen field. She signed up for temp jobs to get assignments at major corporations, including American Express and Merrill Lynch. So she got her feet wet in the world of business, and her ego got a nice boost when some of the firms wanted her to come on board full time.

Tanya accomplished her career change after 11 sessions at the Five O'Clock Club and is pleased with her new role in a new industry. She is a firm believer in positioning and in always being prepared. The Five O'Clock Club teaches that the follow-up calls are critical in the process, and Tanya warns, "Never make calls unless your Two-Minute Pitch is ready, unless you have your resume in front of you."

Career Change: The Value of Follow-Up

Maria had been in the entertainment industry for several years, but in a sales role that she didn't care for. After devoting considerable energy to the Seven Stories, she realized that she was in the right field, "but I wanted to be closer to the entertainment product. I wanted to be in a studio or on a set or working on a show." With no experience in these settings, but possessing a music background, she did Internet research and decided that the most appropriate target was recording studios.

"I did a direct mail campaign. I wrote to about 40 companies asking for informational interviews." She got three responses, one of which was an invitation to come in for a meeting.

The studio was looking for someone with a sales background who could assist with production and handle clients. Maria followed all Five O'Clock Club suggestions for writing "influence letters," after both the first and second rounds of interviews. She even e-mailed the company president whom she had not met and forwarded articles about studios she had come across. Within two weeks she had a job offer. "I had no studio experience at all. I had never been in a studio before. I didn't know what all the little buttons were for." But she had a background in the industry that she was able to leverage. A

direct mail campaign and sophisticated follow-up techniques brought her to a new career.

From Banking to the Arts: Backing Up a Well-Crafted Pitch with Research

"I was determined to follow the Five O'Clock Club methodology," Monique admits—perhaps because she sensed that her search might be a difficult one. After ten years in banking as an executive assistant, Monique was frustrated that her love for art and antiques was not being nurtured. She had taken courses at an auction house, but she knew that moving beyond finance would not be easy.

"I spent a lot of time on the Seven Stories and on refining my goals and objectives." Her coach comments, "Doing the assessment was key for Monique. She was able to focus on aspects of her background that she wanted to bring forward—to change her résumé and her pitch and be able to deal with the questions about why she wanted to move from finance to the arts."

But Monique put just as much emphasis on in-depth industry research and is confident that this aspect of the Club's methodology paid off, too. "When I got the offer, it was a match made in heaven, because I had done all the necessary research. If I had come across the job earlier, I probably would not have recognized what a good opportunity it was." The "heavenly match" was as assistant to the head of a start-up dot.com dealing with the marketing of art and antiques, with good prospects for an expanding role in public relations; the interview had come through a personnel agency.

Monique attended the club for 15 sessions and landed her job the day before Thanksgiving.

Using Direct Contact to Change Careers

Larry went back to college to get a degree in computer science, the first step in moving out of his career in advertising. He gives a lot of credit to his group at the Five O'Clock Club for helping him hone and perfect his Two-Minute Pitch, which was a key as he intensified his networking campaign. He admits that networking didn't yield many hot job leads, "but it helped me get the technology jargon down. The more I did it, the more I could speak to people in their own language." Some of the meetings fell into place because he e-mailed his Two-Minute Pitch—without his résumé—to people at the managerial level.

"I really had to stretch my networking," Larry admits, which meant moving on to using direct contact, that is, reaching out to people whom he didn't know and for whom he had no networking lead. "I went back to the university and began digging in the online alumni network. I found a couple of people in technology who were helpful but who told me there wasn't much going on.

"Then I found someone who worked for a major corporation in Web development. I called him and said, 'I don't want a job. I just want to talk to you.'" They set up a Friday lunch, "and it turned out that they were looking for someone who had a technology background plus experience in a creative advertising environment. He asked for my résumé." On Monday Larry got a call to come in for "a meeting" on Tuesday. "Luckily," he recalls, "I had read all the Five O'Clock Club books! It turned out to be a two and a half hour interview. I met with the head of project management, the head of operations, and the managing director for the New York area."

He was especially thankful for the Club advice about taking notes during interviews. He huddled with his group coach for help to create "influencing letters." "I followed the templates in the books and made a matrix illustrating what they were looking for and what I had to offer. I hand-delivered three letters to the people I'd met and a thank-you note to my initial contact."

The offer he wanted came two weeks later, and, in the meantime, he kept networking and going on interviews. His group coach

commented: "Larry found out that changing careers can be very discouraging, but he never gave up. While he was waiting for that offer, he kept the momentum going—in fact, his attitude is what added to his appeal." Larry was also glad that he listened to Five O'Clock Club advice on negotiating salary. "On the interviews I declined to talk about money. When the offer came it was more than I had been expecting—or would have asked for. I would have shot myself in the foot." Larry attended six sessions.

Doing It By the Book— the 'Cookbook'

Andrew admits that being employed made it rough to execute a career change. "I envied all the people at the Club who were unemployed. Look at all the time they have!" But he also confesses that he had to go through an "attitude change" before he could make much progress. For a long time, he attended the Club on an off-and-on basis, sometimes dropping out for months at a time. "I would call it career frustration. I wasn't doing what I wanted to do. I was a software consultant and a frustrated 'activist.'"

But when the attitude shift happened, "he became the poster child for networking," according to Andrew's group coach. To get ready for networking, Andrew finally did the Seven Stories, retooled his résumé, and decided to follow the methodology step-by-step. "To me it was like using a cookbook. I highlighted sections of the books and just followed all of the directions."

"I had personal sensitivity to making phone calls, but I had to get a business mentality about it: I'm offering them something, they're offering me something. I was familiar with this as a software consultant; I just had to apply it to the job search. And I managed to get 4 to 6 things in the works sometimes, 5 to 8 things at other times. They do fall away through no fault of your own. When something doesn't work, don't take it personally." When Andrew found out about the opening that he eventually was hired for—at a major environmental not-for-profit—he submitted his résumé. "I used all the Five O'Clock Club techniques for interviewing and follow-up letters." He was hired to work on a campaign to protect the New York watershed area from overdevelopment. The frustrated activist had found his niche. "The watershed provides safe water for nine million people. It has worked for over 100 years, but now it's threatened."

In addition to developing the right attitude, Andrew recommends finding a job search buddy—one of the benefits, in fact, of being in a weekly group at the Five O'Clock Club. "I found an 'action partner.' We called each other every two or three days, just to check in, compare notes, keep on track, and stay motivated."

A Move from Publishing to Academia

"I was pleasantly surprised when I found out that my company had arranged for Five O'Clock Club outplacement," Kevin says. He was one of about 300 employees let go by a publishing giant in the summer of 2003. A graduate of New York University's Stern School of Business, he had heard Kate Wendleton speak a couple of years previously at an alumni event, and he had once spent an afternoon at Barnes & Noble reading one of the Five O'Clock Club books. "I ended up reading almost the whole thing in a couple of hours. It made so much sense I bought it a couple of days later."

When Kevin's two-year job at the publisher came to an end and he was assigned to work with a Five O'Clock Club coach and small group, he intensified a self-examine process that was already under way. "I did the Seven Stories, which confirmed what I had already suspected. That is, the track I had been on was surely not in line with my likes and talents. I had been in the private sector, in business and marketing, for over 10 years. I had been asking myself if this

was something I wanted to do long term. I didn't want to look back and claim to have generated tons of revenue and sold lots of products. I know I like kids and I like sports. I realized that I really wanted to have an impact on young people."

With this kind of career change in mind, Kevin realized that he needed to do extensive research on the not-for-profit world. "I was able to get a lot of meetings, and I wouldn't have been able to do it without applying the Five O'Clock Club concepts. I used all four ways to generate interviews, and I did the follow-up required. I am not an outgoing person—not the kind who loves making phone calls. It was difficult, but I learned how to do it effectively."

He also learned what many job hunters discover when they explore a tentative target: it's probably not a good idea after all. "I learned a lot about the not-for-profit world, and I realized that I wasn't cut out for working at a children's not-for-profit in general. But I did narrow it down and decided that a school was a place where I could be very happy."

Kevin happened upon the right contact while taking a class, where he met a school administrator. He was called in for interviews at a New York City independent school and was hired as an admissions officer.

Kevin feels that he is in full possession of career management techniques that will last a lifetime: "The Five O'Clock Club principles have become so engrained. They feel second nature to me now."

New Energy, New Career

When Juliet arrived at the Five O'Clock Club, she had been unemployed for a year, and her morale reflected the frustrating job hunt she'd been conducting. Having specialized in a particular niche in the publishing industry, she was seeking desperately to stay on that career track—despite the odds. "I had been too narrowly focused, and that was a big mistake. In one year I had uncovered only five jobs in the entire industry that were appropriate for me." Since we emphasize that a successful job search—resulting in a position that you really *want,* not one that you'll *settle* for—means identifying 200 positions; new possibilities were the only cure for Juliet's situation. "It was clear the first night that she came," her group coach said. "Juliet thought her situation was all doom and gloom. But with a shift in focus there was more energy, and things began to happen."

As is commonly the case with people compelled to consider new careers, Juliet needed ideas, and she decided to ask for help with brainstorming. One of the most obvious sources for help was her former clients—people who knew the quality of her work and her skills. After just a few meetings, the same suggestion kept emerging: she would probably be well suited for the licensing or promotions industry. She could use her skills in sales and marketing, and she could make use of her former publishing industry contacts.

Juliet attacked the primary problem for any career changer: learning as much as she could about her targeted industry—learning so much, in fact, that she would sound like an insider. "I reached out to anyone. I just kept writing down names of people to contact. I used industry newsletters and did a lot of informational interviews." She soon had a pretty clear picture of the licensing industry and knew the areas she wouldn't want to pursue. And she eventually ended up in an interview where things clicked. "How about if you hire me?" Juliet asked, and the hiring manager said, "I think I will."

Juliet feels she has found her new niche, one, in fact, more to her liking because of the entrepreneurial atmosphere, where she senses much stronger potential for long-term growth. She attended her Five O'Clock Club group only three times, but the change in perspective allowed her to break out from a year of frustration. She landed her new job three months after starting with the Club.

Payoff from a Targeted Letter

The more Samantha researched, the more she kept coming across the name of one industry leader. He was obviously a major player in a field she wanted to pursue. "I really wanted to talk to him. He knows all about what I'm interested in." But because of his level she was reluctant to reach out to him. When she brought this up with Renée Rosenberg, her group coach, she was encouraged to contact him, and they formulated a letter. "We followed the four-paragraph format recommended by the Club. In my introduction I pointed out that we'd gone to the same school and that I'd read his book and articles he'd written."

Of course, targeted letters require a follow-up phone call. "I had to work up the courage to call," Samantha admits. "The first time I left a message, but the second time he actually picked up the phone. He was on another call, but he said, 'Oh hi. I really got a kick out of your letter.' He asked for my phone number, and he did call me back."

In fact, he asked Samantha to come in for a meeting. She met with Renée again to be as prepared as possible for the meeting. During the meeting he praised her again for her letter and encouraged her to keep in touch by e-mail. "Don't send me letters. I don't read letters that come in the mail." Yet somehow, Samantha notes, her letter had come to his attention.

Samantha continued on her job search, but, at a meeting of the Grand Central Branch, she reported this success with a targeted letter. She managed to meet the high-level person she'd targeted and ended with a mentor as well.

Career Change: Creating the Perfect Job for Himself

"When I go to bed at night," Pete Ice says, "I'm so excited about getting up for work the next morning that I can't get to sleep. I sometimes have to get up and watch television to settle down." This is the happy ending that Pete could not have foreseen when he first lost his job in a downsizing. He admits that he was "angry at the world for the first few weeks, and I wasn't very open to coaching." But he agreed to begin working with his coach, Suzanne Harwood. "She didn't want to hear my complaining. She wanted me to get on with finding my next job."

But there was something about the shock of being unemployed that worked in Pete's favor. In short order, he came to look upon this twist of fate as an opportunity. "I wanted to think outside the box. It's too easy to just continue what you have been doing. For 13 years I'd been selling educational products to schools, but my gut said 'there's a bigger purpose.' I was in the field by default because it had been my first job." One thing that emerged from Pete's assessment was his *love for houses*. "Suzanne and I looked at the various industries where this might apply, and we thought I should explore becoming a home inspector."

Fortunately, Pete has a relative back in Minnesota where he was raised, who has been in real estate sales for thirty years. He set up a meeting with her that turned out to be one of those rare life-altering events. "You'd make a fabulous inspector, Pete" she told him, "but most real estate agents already have good inspectors they rely on, and the income will always be in a certain range. Our family has been in this community for 120 years. I'm here to answer questions and be your mentor. You've been a salesman for 13 years—you should think about real estate sales." Pete did think about it, for about six hours, as he recalls. "Then the lightbulb went on . . . 'oh my gosh, this is it,' I said. 'I'm going in this direction.'"

Suzanne's reaction was one of caution, since real estate sales is one of the toughest fields for people to get into—and survive for more than a few months. Pete was determined, but he also saw the wisdom of doing as the Club suggests, namely, *talk to people in the*

industry as a reality check. His relative/new mentor helped him get a meeting with the head of the largest real estate firm in Minnesota, Edina Realty. Suzanne helped him prepare the list of questions to ask: What's it like to be in real estate sales? What do you see in people who are successful? (And in those who aren't successful?) What are your expectations for new hires? "Suzanne coached me on how to approach it all as a consultant, and the interviewer was impressed with how I handled myself. He told me they would love to have me on board as soon as I passed the real estate exams." But Pete wanted other opinions as well. Altogether, he met with eight other real estate agents, some of whom had been in the business for less than two years. "They told me," he remembers, "that they struggled the first year. It's all about hard work."

Pete finished his licensing courses and went to work for Edina. And he remembered the Five O'Clock Club message about the right attitude and correct positioning. "At my first big open house, I *wasn't* saying to myself, 'I am a brand-new agent who hasn't done a deal yet.' Rather my attitude was 'I am the best and the brightest and I'm the top selling agent on Lake Minnetonka!' It's all about confidence." And after his first full year in the business he could look back with satisfaction: "My boss can't believe it," he reports. "I'm on course to triple what is expected of new agents."

Reflecting on his Five O'Clock Club experience, Pete especially credits his work with his coach: "Suzanne was phenomenal. She's the one who picked up on where I was—on the rebel side—and challenged me, got me engaged in the process. I was committed to not just accepting another job. I would tell anyone to use job search as a time to really create a vision for the rest of your life."

Now firmly settled back home in Minnesota—not known for its mild winters—Pete's Website is www.anothericehouse.com, and his firm can be found at www.edinarealty.com.

Career Change in Ten Sessions

"For about a year I had been dissatisfied with the way things were going," Lilly says. "I worked as a financial analyst for a small consulting firm, and I wanted to improve my career. My ten sessions at the Five O'Clock Club were a gift from a friend. I benefited a lot from this experience. For the first time, I really knew what I wanted to do, and I worked hard to get the opportunity. It's one of the best gifts I've ever received."

Lilly was assigned to coach Roy Cohen's group, which usually includes people well along in a variety of financial careers, hence she was able to brainstorm her job search every week with peers and those at higher levels as well. "I got a lot of advice and a lot of help from these people and from Roy. It became very clear that I wanted to make a career change into the fixed income area." Lilly is a careful student; she read the books and didn't miss any of the first-hour lectures.

She landed the first interview in her target area as a result of attending a job fair that she had heard about through an e-mail from the Five O'Clock Club. "I really wasn't all that interested in the company because of its location, but I went on the interview anyway. It was a great opportunity to practice my presentation skills and learn more about the investment industry."

In fact, in another interview she got an even better idea of how much she had yet to learn. "There were many questions that I couldn't answer," she admits. "But I took notes that guided me through more research and study. On the next interview I was able to answer the questions." Lilly was mastering the art of sounding like an insider, so much so that she passed what might be considered the ultimate test: an interview day in which she met with 10 people. This resulted in a job offer. Lilly turned to Roy for help with salary negotiation. "This was difficult, because I was changing careers," Lilly points out. "I didn't have experience in this new area at all." Even so, she managed to get a 50 percent salary boost!

Roy was impressed with her achievement. "She took the Five O'Clock Club methodology seriously, embraced it and ran with it. She is fearless. As demure as she appears, she is an iron butterfly. She would come to the group, then go right out and make the phone calls. She did everything very systematically. Most important, she attended regularly—I think it was almost 10 consecutive sessions."

Helping Seniors: Becoming an Insider in a Specialized World

Changing careers is not for the faint of heart, which is why people often coast along for many years in jobs that wear them down. They coast until they collect their pensions and more than their fair share of regrets. Career change does require courage, but it also requires vision, persistence, and commitment to a proven methodology.

Evan Gansl brought the full measure of devotion to his quest to redirect his career; his vision pulled him along, and he had the Five O'Clock Club at his side to provide the method, the techniques, and the coaching. Evan had begun his career as an attorney, but practiced only three years before moving into financial planning. For nine years he worked as an insurance and financial advisor specializing in long-term care insurance. He loved his clients, but wasn't happy at the prospect of continuing as a financial advisor forever.

By early 2004, working with his private coach, Ellis Chase, his ideal career path for the long term took shape, and it made practical sense because he was targeting a growth industry. "For years," Evan points out, "I had told colleagues that if I ever practiced law again it would be elder care law. After all, the vast majority of my clients were seniors whom I had been advising about estate conservation and long-term care planning. All the demographics were there. Seniors are the fastest growing segment of our population. This will be a growth area for the next 20 years." So while his choice was obvious, he knew it wasn't going to be easy: "My biggest concern was that it had been almost 12 years since I had practiced law, and I had only three years of experience as an attorney. Would this really be viable since I had less involvement in law than a recent law graduate?"

Evan knew that he faced a steep learning curve and that he wouldn't have a chance of being taken seriously unless he could mix and mingle convincingly with leaders in elder care law; in other words, he would have to work hard at sounding like an insider. In such a highly specialized arena, in fact, he would have to *become* an insider before he would get a job offer. He moved ahead on several fronts.

For a rapid introduction into any new career field, the Five O'Clock Club recommends diving into the professional associations. Evan knew that this would be vital. "So I joined the National Academy of Elder Law Attorneys and the Elder Law Section of the New York State Bar Association. I read the quarterly journals of both organizations to get up to speed on the current issues in the field. I joined their list serves and religiously monitored all their traffic."

A second front was formal education, which sometimes is hard to squeeze into the daily routine, but Evan took advantage of all opportunities: "I attended every continuing education seminar relating to elder law offered by the bar association. In total, I took more than 13 courses, including correspondence courses. I listened to the lectures every day to and from work in my car, and I read the written materials during my lunch hour."

With the Five O'Clock Club goal of ultimately targeting 200 positions in mind, Evan also developed his network of lay people and lawyers who could connect him with elder law attorneys. He attended the Club's Grand Central Branch and was in coach Bert Marro's small group. "In the group I refined my Two-Minute Pitch. I had to call attention to my unique combination of skills. I separated myself by

showing that I was different. I could offer things that other attorneys could not: an established base of clients and expertise in long-term care insurance. I also had the insurance and financial planning certifications."

Evan was put onto the trail of the job he ultimately landed by seeing an ad in the *New York Law Journal,* but the process, as it turned out, was not so simple as "answering an ad." He submitted his résumé and got no response. Since the name of the attorney looking to hire was in the ad, he used a referral from a colleague and a letter to arrange a networking meeting with her. "In my letter," Evan says, "I explained why I wanted to see her. When I met with Kimberly she was highly encouraging that I was on the right track and had impressive credentials. Her job opening was not even brought up."

Eager to learn more and broaden his network, Evan attended both the August and October three-day conferences of the Bar Association of New York's Elder Law Sections. At both he met with Kimberly again, and at the October meeting she asked him to join a committee, and he accepted an assignment. By now his networking and newly acquired knowledge were paying off: between August and October he had interviews with five law firms. In November he saw Kimberly's ad again in the law journal. He now knew her well enough to call her and ask to be considered. The person she had hired many months previously hadn't worked out because of a lack of real commitment to elder law.

By this time Evan had several offers in the works, but he accepted an offer from Kimberly. In truth, any competitors pulled in by the new ad probably didn't stand a chance because Evan didn't represent a risk; his commitment to elder law was obvious. "Kimberly had been very helpful and honest with me from the beginning," he observed, "and is giving me an opportunity to gain experience. She will be a great mentor." Much of his success is based on the reputation he worked so hard to build. "Kimberly told me that she recently ran into another well-known elder care law attorney in her building. She told him that she had hired me, and he said he knew of me and had met me at conferences. This has been highly satisfying."

In his experience with the Five O'Clock Club, Evan got help from other coaches as well, including Ruth Robbins, George Hahn, and Renée Rosenberg, and he acknowledges the valuable input from the small groups that he worked with. "In sum, I found out that the Five O'Clock Club methodology works. Because this was a career change, the key was to become an insider—and to be patient and persistent!"

Using the Two-Minute Pitch to Maneuver a Career Change

"Up until the time I lost my job at a bank, I had coasted through my career. This was the first time I had taken control, and the books were a wonderful resource for that." So says Chip Fears, reflecting on his experience working with the Five O'Clock Club materials. His 20-year career in banking came to an end when his employer was absorbed by another company. He took a year off to complete a master's degree in history and came to the Club upon the recommendation of a friend, "although I'd known about the Club for years through the media."

One of the first things Chip discovered in the books was the Seven Stories, and this exercise demonstrated that he would like to combine his skills in finance with his love of education and learning. His exploration of the job market in higher education proved to be a disappointment, so broadening his targets was in order. "One day I just went onto Idealist.org and created a large Excel spreadsheet, trying to identify enough targets in the not-for-profit world to compile a list of 200 positions. I obviously aimed for institutions that sparked my interest, such as those related to human rights and the fight against AIDS." He used his finance background to market himself as a general business manager.

Chip arranged a couple of private coaching sessions with his coach, Dwight Clarke, to get his résumé reworked appropriately. And he pulled some volunteer experience into his résumé positioning statement: he had been treasurer and president of his co-op board, working especially on the roofing and windows committee. This was practical, current, and as it turned out very appropriate information.

Chip also worked hard on his Two-Minute Pitch. "I had the 15-second version, the 45-second version, as well as the two-minute, and I told everyone I ran into." This willingness to spread the word proved to be the key in finding his new job. One day when helping a new neighbor move boxes, he recited the Two-Minute Pitch when he was asked, "What do you do?" She asked for his résumé and passed it on to others; it was eight months later that she informed him of an opening for a business manager at St. Luke in the Fields Episcopal Church, and he sent his résumé. A friend knew someone at the church as well and asked for his résumé. Within a few days Chip was called in for the interview. A week later, he was offered the job.

But by the time he sat down with the church search committee for that interview, Chip had been on about 20 networking and job interviews and had mastered Five O'Clock Club techniques. "I asked, 'Is there anything about my background that would make you hesitant about hiring me?' and I probed for the key things they were looking for in the ideal candidate. I based my follow-up letter on their responses." By the afternoon of the next day Chip had hand-delivered his follow-up letter to the church, along with his list of references. The church acted quickly because the current business manager was about to leave the position, and one of the decision makers was about to leave on an overseas trip. Clearly, however, the church had found the right candidate; it turned out that Chip's co-op committee experience was considered a real plus since the church owns residential properties.

But he had also learned about a new world. As his other group coach, Anita Attridge, points out, "Making the transition from profit to not-for-profit is not easy. Through networking, Chip learned the not-for-profit language, and he learned how to position himself." Most important, he is now aware that career coasting is a bad idea. "The Five O'Clock Club gave me the structure I never had," he emphasizes. "Following the books I developed a plan and a strategy. I'll keep the books forever." And the personal element he found at the Club was vital: "Dwight and Anita brought a delightful enthusiasm to the process. They urged me to keep plugging away. It's work, they always said—there's no magic bullet."

Getting Back on the Farm

"If you had asked me when I was twelve years old what I wanted to be when I grow up, I would have said 'bovine veterinarian.' I spent my summers on a farm when I was a kid." So says Suneet Ashburn, reflecting on her recent major career change. Even with strong science skills, Suneet opted for a business track instead of medicine. She has an MBA with a focus in international marketing.

She spent almost 15 years in a career focused largely on sports marketing, but sometimes with a twist that reflected her love of animals—for three years she did marketing in the thoroughbred racing industry. But by 2004 she knew that sports marketing was the wrong career path.

Suneet is also a veteran of the Five O'Clock Club, and this time around she decided to put a lot of effort into the Seven Stories. Her private coach, Ruth Robbins, recalls that this was viewed as the foundation for a career change: "We knew that Suneet needed to regroup completely by redoing the assessment. The attitude was, 'Let's get a fresh start on this.'" And one target that emerged was the pharmaceutical industry, in the divisions that dealt with animal health. Her strong marketing abilities might prove to be a way in.

Suneet networked relentlessly—even at a wedding. In fact, two important leads came at

the wedding of a friend whose boss's wife turned out to be a director of the animal health division of the company where Suneet was eventually hired. And a friend of the bride knew a lawyer at another pharmaceutical animal division.

She also did exhaustive research and honed her Two-Minute Pitch. "The pitch developed over time," she points out. "It is always a work-in-progress. I became an insider. In fact, when I went in for interviews, I knew more about what was going on with competitors than the people I was speaking with." Eventually, because she was becoming known (after many conversations with the people at the company that hired her), she was called in for an interview for a position in a new dairy initiative. "I met with five people and followed up with slightly different letters to each one," Suneet reports, and a few days later she got the job offer. Suneet was hired to be assistant territory manager of the dairy division for the company's animal health business. She is a sales representative targeting dairy farmers and veterinarians.

Suneet paid attention to small things that contributed to her successful strategy. Since she was working hard to get her career going in animal health, she wanted to add something that could give more weight to her cause. Perhaps a part-time job at an animal clinic might be a good idea. She made a list of all the animal clinics in her neighborhood to call on. At the first one she was offered a weekend receptionist's job! "I did this for just two and a half months. I worked at the front desk and talked to people, assessing whether they should bring their pets in," she says, "and I could talk about this on interviews."

Reflecting on what worked for her, Suneet recommends not skipping any part of the methodology. "The whole is greater than the sum of the parts. I worked on all of it," she points out. "The power is in the whole methodology."

When Suneet reported on her job search at the Club, she mentioned that coming back to the Club to report was a motivator: "I have to get a job because I want to give my speech!" In offering his congratulations, her group coach George Hahn commented, "I don't think I've met anyone else who knew at age 12 that she wanted to be a bovine veterinarian, and she managed to come pretty close to that."

Getting on Course for the Right Career Change

Mario knew he wanted out of the restaurant business. For 20 years he'd made his living building and operating restaurants, and now it was time to move on. He saw himself in a role helping other people set up small businesses, "but before I came to the Club I didn't have a clue as to how I was going to find the right kind of job for me. Well, I found it by using the Five O'Clock Club method—period!"

Mario discovered that the first order of business was the Seven Stories Exercise. "This was crucial," he points out, even though he was clear about his general goal. "I had a lot of unfocused thoughts. Maybe I want to do this, maybe I want to do that. It's a nice thought to want to help others set up businesses, but I needed to make sure I wanted to do this. The Seven Stories, moreover, helped me pick the right targets. In the initial phase of his effort to work the methodology, Mario used a half-and-half approach. "I spent half my time refining my targets, then the other half finding the specific organizations that might have jobs that would interest me. It ended up being a very finite list of organizations. Then I had to figure out how I was going to get in to see them."

The weekly group provided peer pressure to keep him on track. "When I started with the group, I got the message that you're not a real job hunter unless you work at it 35 hours a week. So I said to myself, 'Okay, this is going to be my job,' and I stuck to it. When you do it that way, you really feel like you're getting something done. It's important to commit to this. It puts structure into your search. I knew what I was going to be doing on any given day, and I knew when I came to the group on Monday I would be held accountable. It was like going to school and having to report."

This level of energy and determination proved to be important for Mario in pulling off the career change. Even when responding to ads, he realized that sitting back and waiting would be useless. "When you find a job description," he advises, "figure out how to get to the person who is doing the hiring—then follow up and keep following up. I always got in to see the person." And Mario strategized the interviews. "This is really important. I studied the job descriptions and had a written sheet with me: how my skills matched their needs. But I also knew what I didn't have. I was ready to explain how I would get what they wanted or how my other skills could compensate for what was missing."

As it turned out, a friend knew the hiring manager at one of Mario's targeted organizations and submitted his résumé, which brought about the meeting that resulted in his new job. This kind of luck may tempt some people to say, "Well, that was pretty easy after all." But, as Mario's group coach, George Hahn, points out: "The many months of study and preparation were the key to success when he got in the door for the interview. It all worked so well because he was fully engaged in the process.

Mario was hired by a not-for-profit organization that, among other things, helps people to set up their own businesses. By his reckoning, the career change took five months, and he attended the Club for 14 sessions.

Working Hard to Become an Insider: The Key to Career Change

by Anita Attridge

Susan had worked in the publishing field for eight years. Although she liked many aspects of her job, it was not her desired field. She really wanted to become a librarian.

Susan knew she would need to go back to school to obtain a degree in library science, and she was willing to do that. Her job target was to be a trainee in a library. Although she knew this would be a challenge—after all, most trainees don't have eight-year work histories—she set out on a dual track to achieve her goal. She began informational interviews with the librarians in her town and surrounding areas. She also completed her application to obtain a master's degree in library science. As Susan continued to conduct informational interviews, she was able to network into most of the libraries, share her résumé with librarians, and tell them about her application for a master's degree in library science. Susan was accepted into the library science program.

Susan was now at a point where she wanted to move on another job, even if it had to be in publishing. So she developed her targets in this area. She would spend two more weeks focused on the library positions; however, at the end of two weeks, she would shift to finding a position in the publishing field and would obtain her library science degree at night.

Since Susan was a persistent networker, she contacted each of the librarians she had met, told them of her acceptance into the library science program, and reiterated her desire to work in a library. One of the librarians called her to inform her of a librarian-in-training position that would be opening shortly. Susan contacted the hiring librarian, using the name of her networking contact, and was invited in for an interview.

During the interview, Susan used the consultant approach to learn the needs of the library and how the librarian-in-training would work with the staff. She wrote a compelling influencing letter stating how her current skills and the skills she would be learning would enable her to meet the job requirements discussed. Susan was offered the position.

Later she learned that her networking contact had been a strong supporter. Because of the networking meetings, continuous follow-up, and her acceptance in the library science program, her networking contact saw Susan as a person who clearly understood her goals, was dedicated to achieving them, and had the skills to be a strong contributor in the library field.

From a Corporate Job to Working in a School

By Renée Lee Rosenberg

Marcel had a feeling that he wasn't on the right career track working for a corporation. "I didn't feel fulfilled. I had always loved kids and had enjoyed working in schools on a volunteer basis since college. In my job I was making good use of my talents and skills, but I needed to feel good about what I was doing and had begun to think about how I could make a transition."

As it turns out, Marcel was laid off from his corporate position, and, as he puts it, "My employer was wise enough to send me to the Five O'Clock Club for outplacement, and I hit the ground running."

He immediately began meeting with his small group in weekly sessions, and he started his private sessions with me. We worked on his résumé and cover letter and the overall job search strategy required for a career change. "I talked to as many people as possible, mostly on an informational basis, mostly with people in the nonprofit world, particularly in organizations dedicated to children's causes. Some weeks I met with five or more people. Generating those meetings and going on them was tiring, but I was learning about a new realm and about myself as well."

Soon after beginning this phase of his exploration, Marcel was introduced by an old friend to the head of an independent grade school. As it turns out, this school needed part-time help in its administrative offices. "I jumped at the opportunity," he says. "This was a chance to build on my experiences volunteering in schools, meet a lot of insiders, and get a better feel for what it was like to work in this environment. Although I knew I didn't necessarily want to become a teacher, I thought there could be some other avenues to explore. This allowed me to get the experience that I needed."

A key factor in career change is becoming an insider—or at least sounding like one—and somehow getting one's feet wet. With his experience in the administrative offices, Marcel was getting the exposure he needed: "I began to realize that I could picture myself working in a school. What better place to be around kids and have a direct impact on their lives? I learned that I had skills that could be well suited for some independent school administrative positions, and perhaps I would even have the chance to coach sports!"

We refined his résumé and cover letters further, and he was able to look more seriously at positions in schools. School administrators were also more inclined to put his résumé in the short pile. Using all four ways to generate interviews—direct contact, networking, answering ads, and recruiters—Marcel set out to meet people in a position to hire him. "And meet them I did. Within a few weeks, I accepted the job I wanted at a prestigious independent school. I work in an administrative position, leveraging my business and marketing skills. I will have the opportunity to coach and become involved in the school community in ways I never dreamed!"

CHAPTER TEN

The
Five
O'Clock
Club

Consulting: Perhaps as Transition, Perhaps Forever

Sometimes career-minded people might feel like they're facing the perfect storm: so many mergers and take-overs, so much outsourcing and offshoring of jobs, the globalization of the economy, and the complete disappearance of the ideal of staying with one employer for decades. How do you keep a healthy career on track in such an environment?

These days we commonly advise recent college grads that they can expect to have four or five *careers* and as many as 10 jobs before they reach retirement. Even now most jobs last less than five years. If we meet someone who has been with one company for 10 years, we offer congratulations. Yet we encourage job hunters at the Five O'Clock Club to have a Forty-Year Vision! (If you find that idea too daunting, at least experiment with a Fifteen-Year Vision.)

But how is that possible, people ask, when the employment landscape is in such upheaval? People balk or throw up their hands in despair at the suggestion of a Fifteen-Year vision because they hear "prediction" when we say "vision." We don't expect any job hunter to *predict* what his or her life or career will be like 15 years from now. But if you have a *vision* of what it can and should

be, you'll have a North Star to guide you—as events beyond your control unfold. The long-term vision is *especially* important when we face the prospect of multiple careers, when we know that we are going to be pummeled and buffeted by events and by our own changing tastes and preferences.

The capacity to bounce back or go with the flow—above all, to keep that North Star in sight—will depend on many factors. Being willing to learn and retrain continually is one of the most obvious, but the key in many cases will simply be flexibility, coupled with fresh thinking—otherwise known as "thinking outside the box." This will be especially useful when you face those stretches between jobs—maybe every four or five years. It's in your best interest, both from the financial and career perspectives, to keep the gaps from being *long* stretches. But what if the stretches happen to coincide with a recession or with a traumatic period, such as the years that followed 9/11, when so many jobs and careers got wrecked? Our advice at the Five O'Clock Club has always been: when jobs are scarce and hiring has stagnated, do whatever it takes to keep body and soul together.

For many job hunters this has turned out to mean consulting. "Consulting" used to have a negative connotation—it used to be a code word for "unemployed." Many job hunters shunned or overlooked consulting work because they didn't want any distractions from looking for a "real" job. But when times are hard and the "real" jobs are scarce, keeping body and soul together may mean making the best of opportunities that otherwise may seem less than ideal.

You will read in the pages that follow about job hunters who turned to consulting *as part of their strategies.* Consulting might have an unsettling feel to it: you're settling for something when you know that the ideal job seems to be beyond your grasp, at least for the moment. But Five O'Clock Clubbers have discovered the silver linings: consulting means cash flow even if it doesn't match a previous salary; it means restoring the daily work routine, even if it's a different pattern; it means *not* having to say "I'm unemployed"; it *can* mean adding new accomplishments to your résumé, making you more attractive in the job market; it means that you're back in the workplace, where you might have a better chance of hearing about opportunities for full-time work—especially since people know that, as a consultant, you're available; it means a consulting assignment that might lead, in a few months, to a full-time job; it might mean, as well, that your entrepreneurial fire gets lit, and you're off and running in your own business.

In fact, it should be noted, many people have come to the Five O'Clock Club with the entrepreneurial fire already burning brightly. Over the years, about 10 percent of our attendees have been those determined to launch their own businesses. And the marketing principles that drive a good job search also drive business development. So entrepreneurs have felt right at home in their Five O'Clock Club small groups, strategizing how to promote their businesses.

When you land your next consulting assignment, by the way, be sure to come back to the Club to report. So you've been hired as a consultant—that is, you have been *hired.* It's a success story that people need to hear about. Read on to learn how Five O'Clock Clubbers have made the most out of consulting.

Advancing the Job Search with a Consulting Assignment

Marilyn knew it wasn't the right time to accept a job offer: she didn't have 6 to 10 things in the works! But an interview had turned into an offer, and the hiring manager was eager to have her on board to replace an executive who was retiring. When he called to make the offer, he asked, "When can you start?" She really didn't like the company, the commute was bad, and the neighborhood was worse. Still, an offer is an offer.

But why not propose a deal that would make everyone happy? Marilyn knew that thinking of this job as a full-time commitment would never work. But accepting an eight-week consulting assignment might be a win-win scenario for everyone. For her, it meant cash flow and getting to put a title on her résumé that she'd never had before—although she'd done the work.

She negotiated flextime to ease the commute, allow time for interviewing—and for getting to the Five O'Clock Club on Monday evenings! And the new assignment proved to be a great opportunity on several levels. "I had been in the apparel industry, and just being in this new role outside of apparel showed me how transferable my skills were. In fact, I discovered how much I could expand my targets as I continued my job search. Furthermore, I was really in a crisis-management role during the eight weeks. That can go on my résumé as well." As acting-CFO she was also able to attend several industry meetings and rub shoulders with other CFOs, thus expanding her network of contacts.

Marilyn has attended nine sessions at the Club and used the consulting assignment to give her job search a boost. She later was offered two excellent CFO positions.

Strengthening the Résumé with Consulting Assignments

Unexpectedly in the job market after the death of his boss, Nicholas found the Five O'Clock Club after a narrow and frustrating job search for a public relations job. "I had answered a lot of ads and contacted headhunters. Absolutely nothing came of that." Nicholas feels that two aspects of Club methodology especially helped get him on track. He put a lot of effort into targeted mail and took to heart our message that "acting like a consultant" can play a role in getting ahead. In his targeted cover letters, he decided to stress that he was open to full-time or consulting assignments.

His targeted mailing soon led to a two-month consulting assignment, and others followed. Nicholas is enthusiastic about the role of consulting in helping career-minded professionals. "If you're not sure of your next step, consulting gives you an opportunity to work again and get new experience. It restored my routine of getting up, going to work, getting a paycheck. It also gives your self-confidence a boost and gives you flexibility for exploring the market and going on interviews."

Nicholas's group coach played a role in helping him face what he regarded as the most painful aspect of targeted mailing: making the follow-up phone calls. "When do you plan to make the calls?" she asked. He admits that he hadn't planned to make them at all, but he managed to blurt out, "Well, tomorrow." "What time?" she responded. "One o'clock," he said. "Good, you call me after you've made those telephone calls."

"It worked," Nicholas says, "I felt like I was in third grade—admittedly—but it really worked. One of those calls was to a CEO I'd written to two weeks earlier. I got him on the phone and we met for two hours the following week. The painful follow-through is so important. It can yield valuable results."

Nicholas ended up on a long-term consulting assignment with a Fortune 500 company; he attended nine sessions at the main branch in Manhattan.

Follow-Up Is Crucial for Another Consultant

Anthony decided to go the consultancy route after losing what he describes as "the job from hell." His morale was low because of the loss of income and damage to his self-confidence. He also realized that he wasn't sure what direction to go in. "I needed time to decide what I wanted to do next. Interim consulting was a natural. It was a way to make money, and I felt under less pressure in looking for a full-time position."

Anthony applied several Five O'Clock Club principles in his approach. On one interview for a consulting assignment, it soon became clear that the company didn't even know what it needed. "I realized that I had to tell the client what was required. I got the assignment because I took the initiative and made a proposal on what to do to go forward. They accepted the idea and hired me." He landed another role because of persistent follow-up. The interviewers had stressed their urgent need to get help, yet he didn't get a call on the day they promised to get back to him. Anthony realized that they were probably swamped, so he started trying to reach them, taking to heart the Five O'Clock Club rule that it will take eight attempts to get through. Also, he didn't call to "check on the status." When he finally reached the hiring manager (after more than eight tries), he asked if there were any issues about his candidacy that might be troubling them. The answer was "no"—they had just been too busy; they appreciated his persistence and made him the offer.

Both of Anthony's consulting assignments were at high-profile, high-prestige firms, which gave more weight to his résumé; he attended four sessions of the Five O'Clock Club.

Taking Advantage of Professional Associations

Kurt came back to report at the Club after landing a consulting assignment, and he made

161

no secret of his goal: "I'm doing everything I can to turn it into a permanent assignment." He had spotted an ad on the website of the prestigious professional association that he belongs to. An investment firm that caters to high net worth individuals had posted a full-time position. But as he went about putting together his cover letter to respond, the ad puzzled him. He noted everything they said they wanted, then listed his qualifications accordingly. He was struck by the fact that they seemed to be looking for an odd blend of entry-level and senior skills. He was called in for the interview and was ready to express his puzzlement, but the hiring manager beat him to it: "I'm really of two minds about this job." She also made a suggestion that Kurt had been prepared to offer himself: why not consider coming on board as a consultant while they decided what to do in the long run.

He was careful to do the appropriate follow-up. While e-mail has become a follow-up method of choice these days because of the immediacy (and most people seem to prefer it now), in this case he sent a handwritten note. "Servicing high net worth people is a very personal business. I still favor the personal touch."

Kurt's approach in his consulting role is to remain proactive. He was asked to come up with a plan for a new line of business for the firm, and he welcomed the opportunity to become involved. He also followed Five O'Clock Club advice about surrounding the hiring manager; through the professional association, he was able to identify other people who knew key decision makers at the firm, and he reached out to become acquainted with them.

Kurt is also a firm believer in having as many things in the works as possible. Even as he was getting close to a formal offer for the consulting position he took, another situation he has been pursuing fell through. "It certainly helped my morale when it wasn't the only thing I had going." Since membership in a professional association proved so helpful to Kurt, he urges other job hunters to follow his example.

"Whatever your field is, find out the appropriate organizations and get involved. This will be invaluable to you throughout your career."

Kurt had attended the main Club for more than 10 sessions and was eligible to take part in the Advanced Group during the first hour lecture. One of these sessions covered how consultants can price their services, which proved to be valuable guidance as he negotiated the terms of his new role. The spirit of collegiality that comes from taking part in an association appears to inform Kurt's approach to others in general. His coach commented, "In the group he was always positive. There were a lot of things that went wrong, but he never whined. He just kept on going."

The Danger of Having One Thing in the Works

Marcel decided to take the summer off when he lost his music industry job in May 2001. When he was ready to get serious, the employment market in New York was taking a beating in the wake of September 11th. "For the next year I worked where I could. I managed a bagel shop, babysat, walked dogs, painted houses. By the end of 2002 I was really down on myself. I knew I had to think seriously about a career change, because I didn't want to go back into the music industry. I went to the library to look in the career section and found the Five O'Clock Club books." And he took the next step of joining the Club.

His first move was to get help with his résumé from his Five O'Clock Club coach, but then he took a giant step backwards. After interviewing with seven people at one firm, and sure the job was his, he stopped searching. "I made the classic mistake of assuming I was going to get the job. I went on vacation. They strung me along for four and a half months, and they didn't hire me."

Marcel then launched an intensive networking and direct mail campaign—so much so that his coach described him as a "elocomotive of action"—and secured a temp-to-perm job at an event-marketing company. At least temp-to-perm was the promise; Marcel came back to the Club to report on his search after starting in the new position. "The targeted mail campaign really worked for me," and this time he vows to "keep the wheels moving at all times," trying to line up as many more interviews as he can, in case the move to permanent doesn't come to pass.

Another Career Boost from Consulting

When Emory arrived at the Five O'Clock Club for the first time, five years earlier, he had seen "the worst possible scenario" come true. He had been the national public relations director for an MRI firm, and his boss had died. He was fired by the new boss. "I was devastated and went about a job hunt the way most people do—I answered ads and went to search firms."

Focusing on public relations and health-care firms fairly close to home, he launched a targeted mail campaign and got interviews for short-term consulting assignments. He accepted one with a Catholic organization, but "short term" in this case was two years.

Four months before the two-year contract was up, Emory returned to the Club and launched another targeted mail campaign—this time covering an expanded geographical area, anything within two hours of his home. Since he had worked for a Catholic organization, he decided to include similar groups this time around. He sent out the letters and made the follow-up calls. The organization that turned out to be his next consulting client welcomed his initiative: "We've been waiting for your call," and he was asked to come in. "I submitted my proposal, and we came to terms." As much as targeted mailing has worked for Emory, he admits that the requisite follow-up is no fun. "Making the telephone calls is crucial, of course, but I just hate it."

But he remains enthusiastic about consulting. "Even if you're focused on getting a full-time job, if you get a consulting offer in the meantime, take it.

It gets you out of the house. It gets you working again, mixing with people, and earning a paycheck. But, even more important, when I have a consulting position I can position myself differently. I can say, 'I'm a consultant available to other customers,' rather than 'I'm a guy out of work looking for a job.' It made me more confident."

Emory also discovered that consultants don't seem to face age discrimination as much as others might. You're a consultant—you're there *because* you're older and can bring your wisdom to bear on a situation. "When I was consulting for a public relations agency, a younger person said to me, 'It's good to have a senior person around.' In fact, you can put that in your Two-Minute Pitch: 'It's good to have a senior person around.' And I found that with the Catholics, age isn't a factor, because they're focused on eternity—so I didn't have to worry about it!"

Well Positioned . . . to Hire Himself

Chandler came to the Five O'Clock Club intent on finding a new job. After 13 sessions, however, he was able to say, "I hired myself." "I really found that coming here helped me a lot because it helped pull a lot of things together that I couldn't have done on my own." He praised the Seven Stories especially for confirming his interest in training and teaching, but also for helping him to realize that he prizes his independence. Hence he came to see that he didn't want a new job—in the sense of being hired by someone. He realized he was giving such signals when an interviewer commented: "I know you can do this job. The question is, Do you want to do it?"

Chandler met a woman at the Club who helped him hook up with an assignment that proved to be a valuable foundation for launching his own consulting practice. He felt that his small group was helpful in keeping him focused, and he credits regular attendance with "keeping me on track." Chandler's experience illustrates the truth that the Five O'Clock Club methodology is valid for consultants as well as traditional employees—that it is about life management as well as job search and career skills. After his 13 sessions at the Club, Chandler said, "I don't see myself being retired. I want to work close to things that are important to me. I feel like I've taken this really giant step forward toward doing that."

Deanna Dell, Health-Care Consultant

"I wish I had connected with the Five O'Clock Club all along. I always thought about my organization and the people in it more than I thought about what was happening to me. I never thought about: what's right for my career?"

These reflections came after Deanna had spent 28 years working at a community hospital in Maryland. She had begun her career as a registered nurse, but her talents for management were soon recognized by the hospital administration. Over the years she was promoted many times: to supervisor of nurses, to head nurse of intensive care, to vice president of nursing, and eventually to chief operating officer of the hospital itself.

"I didn't even have a résumé," Deanna recalls, because she'd never even thought about moving elsewhere. But after 28 years with one organization—in the increasingly turbulent world of health care—Deanna realized that it was time to move on. To be fair to herself and her career, she needed to consider other options.

One of Deanna's obsessions throughout the years has been management by team-building and mentoring. So, after leaving the hospital, one of her first approaches to exploring a new career was an intensive self-study program on leadership. "I went to the library, and, over the next few months, I read about 35 books on leadership and excellent organizations. When I was at the hospital, I had always tried to bring improvements to the delivery of health care by looking at what good companies do."

It was at the library that Deanna discovered the Five O'Clock Club books. "I realized I needed

help, and when I found out about the Club, I called the main office in New York and was referred to Harvey Kaplan's branch in Rockville, MD."

Deanna arranged for a private session with Harvey to help get a résumé put together, and she took his advice to do proper assessment. "I took the homework very seriously. I spent a lot of time on the Seven Stories, which helped me come to understand what it is about myself that gives me the greatest satisfaction: my passion for improving health-care delivery—wanting things to be right for the patient."

Deanna attended weekly sessions of the Five O'Clock Club for well over a year, treating it as an ongoing support system as she went about forging her new career. Five O'Clock Club coach, Jim Dittbrenner, who assists Harvey at the Maryland branch, also worked with Deanna, and both coaches encouraged her to move in the direction of consulting, based on her wealth of knowledge of the health-care world—and her own vision of the future. Deanna had also done the Forty-Year Vision: "I wanted more control of my life. I wanted to make a greater impact on the quality of health care, to align myself with professionals who share the same vision and goals and still have some balance between career and personal goals."

Another attendee of the Five O'Clock Club actually played a key role in helping Deanna become an independent consultant. She knew that health-care clinics in the region needed help with improving practices and implementing quality assurance, and she made the introductions that helped Deanna land an assignment. But Deanna believes that a good lead has to be considered in the context of working the whole method: "I used every facet of the Five O'Clock Club process. I had already been identifying targets: I had targeted five major health-care systems and had been going on informational interviews." Deanna ended up helping public health-care clinics develop tools for assessing the quality of their services, and she discovered how much she enjoyed her new role: "I found that I really liked being a consultant: I get the job done and I'm able to coach the team and see results—and then I get to help the next client."

The next big step came when Deanna was contacted by a woman she'd known for years who consulted for physicians in the process of setting up ambulatory surgical centers. She actually was looking for someone to partner with, in order to scale back her own role in the business. She was delighted to find that Deanna was on her own—and available.

The consulting practice now actually bears her name, Deanna Dell Associates, and she is doing what she loves, working toward the goal of excellence in health-care delivery. "The doctors say to me, 'I don't have the time for the paperwork and detail it takes to get things up and running. I want to practice medicine.' From start to finish it takes about 14 months to two years. I'm doing all the things I love to do—hire the best talent, put the best practices in place in the best physical environment, get the centers operational, and ultimately affect the quality of health care for a lot of people."

Deanna's only regret, as she is well under way in her consulting practice: "I should have done career planning much earlier. I should have left the hospital about *five* years earlier!"

Gary Stine, Executive Leadership Coach

"I wonder if you can imagine yourself the way I already see you?" This is one of the questions that Gary asks as a consultant to senior executives. "I watch executives interacting with people for five minutes and can see what kind of leaders they are. I ask them what they want their legacies to be."

Gary is now almost five years into his successful career as consultant to senior corporate leaders, and he acknowledges that the Five O'Clock Club played a pivotal role in getting his business off the ground. He had already made the decision to become a coach when he arrived at the Club. He had recently completed a degree

in landscape architecture—after twenty years as an actor, primarily in regional theatre. But he realized that his new degree would be taking him in the wrong direction.

"I knew I should be coaching people and had had one big client, a public relations firm, but that came to an end. I realized I really didn't know how to look for work. I didn't understand the process."

Gary's wife referred him to the Five O'Clock Club. "I was startled to see so many accomplished people who shared my plight—people who knew how to do their work, but didn't know how to *find* work, didn't know how to set themselves off from the pack."

He attended faithfully, learned the Five O'Clock Club process, and benefited fully from the group. "I needed to have my energies channeled. The group is there to support and prod. You'll achieve the desired results if you do the work that the group suggests."

Gary benefited most from the Five O'Clock Club understanding of networking as the ongoing process of forming lifelong relationships. "The outcome was that I got work, lots of it, by knowing how to network. I learned how to ask for what I wanted. It was difficult for me, but I learned how. I got an introduction into a major firm, and that led to more and more referrals." Initially focused on coaching presentation skills, Gary worked with television anchor people to hone their skills, with executives who wanted to get better at seminar presentations, and with the Five O'Clock Club career coaches to improve their public speaking skills. His role has broadened considerably to include coaching on executive leadership skills.

As Gary was getting his new business off the ground, he attended seven Five O'Clock Club sessions. "I stopped coming because I was getting so much work."

Remaining His Own Boss

Originally Dennis got a boost from the Five O'Clock Club during the dot.com boom a few years back. At that time, after attending his weekly group for 12 sessions, he landed in a fairly intense dot.com environment. "It lasted about 18 months. It was fun and it was interesting, but the workload was too much. I got laid off along with about 40 percent of the staff. Actually that was fine by me. I wasn't all that happy."

The post 9/11 environment wasn't conducive to finding on-payroll jobs, so Dennis welcomed consulting work, especially a role that allowed him to exploit his prior *shopping* experience. Not shopping as most of us think of it, nor even as the typical corporate buyer might have in mind. "You've all seen my work," Dennis told the Five O'Clock Club meeting in New York. "I worked for the Transit Authority. I bought railway cars, the new technology trains. I also bought the telephone and radio equipment for the system." Based on this experience Dennis was hired by a firm as a consultant—a strategic sourcing consultant.

And he remembered his Five O'Clock Club training. He went back to our book on salary negotiation and followed all of the suggestions for launching and pricing a consulting business. After more than a year on his own—turning down payroll jobs to remain his own boss—Dennis generated about $150,000 cash flow. "I'm having fun, it's my company. I'm doing things that are in the book. I'm out there promoting, I'm interviewing while I'm working on my current four or five contracts, looking for the next assignments." Going by the book means connecting with industry associations, and, for Dennis, that means attending meetings of the National Association Purchasing Managers. "I got to know the president, and I'm writing an article with him."

Dennis had originally reported at the Club when he landed the dot.com job in what now seems another era, but he asked to come back to report on his successful consulting practice to give encouragement to others. This is not surprising, according to his coach, who recalled that Dennis "really followed the methodology and he was very helpful in the group."

Nothing Goes to Waste: Explore All Options

As an officer-level information technology professional in the retail industry, Lester felt the impact of 9/11 acutely. Not only was his job eliminated, but the job market itself for people with his skills went into a recession. "Jobs were scarce, and my search for a full-time position was not successful," Lester admits. On the advice of friends, he joined the Five O'Clock Club and initially worked with a coach privately to develop a better résumé and a marketing plan—the component of a good job search most commonly neglected by job hunters. Getting professional help one-on-one is a smart move, but one that many job hunters commonly neglect. "But private coaching was great," Lester says. "I found it very helpful."

The marketing plan was Lester's catalyst for launching a major targeted mail campaign. "I sent out 100 letters, aimed at specific people, and I ended up meeting with about half of them at the chief information officer, vice president, information technology level. They were interested in speaking with another vice president-level person, and we had nice conversations."

Unfortunately, the field was not open. When this is the message gleaned from intensive primary research (i.e., talking directly with people in your targeted areas), any job hunter is well advised to develop additional targets. After 9/11 one of our most common pieces of advice to job hunters was, "Do whatever you can to keep body and soul together." Lester intensified his efforts to identify consulting assignments.

He posted his résumé on www.dice.com (for technology professionals) and www.hotjobs.com. This brought interviews that resulted in a six-month project, then in an open-ended assignment. In reflecting on this outcome, Lester pointed out that the lesson from his experience is: "Try everything. The Club says that there's only about a 1 percent chance of a posted résumé resulting in a job." And it's a good bet that Lester interviewed well for the consulting roles—which he landed—precisely because he had met with several dozen chief information officers and vice presidents, information technologists during the previous few months. As his group coach, Ruth Robbins, pointed out, "If you haven't been meeting with a lot of people, it's a lot easier to flub important interviews." She praised his whole approach: "He ran a very good, methodical search." Lester also credits the lectures at the Club, especially on interviewing techniques: "It all helps." Although he came to a Club meeting to report on his success in landing the long-term consulting job, Lester has no intention of neglecting the marketing plan. He will continue the search, now from the strength of additional experience on his résumé and a little more peace of mind from a steady cash flow.

CHAPTER ELEVEN

The Five O'Clock Club

Powering Through the Emotional Roller Coaster: Ten Ways to Confront Job Search Stress

This chapter is based on a panel presentation to the December 11, 2003 training workshop of Five O'Clock Club coaches in New York. The panelists were three of our senior coaches, Bill Belknap, Renée Lee Rosenberg and Mary Anne Walsh, who have extensive experience counseling clients through the stress of job search.

"In this world," Ben Franklin wrote in 1789, "nothing is certain but death and taxes." That was before the invention of the income tax—and the government's practice of grabbing part of everybody's paycheck!

But in our far more complex world 215 years later, most people are probably aware of another inevitability: occasional job loss has also been programmed into our lives. Death we owe to the Creator, for taxes we can blame the government, and occasional job loss seems to be a byproduct of the modern global economy. Job churn has been a relatively recent development; even a couple of generations ago people were accustomed to remaining with an employer for two or three decades or more. Today, of course, most Americans stay in their jobs, on average, for only about four and a half years.

In fact, college graduates in 2006 can anticipate having four careers and perhaps as many as a dozen jobs during their lifetimes. In other words, everybody had better get used to being unemployed—for a few weeks, a few months?—every four or five years.

Get used to it? Anyone who has been through unemployment will tell you that getting used to it is not likely to happen. In fact, there are few

experiences of modern life that are more stressful than losing a job, even if the job wasn't a very good one. We can name at least six sources of the stress. Do any of these sound familiar to you?

1. **The Loss of Income** Few Americans are probably ready for the paycheck to stop, that is, there's not a lot in the bank for a rainy day. There may be a reserve to cover a few weeks or months, but getting along from paycheck to paycheck is the reality for millions of wage earners. Severance and unemployment may ease the burden for many, but when the paycheck has stopped, the end is in sight: we can look at the calendar and see when severance and unemployment will run out. Add to this stress the ugly truth about consumer credit card debt, now at record levels. All too often, people who are out of work can pay only the monthly minimums and watch late fees and interest charges pile up.

2. **The Loss of Self-Esteem** When you have a job it's easy to tell the world what you do: "I'm a divisional controller at Roland Chemicals," "I'm an administrator at St. Matthew's Hospital," or "I'm a marketing manager at Southworth Paper." But when you don't have a job, "So what do you do?" becomes a dreaded question. We resort to a

euphemism, "I'm between jobs." Somehow it's very hard to muster the words "I'm unemployed, because these words seem to carry the meaning (or so we're afraid): "I'm damaged." We probably overidentify what we do with who we are, because we tend to devote so many waking hours to the job. Hence the core of our being—dipping into philosophical terms—becomes vulnerable when we're out of a job. Ironically, the problem for many folks is that they don't really believe they're between jobs; which is absolutely the truth. More about that later.

3. **The Loss of Friends and Colleagues** Of course people don't stop being friends with people they used to work with. But now the daily camaraderie is gone. "Let's get together for drinks one of these days" is now the reality instead of seeing Mark or Helen at the next desk every day and sharing news of daily life as well as of the work to be done. If coworkers have been a part of the daily routine for several years—and have become friends—we can, in fact, speak of the grieving process as people are removed from such an environment. For many people, a painful part of not getting up and going to work every day is missing people who were fun to be around.

4. **Envy and Resentment** In some cases, part of job search stress can be traced to the knowledge that life at your old office goes on without you. You may have been one of five, six, or ten people cut from the payroll, but 30 people are still there. Maybe some of your favorite people are still there—and some of the people you know aren't especially competent. If it were not for some arbitrary executive or budgetary decision beyond your control, you would still be there. Why me?

5. **The Fracturing of Routine** One outplacement client commented recently to her Five O'Clock Club coach after a few weeks of unemployment, "I am in a dream, and I know I'm going to wake up and be back in my office." After many years of catching the 7:35 train and putting in eight- or ten-hour days, the lack of

that routine can be disorienting. As much as we wish we could sleep late more often, as much as we welcome three- or four-day holiday weekends, our lives are structured around work schedules, whether it's nine-to-five or some other shift. When people are robbed of such routines, they can feel that they've been cut loose. Their comfort zone has been destroyed, and they can feel that they've lost control over their lives. This is similar to the uprootedness that retirees feel if they don't know what to do with all of the "empty" hours and days. Even if an unemployed person knows that there are things to be done to find a job, such as scanning the want ads and sending résumés, the lack of structure (i.e., not having to catch the 7:35 train) can be debilitating. Aimlessness sets in and people may park on the couch for days or weeks. It's not that they're lazy . . . it's more a matter of shell shock.

6. **The Impatience of Family and Friends** Those around you are stressed as well. They're not accustomed to having you around the house; their routines are disrupted too. Spouses and offspring are worried as they see the strain on the family finances and perhaps even resentful as lifestyles are trimmed to conserve resources. They're not used to dealing with the breadwinner's drastic morale swings when a job hunt drags on and on, with hopes raised and dashed. It may not be said in so many words, but the message soon becomes, *snap out of it*. And the impatience is often accompanied by mindless advice that damages morale even more: "Look at all those ads in the newspaper. Haven't you sent your résumé yet?" or "Why not try handing out your résumé at the train station?"

Getting Over, Around, or Through the First Brick Wall

The first major Five O'Clock Club book (1992) was called *Through the Brick Wall: How to Job-Hunt in a Tight Market*. The topic was overcoming the odds in a difficult job market, and the primary question posed was: "How much do you really want that job? Are you prepared to go through a brick wall to get it?" The book outlined smart job-hunting techniques to outclass the competition and get the prize.

But the six factors listed above tell us that there is often another brick wall that people sometimes need to get through before an effective job search can begin. Whether we call it stress, depression, or bad morale, that's the first brick wall. "I'm not in the mood to job-search" can be a major hurdle.

Of course you've got to snap out of it. But how? Obviously there's a big difference between situational and clinical depression. In the case of the latter, a person should be under medical care and on medication—those are the first steps to getting better and regaining control of one's life and destiny. But situational depression means, as we sometimes say at the Five O'Clock Club, "You'll feel better when you have a job." However, you've got to feel better in order to get off the couch and do the work required to find a job.

Here are a few suggestions for *powering through the emotional roller coaster.*

1. Job Search Is a Transition: Keep It in Perspective Don't believe the negative inner voice that may tell you, in your darkest moments, "I'll never get a good job again." When you tell people, "I'm between jobs," you assume they believe you. *Believe it yourself.* Even if you've just been turned down for three jobs—a day like that can plunge anyone into self-doubt—remind yourself that you got three interviews and you can get three more (if you're working the Five O'Clock Club method, you probably already have three more or know how to get them). One of the most memorable sermons preached by Harry Emerson Fosdick, founder of Riverside Church in New York in the 1920s, was on the topic, "When You're at the End of Your Rope." One of his main points was that you've probably got a lot more rope left. Whether you believe it or not, you're not really at the end of it at all.

2. Despite the Worries, Being in Transition Can Have a Plus Side Being freed from the nine-to-five grind, including catching the 7:35 train every morning, means you have time to take stock. Many people realize that they have been charging ahead so intensely, so relentlessly for so many years that they haven't noticed they've been off course. Or they've been putting up with demands and environments that drag them down. Unemployment can be a time to think and plot course corrections. Here are some questions to be considered as you claim R & R time and test the job market:

- What matters to me the most?
- What do I want to do differently?
- What hasn't worked for me in the past? (that is, dissatisfiers I've put up with)
- What was my own role (if any) in my job loss? What can I do better the next time?
- How am I taking care of myself?

Serious deliberation of these questions can be liberating and energizing.

3. If You Need to Vent, Vent! If you're angry, frustrated, feeling betrayed—whatever—find people to talk to about what has happened. There's only so much your family wants to hear, so find a support group. "Getting it all out" does have healing power, and there is nothing especially heroic or brave about trying to go it alone. It will take only a little snooping on the Internet or in your local newspapers to find support groups at churches and synagogues, libraries and community centers. You'll find people who will listen and whose stories will help you feel less isolated. The weekly job search strategy groups at the Five O'Clock Club serve another purpose altogether—for that, see the last point, Number 10.

4. But . . . Surround Yourself with Positive People and Things! Obviously, circumstances differ greatly, but job loss can mean you're far more fragile and vulnerable than you realize. The stress and uncertainty of the situation impact your response to the world. As we've often said, job hunters lose wallets and walk into walls. So it's especially important to manipulate your environment in your favor as much as possible. Make *protecting your morale* a daily obsession:

- Avoid toxic people—the naysayers, pessimists, and cynics. Some job hunters have told us they shun some of their friends who turn out to be too negative. Associate with people who tend to see that the glass is half full. Stop going to a support group if there is too much venting and negativity.

- There's no law that says you must watch the local news. Even if it's been a lifelong habit, ask yourself why it's necessary to hear every night about babies that fell out of windows, little old ladies who got run over, or the serial rapist who's still on the loose. You know that bad things happen to good people. What's the point of being reminded when you're emotionally vulnerable?

- If you see headlines, "Jobless Rate Hits Six-Month High" or "Ace Electronics Announces 2,000 Jobs to Be Cut," *don't read the articles.* They'll get you down, and, chances are, they have nothing to do with your situation or your job search. You can be sure the article will not point out that Ace Electronics hired five people last week.

- While it's important to have fun (more about that later), protect yourself in this respect as well. Going to the movies is a great idea, but don't watch depressing movies. If you see that *Deliverance, Schindler's List,* or *Saving Private Ryan* are on cable, pick something else. Not that you should stick with the Disney channel, but pay attention to input. Now is not the time to get a full dose of reality about the dark side of human nature. Treat yourself to *Analyze This, My Big Fat Greek Wedding,* or *Shrek,* even if you've seen them before.

5. **Accept that the Emotional Roller Coaster is Part of a Job Search—and Life!** There's no use kidding yourself—you will have bad days. Just don't fall into the trap of believing that the bad days are the norm. The real world will hand you the good days as well, and you should do your part to make them happen.

Remember that you had good days and bad days when you were on the job! The ups and downs aren't part of life just when you're unemployed. One of our coaches who leads groups reports that, according to one survey, the number one thing that gets people down is unreturned phone calls. But keep in mind that persistence does pay off (i.e., it takes an average of eight follow-up phone calls to reach people), and the payoff means that morale swings up again. Make more phone calls. That's part of the process. And morale, in fact, can get a big boost when your phone calls put you in touch with people who are eager to be helpful. They welcome you to come in for a networking meeting, refer you on to other people, or simply take a few minutes to give you pointers and suggestions. Many Five O'Clock Clubbers have reported on how nice people have turned out to be.

6. **Look at Your Unemployment as a Business Problem** When you had bad days at work, you analyzed the problem, marshaled resources and people, and came up with solutions. In the wake of a job loss, your emotions—hurt or anger—may be blocking this kind of response. But think of getting hired again as a business problem—you've rarely been stumped before, why now? Obviously you may need to master some new skills, especially if it's been a long time since you've been in the job market. But the Five O'Clock Club methodology is not rocket science. Once you have the tools, job-hunting can be treated as a business problem: tracking down the people who are in a position to hire you, positioning yourself appropriately, offering proposals to meet their needs, and turning interviews into offers.

7. **Try to Get Short-Term Successes** Break this business problem down into manageable components. When you get up in the morning, don't say to yourself, "I'm looking for a job again today." Rather, have a realistic agenda for that day, things that can be accomplished in a day: write five more targeted letters, identify ten more

companies to contact, make 10 follow-up phone calls, get one or two networking meetings set up. Some of the activities will pay off—you land a meeting, you get suggestions on good companies and people to contact. These are the short-term successes, and they feed good morale. Many people have found that one of the best short-term successes is retooling the résumé after finishing the Seven Stories Exercise. Their old résumé was a boring recitation of past job descriptions, and it can be very invigorating to see one's strong points and accomplishments stated brilliantly at the top of the résumé: "Gee, I didn't realize I was this good." This creates confidence and energy for moving forward.

8. **Keep on Top of Your Game** So you don't go to the office from nine-to-five like you used to, but that's no excuse to let your skills and knowledge slip. You always want to be perceived as a valuable commodity. You always want to sound current and sharp when you interview. Use some of your time now to catch up on reading journals and attending meetings of your professional associations. You may feel a little awkward showing up and saying you're between jobs, but rubbing shoulders with the people in your field helps you feel you're still part of the scene. And, of course, you're there to network, too. This would be a good time to volunteer for one of the association committees. This helps people see that you're still in the thick of things, at the top of your game. The fact that you're between jobs becomes irrelevant. Volunteer in other contexts as well, even if it means helping a friend in his/her business. That experience can go on your résumé as well. Nobody is going to ask if you got paid to do it.

This might also be the time to take a course, one that you could never find the time for when you were employed. This could be a great selling point on your next few interviews. Or you could teach a course, which obviously makes you look more valuable.

Temping or consulting is also a way to stay current. It brings in cash, keeps you focused and calm, can add more heft to your résumé, and introduces you to new colleagues in your industry—and it could turn into a payroll position.

9. **Keep Physically Fit and Have Fun** Bad habits usually have a bad payoff. Watch your smoking and drinking. People tend to abuse these habits when life is disrupted. If you're depressed, it's probably easier to order takeout or go for fast food instead of cooking, but this is not the time to neglect good nutrition. So try to maintain the good habits you're used to.

If your routine includes going to the gym, keep going if you can afford to. Or find some other way to make physical exercise part of your daily regime. It is a fact that regular physical exercise helps to reduce tension and stress; a half-hour walk every day is the way to do it on a budget.

And we're not kidding when we order Five O'Clock Clubbers to take a break from job-searching to have three hours of fun a week. Laughter is good therapy. When you're unemployed you have more flexibility in booking the hours for fun: go to your favorite museum on a Wednesday morning or take in an afternoon ball game.

10. **Five O'Clock Club Resources Are Your Booster Shot!** It's a huge stress-buster for people to see progress in their own searches and in the searches of others in their small groups at the Five O'Clock Club. Countless times people have arrived at the Club feeling thoroughly defeated, convinced that their situations were almost hopeless. In a matter of just a few sessions, they undergo a transformation because they see the methodology working. They see others getting interviews, strategizing follow-up, and landing offers.

The tools are there to help you overcome stress and paralysis:

- Do the Seven Stories Exercise and the Forty-Year Vision.
- Get into a weekly job search strategy group.
- Read the books, and reread crucial chapters.
- Read the inspirational quotes sprinkled throughout the books—they're there for a reason!
- Relisten to the recorded lectures (on CD) that apply to what you're going through right now.
- Review one of the handouts we've been using for years, "When You've Lost the Spirit to Job Hunt." (included at the end of this chapter)
- If you don't feel like attending your small group this week, force yourself. That's when you should. You need a booster shot!

The Twenty-First-Century Career Continuum

So where are you in the scheme of things? On your second or third career? On your seventh job? Between your fourth and fifth? Yes, you've got to go through this again.

Getting used to unemployment and job-searching will probably never happen. But each time you go through it you learn a little bit more about how to cope and conquer. Learn the fundamentals of an effective job search, build your network relentlessly, and recognize that the maelstrom of emotions is perfectly normal.

And try not to forget that, chances are, you've always got plenty of rope left.

CHAPTER TWELVE

The
Five
O'Clock
Club

Forging *Career* Security: Ten Things to Do When You're *Not* Job Hunting

It's not a big surprise that most citizens of the modern workplace worry a lot these days about job security—much more so than their parents did. Employers used to be concerned about hiring people who would stay put for years (beware of job hoppers!), but now candidates are eager to find the companies that won't shuffle them out of a job in two or three years. People know that job security has almost become a fiction; who is surprised when the next merger, corporate takeover, relocation, or outsourcing is announced?—followed by headlines about how many jobs will be eliminated.

With job security on the decline, it is important for people to be even more vigilant about *career* security. Isn't it pretty obvious that losing your job every five years could wreak havoc with your career plan? Maybe you don't even have a clearly formulated career plan—members of the Five O'Clock Club know that's not a good idea—but it's just good strategy to think about the consequences of forced job moves and minimize the impact of disruptions; obviously a derailed career can dash your hopes, plans, and goals. A recent caller to the Five O'Clock Club lamented how many wrong turns he had made. At age 59 he was facing the grim

truth that *he would never be able to retire.* He might have failed to do proper financial planning (and saving!), but he was calling the Club because his *career* was a train wreck.

Let's consider some of the steps you can take to protect yourself. Career security—not just job security—should be one of your top priorities.

But what do we mean by *career security*? Let's give some specific content to the term. Successfully forging career security means:

- Being able to remain on track with your career goals even if your next job lasts two years instead of ten; even if you're suddenly out of a job when your company is sold; even if your new boss turns out to be toxic and blocks your advancement. In other words, having strategies to help navigate the unforeseen.
- Minimizing the time you spend in the job market, that is, reducing your "in-between-jobs status" during a 20- to 25-year period. If you can put things together in such a way that periods of employment are brief, you're more likely not to be diverted from your goals. Long periods of unemployment often prompt job hunters to settle for jobs that are *off strategy.* Career security means not having to *settle.*

175

People tend to think about job hunting and career goals when circumstances force them to; that is, when they're about to be out of work and they have no choice. But that's a bit like shopping for fire insurance after your house has started to burn down.

We like to say that the Five O'Clock Club is for "career-minded people" and indeed, over the years we have found that the people who enthusiastically embrace our methodology *do* want to think long-term (which is implicit in the very word "career"); they *do* want to give the Forty-Year Vision a good shot. But, guess what? This can't be done just when you're unemployed or about to be! It can't be done sporadically or on an emergency basis. Attention must be paid *all the time.* Hence, there are plenty of things you can do while you're *on* the job, hopefully for a period of several years; there's much to be done when you're *not* job hunting. Here are ten suggestions; some of them may not apply to you . . . but you would have to come up with a good argument why any one of them doesn't!

1. **Nurture the Network** If you worked the Five O'Clock Club methodology properly during your job search, you constructed a marketing plan designed to help you contact people who represent 200 positions in several targets. The Club's mantra is "aim for 200 positions," to get a lot going and get multiple offers. By the time you land your new job, you may have contacted 100 people—or maybe it was 50, 75, or 125. But when you hear those thrilling words, "You're hired!" what do you do with the marketing plan? If you're thinking about career security, you don't put it in a file and forget about it.

Look at it this way: in the process of your job hunt you managed to tell at least a few dozen new people about your skills, accomplishments, and goals, and these are people to maintain relationships with forever. That's what we say networking is: *building lifelong relationships.* Chances are, quite frankly, some of these people could play a key role in helping you stay on track *years from now.*

One Five O'Clock Club graduate, a senior bank auditor who hadn't looked for a job in 25 years, went through a long stressful search. He admitted that he was shy and job-hunting didn't come easily. But where did he eventually get the lead that resulted in his new job? He contacted a former colleague with whom he hadn't been in touch *for more than ten years.* But the former colleague had a very positive memory of his work and character and happily gave him the recommendation that paid off. In other words, it's likely that he wouldn't have had a long stressful search if he hadn't been *out of touch* with important people. If you make a point of keeping in touch with former colleagues and new contacts forged during your job hunt, the outreach during the next period of unemployment won't be such an uphill battle, and it is much more likely to be brief.

Keep reviewing your marketing plan and use it as a blueprint for your *ongoing* networking efforts. These days there are so many electronic techniques to keep you mindful of calls or contacts to make every week or every month. But you don't just need reminders: build a database of your contacts and work to maintain and grow it; use an electronic format of some kind—Lotus, FilemakerPro, Act, for example—instead of a collection of business cards or a little black book. You should have good written notes in this database on all these people (their projects, interests, areas of expertise), so keep feeding them information that may be helpful. Keep reminding people in your chosen career field where you are and what you're up to. Nurture the network by letting people know *you* are a resource and that you're at the top of your game (or working hard to get there!).

2. **Get Out of the Office: A Starring Role in Your Professional Association** We know that attending meetings of professional associations can give a boost to networking; and we have always urged career changers to get involved in associations to speed the process of being perceived as insiders. Thus job hunters are well

served by showing up at monthly association meetings and pressing the flesh. But consider the impact that association *participation* can have on career security. It's one thing to attend from time to time—and it's very easy to argue that you're too busy to go to meetings—but career-minded people want to be seen as leaders, not just in their own companies but in their fields. Join associations, accept leadership roles, and volunteer for projects and committees. Obviously this means a commitment of time, energy, and enthusiasm, but this can be part of your *career security* strategy. Is it worth it from that perspective? At the very least, your name, title, and photo show up in the association newsletter or magazine—hopefully on a regular basis. Your boss and peers will see it, as well as executives in other companies. And you can add descriptions of your association accomplishments to your résumé.

One of our favorite case studies of the use of associations comes from Evan Gansl, a Five O'Clock Clubber whose story was featured in the May 2005 issue of our magazine, *The Five O'Clock News*. As part of his intensive effort to move his career into elder law practice, he became active in a professional association. He signed on to work on a committee that included a woman—a leader in the field—who eventually was looking to hire someone for her firm. He applied for the job, and hiring Evan was a relatively easy decision; because he was fully involved in the association, she knew him and the quality of his work.

You can become a star in your own company, but it would be nice—it would be strategic—if others in your industry can see your value. If you become easily recognized as an industry player because of your high profile in an association—appreciated for your hard work, perhaps on a research project or arranging a conference—it will be a lot easier in future interviews for hiring managers to recognize your commitment and contribution to the field.

3. Get Out of the Office: Building Your Reputation by Public Speaking How about

being the featured speaker at an association meeting? Or the keynote speaker at the annual conference? What better way to gain recognition as a "thought leader" in your field? You don't have to wait for your company to anoint you as a media spokesperson—that privilege actually falls to very few. In fact, if you end up speaking on topics of interest in your field, whether to industry associations or even to general audiences, you usually *cannot* appear as a representative of your company (unless authorized to do so). Rather you can present as an expert in your field, perhaps on trends in the music recording industry, new reporting regulations for banks, the growing balance of trade deficit, or the areas of the biggest expansion expected in the hospitality industry.

The best protocol is to let your boss—and your company's public relations department—know what you're up to, even though you are not speaking on behalf of your employer. In fact, you *want* your boss to know. Remember, this is part of your career security strategy; you want to enhance your reputation as a specialist and an expert. And the more speaking you do, the more you will be in demand.

Six times a year, the Five O'Clock Club sponsors the Human Resource Network Breakfast seminars for human resources officers in the New York area; we look for three panelists for each event, people who have built solid reputations as specialists in their fields and with a knack for communicating well with audiences. A summary of each panel presentation appears in our monthly magazine, *The Five O'Clock News*, along with photos and bios of the panelists. This all helps to build career credibility for the presenters. Bear in mind that the goal of your marketing plan (when you were job hunting) was to talk to dozens of people (representing 200 positions) who might ultimately be able to hire you. If you give speeches on hot topics in your field, *people will be lining up to meet you.* This will help you develop a wide network of professionals in your field.

It's very common for shy people and introverts to shrink from the idea of public speaking, and they may be tempted to take a pass on this technique for building career security. But introverts can be inspired by the example of James Brown, a spokesman for the New York State Department of Labor. Mr. Brown addressed the annual dinner of the Five O'Clock Club Guild of Career Coaches in February 2005. He began by admitting that he is a shy guy and that the public speaking role was thrust upon him by his superiors. So he had to do what he had to do. *But he is in demand as a speaker.* His key for success is his amazing knowledge of the New York economy and labor market. His expertise allows him to get up in front of a roomful of people and talk from the heart to his audiences.

Maybe you sense that you are not high enough on the corporate ladder to have anything to say or command attention. But one way to move up the ladder is to build your expertise and *become* known as someone who has something to say. The next time you hear a presentation at an association meeting you should make a point of chatting with the speaker afterwards: "How long have you been doing this? How did you get into public speaking?" Maybe public speaking can become part of your plan five or ten years from now.

4. **Build Your Reputation by Writing** One way to get *asked* to give speeches is to become known as someone who has a message or—like James Brown mentioned earlier—just a lot of useful information in any particular field. You can do this by *writing for publication.* Very few executives actually write books, so that is not the goal here. It doesn't take long to identify industry newsletters that may be an appropriate outlet for anything you may want to write. Gale Research's *Newsletters in Print* lists "11,600 subscription, membership, and free newsletters, bulletins, digests, and similar serial publications in the U.S. and Canada." This clearly is a major resource. But if you're at all aware of what your boss or CFO is reading, you'll know the industry newsletters you

should be targeting. We mentioned earlier that your name, title, and photo will end up in an association newsletter if you're simply active on committees or at conferences; the same will happen if you're a contributing author.

Recall that a good networking technique is to send copies of articles to people you've met with. It's a plus for you if people are sharing *your* article in professional circles. We also recommend contacting authors of articles; here again is a way to get people to reach out to you—people who can become part of your expanding network of industry contacts.

What about writing a book? Because writing a book requires so much work and pays so little, it's not really a practical option for most people strategizing career security. There are clearly cases when it provides a boost. Five O'Clock Clubber Anthony Politano is the author of *Chief Performance Officer,* which enhances his stature as an expert in his field. He was invited to be a panelist for the May 6, 2005 HR Network seminar on "HR Metrics: What Your Board and CEO Want," and there was a long line of human relations executives at the end of the session to get his book. Hence at just one event he impressed a lot of people and expanded his network of contacts. The next time he looks for a job, securing interviews won't be a struggle, and he won't have trouble adopting the stance of a consultant.

The goal of writing for publication obviously requires knowing how to *write well.* Try writing an article or two and ask an editor—maybe the editor of your professional association newsletter—to review and critique it. If it comes back to you covered with red ink and suggestions for rewrites, you know you need to work hard at learning how to write for publication. This will be well worth your time, because strong writing skills can enhance your career on several levels.

5. **Take Courses or Teach Them, but Continue Learning!** If your company pays tuition reimbursement, take full advantage of this benefit. Even if your company doesn't, then

consider paying out of your own pocket. Be on the lookout for courses offered by colleges, learning centers, and professional institutes. It may almost sound like a cliché now to say that you should be "on the cutting edge," but you do want to be on top of the latest knowledge, trends, and technology that impact your field. There's also a lot of talk these days about the importance of "thought leaders," and pushing yourself to be perceived in this way can be a part of your career strategy. Being current and innovative—and taking the initiative to remain so—makes you a valuable member of your staff or team.

Coursework also looks good on your résumé, especially if the topics relate directly to important trends in your field. Effective interviewing, after all, is a matter of outclassing the competition, and you will have an advantage if you can list several recent courses that you've taken.

Naturally, teaching a course is even better. The hard work and research required for course preparation (reading a half-dozen books and probably many more articles) will push you to master new material and deepen your own understanding. What better way to achieve a reputation as a "thought leader"? Even if you don't take or teach a course, don't neglect the learning required to stay abreast in your field. Have there been five or six new books published in your field in the last six months that relate to your function and your goals? You want your peers and bosses to look to you as a source and a guide. *Being very well read is a step in this direction.*

6. **Taking Stock: Reviewing Your Résumé**
If you've been through the Five O'Clock Club group process, chances are a lot of blood, sweat, and tears went into transforming your résumé into an effective accomplishments-based marketing tool. Most people find the job search process so stressful that they just want to put the résumé away for a few years. Now that they have a job, why not?

One of the best reasons *not* to neglect the résumé is that jobs aren't permanent any longer!

Of course, you may have every hope and expectation that a new job will last for five years or more, but we all know that job security isn't what it used to be. Hence, always keeping one eye on the résumé isn't a bad idea. "I haven't looked at my résumé in years" is a common refrain heard from people who have enjoyed a long run with one employer, but any Five O'Clock Club graduate should know that the résumé is a marketing tool to keep fresh. Get in the habit of reviewing your résumé every few months.

Presumably you were hired *to do something.* A great interview question is, "If you were to hire me, what would you like to have me accomplish in the first three months?" Or: "Is there something keeping you up at night that you want me to help solve?" After you've been on the job for six months, there should be new accomplishments to put on your résumé. If the months or years go by and you're not adding fresh accomplishments and skills to your *marketing document,* you may be stagnating. You may not be building the kind of expertise that underwrites career security. In other words, frequent résumé review is a way to gauge your career progress.

Having your résumé current and fresh is a way of staying on the offensive. You should always be saying to yourself, "If I had to market myself tomorrow, would I be ready?" Remember the importance of keeping job search periods as brief as possible. You never want to have to *dust off* your résumé.

7. **Taking Stock: Reviewing Your Vision**
Many people wander from one unsatisfying job to another because they skip assessment. Five O'Clock Clubbers know that we have tools for evaluating the past (the Seven Stories) and for figuring out where to go (the Forty-Year Vision). These are most commonly done when people are gearing up for a full-scale job search, but assessment can help people who may simply feel that they're in a rut, whose careers seem to have gone into a blind alley. The Seven Stories often

drive people to a realization that they are simply in the wrong career, and something's got to give. A number of years ago a partner in a law firm realized he was off course when his Seven Stories revealed that his most recent enjoyable accomplishment was in *junior high school.* More recently, Five O'Clock Clubber Rigo Martinez (whose story was reported in the May 2005 issue of *The Five O'Clock News*) was reminded by his Seven Stories that he liked teaching. He went back to school to get instructor certification and is expanding his job to include training responsibilities.

Reviewing satisfying accomplishments isn't something that needs to be done every year, but the Forty-Year Vision is clearly more fluid and deserves repeated reviews, in light of how your life is actually unfolding. We always say that you should take the job that positions you best for the future you envision for yourself. At every anniversary of your start of a new job, you should review the vision, which should be in written form. Are you being promoted according to plan? Are you taking on new assignments that move you in the right direction? Career security means paying attention to these issues on an ongoing basis, especially if your tenure in the job continues past the typical four-and-a-half years that people expect these days.

8. **Taking Stock: The Annual Checkup with Your Career Coach** This may not be something that you've given much thought to, but all of our coaches are *certified by the Five O'Clock Club.* That is, they are all graduates of *our* rigorous training program that ensures that they've mastered the unique Five O'Clock Club method. We don't entrust our clients to "generic" coaches. So it's no surprise that we get rave reviews about our coaches—those who lead the small weekly groups (either in person or by phone) and those who only see clients privately. The overwhelming testimony of successful Five O'Clock Club job hunters is that the coach played a central role in seeing them through to the desired results.

A powerful lesson to draw from this is the importance of *staying in touch with your coach.* Once people land in new jobs, however, the tendency is to want to forget about the job-hunting struggle: "It's behind me now. I should get on with my new job and hope that it lasts a good long time." This commonly translates as well into *complacency about career security.* But the coach who provided such reliable guidance during the hard days of the job search should remain a resource. Just as it's a mistake to put the résumé in a file, it's a mistake to neglect thinking about and evaluating your career—*in the company of an expert.* Within a year after starting your new job, meet with your coach to review the long-term plan. Talk about complications or issues on the new job that may be pushing you off course—or those that may have opened up some new possibilities. Using your coach as a professional sounding board can help you achieve perspective. Most of us are surrounded by professionals that we rely on to keep us sound and whole: an accountant, lawyer, doctor, dentist, pastor or priest. It's a good idea to add your career coach to this roster and arrange for a checkup from time to time to guarantee that you'll give a few hours of focused attention to your career. And by all means, if you run into rough sledding on the new job, get in touch with your coach again.

If your company purchased Five O'Clock Club outplacement for you, you may well have a few unused hours of private coaching—be sure to use them!

9. **On the Job: Being Tuned In** Five O'Clock Clubbers are familiar with one piece of advice about acing the interview: be nice to the receptionist or secretary when you show up for a meeting, because his or her opinion could very well carry weight with the boss. The important lesson for the long run is that you usually have to get along with everyone in the office if you want to get your job done. In other words, pleasing the boss isn't all that counts: how you relate to subordinates and peers is important as well; in

fact, these people can make all the difference in the world. So part of building career security is being aware of your impact on those around you. If morale is bad because of your management or work style, if people are less than enthusiastic about helping on vital projects because they can't stand you—you've got a problem. Most of us have had to deal with the toxic boss; most of us have war stories about the colleagues whom we describe with four-letter words.

But what if *you're* the toxic boss? What if *your* colleagues launch expletives behind your back? It's obvious that your career can suffer if this is the case. So it's vital to be tuned in: how *am* I perceived by bosses, peers, and subordinates? One of the most important assets in trying to accomplish your goals on the job—and, ultimately, your career goals—is the morale of those around you. So work hard at self-perception, and develop your skills for listening and encouraging others to speak honestly and offer candid feedback.

10. **On the Job: Being a Good Advocate for Yourself** Let others know what you're up to—in a positive way. Being boastful or claiming credit for work done by others won't win any points, but you can advance the cause of your career by speaking up about your accomplishments. For example, we recommend what we call the Eight-Word Message; it's a technique for making the most of unexpected opportunities. When you run into your boss's partner in the elevator, after she says, "Good morning," it's natural enough to say, "Good morning. Isn't it great to see an end to all this rain?" But you'll do yourself more good by saying, "It *is* a good morning! Last night we finished the Frankfurt project." This helps build a perception of the kind of work that you do. You're building career security when peers and bosses—who need to know who to tap for future assignments—appreciate what you do.

These last two items, by the way—9 and 10—are just tips of the iceberg. They are aspects of the very broad topic of how to tend to your career every day on the job. This is treated at much greater length in the 30-page Five O'Clock Club publication *Managing Up, Down & Across,* which is available from the Club for $6.50 + shipping.

CHAPTER THIRTEEN

The
Five
O'Clock
Club

The Holiday Job Search: Full Steam Ahead! Burying the Myth that the Holidays Are a Time to Slack Off

Nobody likes to job search. Thus, it is so tempting to put off doing the things you need to do to land your next position. Even people who have very compelling reasons to get a job as quickly as possible (low bank balance, a panicked spouse) commonly find compelling reasons why they can't look for work *today*.

For chronic procrastinators, what could be better than having an excuse that lasts for almost two months? The year-end holiday season, framed by Thanksgiving and New Year's, is commonly viewed as a bad time to look for a job. Indeed, we sometimes hear that November– December is the worst time of the year for job-hunting. The usual refrain is, "Well, nothing's going to happen until January, so why bother? I might as well not waste my time." That's the conventional wisdom—we begin hearing it as soon as people have taken off their Halloween costumes. *But it's wrong.*

Let's review four reasons why it is wrong. There may be more reasons, but these are enough to nail the coffin firmly shut. Then we'll turn to several suggestions for what to do during your unrelenting holiday job search.

1. One of the biggest reasons that slacking off during the holidays is wrong is that other, less savvy job hunters don't know that it's wrong. They retire from the battle and leave the field wide open. Of course, it's not true that *everyone* stops job hunting, but thousands of people who ought to be out there interviewing decide to kick back and coast through the season. They believe the misinformation! What more could you want? This makes it easier for you. The last thing you want to hear at the end of a terrific interview is, "We have five more candidates to interview." You don't want competition. We focus a lot at the Five O'Clock Club on strategies to outclass the competition, and this is a lot easier if there aren't a lot of people in the race. You'll rarely have the field all to yourself, but in November–December it will be a lot less crowded.

2. During the final months of the year, department managers are planning ahead; and they're not waiting for January to get things moving. Budgets and head counts have been approved, goals for the new year have been set, and steps are already being

taken to carry out plans for the next six months. If managers want new people on board in January, they know that January 1 is too late to start interviewing. Traditionally, January has been one of the highest hiring months for Five O'Clock Clubbers because department managers *interview in December.*

3. This is not rocket science: You may have noticed that business does not shut down during the last six weeks of the year. The stock market doesn't close for November–December, banks don't stop taking deposits, and salespeople continue right on making calls and closing deals. So does anyone really think that hiring managers won't read new résumés that land on their desks ("Well golly, I can't look at these until January")? Of course not. It's business as usual, holidays or not. Certainly there are distractions, but office parties and holiday shopping remain extracurricular activities. If there is hiring to be done, it will be done.

4. You don't want to lose momentum! If you have a great job search going on in October—or even a tentative one—November is not the time to go on vacation. It would be a disaster to let the momentum dissipate. The failure of momentum, in fact, is the great saboteur of the job hunt process at any time of the year. When people fail to have lots of things in the works, they concentrate on the one great job that they really want, and they're devastated when they come in second or the company puts a freeze on hiring. It takes two or three weeks to dig out of depression, because one is in a dead calm. Putting all hope and effort on that one great job means that you can have no momentum. Don't let anything—especially the season—cripple momentum.

Your Best Friend in Strategizing the Holiday Job Search . . .

If you're reading this chapter in October (or in May—more on that later), remember that the weeks ahead are precious, so you want to make them count.

Wouldn't it be great if you had some way to figure out if you're conducting a good search? Obviously, when you land a job you can say, "My job hunt techniques worked"—but as you're slogging along week after week, *then* is when you need to know if they're working. Are you doing the right things? After all, many people end up with jobs *despite* making false starts and needless mistakes. "I landed a job" is not really the true test of having done a good, efficient, and effective search. Some people just get lucky—by which they mean they landed a new job—all the while admitting it's not really the right job or a great job.

The good news is that the Five O'Clock Club *does* have a tool to help you assess your search. We call it Stages 1, 2 & 3, and it can be your best friend. Before we discuss what you can do in your job search during the holidays, it's a good idea to describe Stages 1, 2 & 3, so that you can frame your strategies accordingly.

What do the stages mean? It took several years for the Five O'Clock Club to hammer out and perfect this assessment tool, so it's worth mastering. It could mean all the difference in making the holiday season pay off!

Simply put, you have achieved Stage 1 when you are in touch with *6 to 10 people in your target markets on an ongoing basis.* This is simple, but it's also tough. You might be surprised at how many people arrive at the Five O'Clock Club after many months of a stalled search, and we point out to them that they're not even in Stage 1 yet. They're shocked and annoyed by such a thing! We might hear that they've sent out hundreds of résumés and networked with dozens of people, but they're frustrated and exhausted because "nothing's worked."

The clouds begin to clear when we point out that many of those résumés haven't really been aimed at clear and realistic targets and the job hunter failed to keep in touch with all of those networking contacts on an ongoing basis. It turns out that getting to Stage 1 requires a lot of focused effort, because you need to use all of your ingenuity to find reasons to *stay in touch* with people so that they can be included on your list of Stage 1 contacts. Many months of job-hunting labor, the kind claimed by distraught and frustrated newcomers to the Five O'Clock Club, may simply be unstrategic—or even mindless busywork—and thus is not as impressive as it sounds. When you can genuinely say that you have a healthy Stage 1 going, things can begin to happen.

You have achieved Stage 2 when you are in touch with 6 to 10 people in your target markets on an ongoing basis, *and* people are saying to you, "Gee, I wish we had an opening right now. I'd love to have someone like you on board." In other words, you're getting affirmation that you're doing the right things. You are (1) meeting with the right people at the right levels, and (2) positioning yourself correctly. You're on the right track!

But if you go on meeting after meeting and *don't* hear that people would like to hire you, then *something is wrong*: your targets are wrong, your positioning is wrong, or you are interviewing poorly (failing to act like a consultant is one big mistake). Something needs to be fixed. Thinking in terms of what it takes to achieve Stage 2 helps you to identity the mistakes that may be sabotaging your search.

You have arrived in Stage 3 when you are in touch with 6 to 10 people on an ongoing basis who are discussing real jobs with you or the possibility of creating a job for you. Don't obsess

about Stage 3. It will take care of itself if you obsess about Stage 2.

The full worksheets to help you visualize and track your Stage 1, 2 & 3 efforts can be found in the chapter, "How to Control Your Campaign" (pp. 187–202) in our book *Shortcut Your Job Search: the Best Way to Get Meetings.*

How to Improve Your Job Search during November and December

So, what to do during these final weeks of the year? All of the four suggestions discussed below can have a large payoff; they're all practical and realistic. In no case can you say, "You expect me to do *that* during the holidays?"

1. **Reconnect with everyone during the next few weeks** Remind people who you are, what you do, and what you're trying to accomplish. Notice that a constant theme in Stages 1, 2 & 3 is being in touch with people "on an ongoing basis." This is crucial to success. If this element is missing, you're in trouble. Many job searches stall because people lack the discipline to keep in touch or just lose interest in doing so. One Club member sent out "gratitude e-mails" in December to everyone whom he'd networked with during the previous months. This prompted one of his contacts to forward his résumé to someone else, which resulted in an interview and his new job. The simple truth is that people forget about you if you slip off the radar screen. The holidays are, in fact, an ideal time to touch base with everyone to extend good wishes—and give an update on your situation.

2. **Devote a few hours each week to expanding, defining, and refining your targets** This takes time and hard work, and there's nothing happening during the holidays to

impede this. The excuse that "Everyone out there is too busy" should have no bearing whatever on your ability to hunker down at the computer and do more research. Remember you're aiming to identify 200 positions ending up with multiple offers and a great job (not just one you'll settle for). This usually requires expanding your targets: Our coaches are always urging and prodding clients to do this. Your job search will be hobbled if your targets are skimpy or sloppy.

You can expand targets by (1) reviewing your assessment exercises—maybe there's something you've overlooked; (2) brainstorming with your job search buddies and your group; and (3) doing more Internet research that can include identifying more second- and third-tier companies to contact. Many people are amazed to discover companies they never knew about—organizations that aren't rich and famous, but may be great places to work. If you can end up with a map of 200 positions spread over several targets, you'll be getting closer to achieving a healthy Stage 2 in which you're talking to 6 to 10 of the right people at the right levels. If you have a weak Stage 2, refocus on the breadth and depth of your targets. By expanding your targets, you will be able to reach your goal of identifying 200 positions. You can put a lot of holiday time into building your target map.

3. **If you've neglected one or two of the ways to get meetings, work on all four:** ads, search firms, networking, and direct contact. We know that job hunters tend to favor ads and search firms, so we usually urge them to get better at networking and, toughest of all because it is labor intensive, reach out directly to companies—as many as your research uncovers. Hence, launching a targeted mail campaign is an ideal holiday pursuit. It takes time to research companies, create intelligent cover letters, and make the follow-up phone calls a few days later.

There are five weeks between Thanksgiving and New Year's; imagine the impact of sending out 10 targeted letters each of those weeks. You

will have a very busy holiday job search if you do this, and it would be remarkable if you don't end up with a healthy Stage 2.

Maybe, however, you've slighted the newspaper ads because responding to ads has never worked very well for you. Spend a couple of hours scanning the ads anyway, but not just to look for openings. People *do* get interviews through the ads (especially if they follow the Five O'Clock Club template for cover letters), however you may spot trends in the kinds of jobs being advertised and the salaries offered. You may also see ads placed by companies you've already been targeting, which should prompt you to use your own networking contacts to get an introduction to the company.

4. **Attend your weekly group at the Five O'Clock Club** *consistently* One of the primary goals of your group is to make sure your search is moving forward. Skipping sessions works against this purpose. When the coach asks, "What's happening in your search this week?" the right answer never is, "Well, I don't have a job yet." A right answer is an evaluation of your progress: "I have 12 Stage 1 contacts, 6 good ones in Stage 2, and I'm working to get a couple of those into Stage 3." *The group wants to hear an honest assessment* and will help to brainstorm how to get more things going in each stage. With this goal in mind, everyone leaves with an assignment to help maintain his or her momentum. Attending your group throughout the holiday season, either at one of the in-person or telephone branches, will help sustain the momentum. Remember: You're looking for the January payoff.

Looking Ahead: There is No Such Thing as a Bad Holiday

If procrastinators are fond of excusing themselves from a year-end job search because hiring supposedly goes downhill after Halloween, then their favorite time of the year is probably summer. June, July, and August combined are frequently declared the summer holiday, and we hear that "nothing is going to happen until after Labor Day."

Accordingly, a lot of people head for the beach, telling themselves that they'll get back to the job market when the season changes. Of course it's a good bet that there'll be another excuse when the Tuesday after Labor Day arrives. Setting an arbitrary date when you will finally tackle an unpleasant task invites only dread and more delay. In fact, there is no bad season for your job search. No matter what month it is, there are always things you can do to move yourself through Stages 1, 2 & 3 and end up in your new job. In the good old summertime, with most of your competition relaxing at the beach, you can work the job market productively.

When to Use the "Holiday Excuse"

There is one time, however, when you can play the holidays-are-bad-news card. If you lose your job as the holidays are approaching and you're negotiating for the best possible severance and outplacement deal, be sure to tell your department manager or the human resources officer that it's a tough time to be looking for a job: "You know, with the holidays just around the corner, it's a rotten time to send out résumés. I'll be facing an uphill battle, and nothing will happen for months." Since *nearly everybody believes this,* you might be able to pump up your departure package.

But *you* know that you're just being a good negotiator, and you also know that the holidays are a great time to be in the job market. In other words, full steam ahead!

CHAPTER FOURTEEN

 The Five O'Clock Club

How to Get Fired: A Review of Smart Exit Strategies

Let's see, you could throw a drink in your manager's face at the company picnic. Or perhaps arrive at the office wearing your pajamas. Every morning at your desk, before taking a half-hour coffee break, you could spend a couple of hours surfing the net looking for your next vacation destination. Or during your annual review with your boss, say, "You were *serious* about all those goals for last year?" In the film *Nine to Five,* when Lily Tomlin's character thinks she's poisoned her boss (Dabney Coleman) by mistake, she laments, "I just killed the boss. You don't think they're not going to fire me for something like this?"

These are surely ways to get fired—or at least come very close. But this chapter isn't really about how to get fired—who needs that kind of advice? We want to review a few of the things you can do to survive the process of being fired. That is, how do you survive with dignity and with as little damage as possible?

This clearly is a topic most of us don't even want to think about. But bear in mind that jobs don't last forever in the modern economy. A generation ago, job security was built into the system. These days, however, it's *built out* of the

system. Jobs last an average of 4.5 years. That's why it's important to be very aware of career planning—and it's important to be savvy about being fired. Chances are, you will have to go through it once or twice.

Of course, employers and termination policies differ greatly. We've all heard horror stories about employees being treated like criminals when they're asked to leave. We also know that some organizations get high marks for handling people with care and sensitivity when there's a forced departure. And it's hard to know when you take a job how things may play out when you leave the job.

But it's also very true that employees commonly aren't as skilled as they could be in handling forced exits. There usually is a degree of trauma, confusion, and anger—the latter especially, if the circumstances seem to be unfair or arbitrary. Even people who have been through this harrowing experience give far less thought to the process of leaving a job than getting a job. Naturally at the Five O'Clock Club we focus far more on job search strategies. But we encourage people to look upon being fired as a crucial time for self-protection instincts and strategies to kick in. Being fired may be inevitable now and then, but you don't necessarily have to take it lying down—as in, being run over.

Circumstances will vary enormously, but we're going to review a few key principles to bear in mind. Some of these may apply to your situation, others may not, but keep this list on file to review if it happens to you.

Find a Coach

Why try to fly solo through an experience that has the potential to cause you damage and loss? Getting good advice can save you a lot of grief.

There are coaches who have helped hundreds of people go through this, and their words of wisdom and emotional support can be invaluable. The rate for such coaching is usually in the $125 to $150 per hour range, but the return on investment can be huge. The strategies, suggestions, and scripts offered by a coach could mean that you will walk away with a few thousand dollars more or a few more months of insurance coverage, as well as other substantial advantages. After just a few minutes into a conversation with a coach, you may find yourself saying, "Gee, I never thought of that." It's the things you don't think of that can mean big trouble.

At the end of this chapter we will return to the topic of getting help—in the form of employer-paid outplacement services.

Distance Yourself from the Emotions of the Situation

Depending on your temperament, you might react smoothly or hysterically, or anything in between, when you hear the words "you're fired"—even if it's not put that bluntly. But most people can assume that their judgment will be clouded when they get the word that their job is over. By all means, avoid making decisions or signing anything until you've had time to distance yourself from your first reactions.

One of the most difficult emotions to handle is panic, because job loss may feel like the end of the world if you haven't looked for a job in ages, if you live from paycheck to paycheck, or if your plate is already full with personal problems at home. But panic will work against making the best of a bad situation. Simply reviewing the other points to follow in this chapter can help you see that there are constructive steps to take and the situation probably is not as bleak as it may seem.

There may be a lot of anger, too. One Five O'Clock Club client was so filled with rage when she was fired that she couldn't even bear to meet with her boss to work out severance. With the help of her coach, she crafted carefully worded e-mails to present her case; that is, she made sure that her rage and anger didn't come through in what she wrote. In this way she doubled the payout that the company had originally offered. If you try to negotiate from anger, you're probably building toward a lose-lose situation for everyone. Which brings us to the next point.

Try to Be as Nonconfrontational as Possible

One of the most natural reactions to being fired is one variation or another of "After all I've done for this company. . . ." Almost everyone, on one level or another, wants to think that he or she has done a good job and doesn't deserve to be fired. Even if an employee is being terminated for performance reasons, there is likely to be disagreement with the boss on the quality of the job done. But it is usually pointless to try to argue your case. For every wonderful accomplishment you can claim, your manager is likely to counter with an example of something you failed to do or how you fell short. An argument about performance is the last thing that will advance your case at this point.

Believe it or not, most employers want to make the exit as graceful as possible to keep stress as low as possible for all parties concerned and to protect the reputation of the organization.

So just accept the fact that there will probably not be agreement on whether or not you deserve the forced exit and focus on negotiating as calmly and pleasantly as possible. As much as anything, a feeling of goodwill (even if it seems strained and artificial!) increases the chances of arriving at a win-win solution. You are vulnerable to damage in these situations, and you want to minimize damage as much as possible.

So how good are you at making nice?

Sharpen Your Acting Skills

At the Five O'Clock Club we tell job hunters that interviewing is showtime. Even if you don't feel confident and on top of the world, try to act as if you do. Performance is half the battle in landing a job offer. The same advice applies when you're presenting your case for the best possible exit package. Of course you need to huddle with your coach to plot strategy, perfect your script, and note all the points that need to be covered. Have your list of needs and desires (not demands!), and focus on the realities of your situation and the job market. We prod job hunters to perfect their Two-Minute Pitches, and you need a variation of this for the meetings with your boss or human resource manager to discuss the terms of your departure. Rehearse it with family members and your coach. This is meant to be a framework for your presentation, but you will act the part when the time comes if you can remember to talk from the heart. If you have firmly in mind the reasons why the package you want makes sense, it will be easier to do that.

It's Not a Done Deal Until It Is Signed: Gear Up to Negotiate and Influence

Being an employee usually means being in a position of minor or inferior power in comparison to the corporation or boss. The feeling of having power stacked against you usually is intensified by being forced out of a job. It's very common to feel that you're in a take-it-or-leave-it situation. But you'd be surprised how many people get more by *asking* for more and by simply being persistent about it. The Five O'Clock Club mantra for finessing salary negotiations, that is, keeping negotiations going while building the case that you're the best person for the job, is "You're a fair person, I'm a fair person."

That can be your opening volley every time you come back to your employer to try to get more. Most employers assume that people will just go away when the terms of separation have been announced; after all, who (supposedly) holds all the power? But you can come back with reasoned arguments about why the package isn't all that it should be. To put it bluntly, this can be a matter of guts. How often are you willing to go back to the table? They think they've gotten rid of you, but you refuse to go quietly: "I'm a fair person, you're a fair person, and here's what's fair." Don't forget that things don't have to be rushed. By law you usually have 21 days to work out an agreement.

Clearly, if you happen to be part of a massive layoff of dozens or hundreds of people, there may be little room for you to maneuver; company policy that applies to everyone may appear to be written in stone. But can you make the case that your situation is unique? Have you been on the payroll only a short time, after being recruited away from a ten- or fifteen-year job somewhere else? Did you relocate from a great distance to join the company? Did you play a key role in a major project? Your career coach can help you build the case that you deserve more than is being offered. It may also be good strategy to find allies within the company who are willing to remind management of your contributions and accomplishments; especially if a manager or boss is losing you because of a merger or reorganization. Now is a good time to call in the favors that people may owe you.

Go into negotiations with a firm idea of your priorities and have the numbers carefully worked out. "I want to remain whole" is a strong argument to make with fair-minded people as you initiate negotiations. That is, as you transition to a new job (and you usually have no idea how long that may take), you don't want your finances or family life to take a hit. Hence, you should know all of the numbers and be prepared to discuss items in order of priority, for instance, severance, health insurance coverage, unpaid vacation days, the laptop you'd like to take with you.

When to Get the Ball Rolling Yourself—Without Quitting

It's not uncommon for people to see the handwriting on the wall. Perhaps there's a new boss or a change in management in general. Or the newspapers may be full of stories about an upcoming merger that will impact your company; so it's no secret that jobs will be cut. For a variety of other reasons you may sense that your days on the job may be numbered; you might have been put on warning for failing to meet goals, to master a new process or procedure, or to fit in with the corporate culture. In such cases the daily mood at work can be strained; if you sense that you're just marking time, it might be appropriate to be proactive. The boss or manager might be relieved to hear that you're looking for a separation that will make everyone happy. Here are some of the possible scripts:

- "Janet, you know this is not working, I know it's not working. Why don't we work something out."
- "Tom, after really thinking about this situation, I'm afraid that I won't be able to meet these expectations. I'd like to work something out that makes sense for both of us."
- "John, this is not the job we initially discussed. I'm not as motivated as I thought I would be. Maybe we'd better discuss how to bring this to a conclusion."

Obviously situations and reasons differ enormously, but if you've arrived at the point of hating to get up and go to work every day, it may be time to maneuver an exit, without quitting. Resigning because you hate your job can be a very risky strategy; in fact, if it's not thought out carefully, it's an impulse, not a strategy. This chapter is aimed at helping you be fired and working that process to your advantage. Unless you have solid backup plans A, B, and C (which include, for example, money in the bank and the means to provide health insurance), quitting is not really an option.

The scripts suggested above should be tried only after gauging the political situation at work, which means talking to trusted coworkers to get a reading on how the powers-that-be react to employees who ask for exit packages. Chances are, these waters are not entirely uncharted, and finding out about company history can be useful. And absolutely nothing of this sort should be attempted without talking with your career coach.

Get a Written Statement

At the Five O'Clock Club we advise job hunters to get good at explaining why they left their last job. Anyone who asks you on a job interview why you left your last job doesn't really want too much information—in the sense of "all the gory details." Interviewers want a brief explanation that makes sense and reflects well on you. They don't expect you to give them names of people (as references) who are going to say bad things about you. They expect to hear good things about you. That's why it's important to build a list of former bosses and colleagues who will sing your praises.

And part of a good exit strategy is to get something in writing. Especially if you're leaving a job for performance reasons or because the job turned out not to be a good fit, it's wise to get a written statement that accentuates the positives you brought to the job. Even if your employer doesn't want to write a glowing recommendation, negotiate a statement that will help satisfy curiosity in a positive way about why and how you left the job.

You can show this document to the people you have asked to be your references. That will help them say the right things when people call them to ask about your personality, reputation, and work history. Of course, if you're a student of the Five O'Clock Club methodology, you know that your references should be thoroughly briefed about each job you're a finalist for so they can better describe you in terms of the position.

A letter of recommendation or reference from your employer should be kept on file permanently. Ten or fifteen years from now, it may be impossible to find former bosses and managers, so the letter can substitute for talking to the people who have disappeared.

To Sue or Not to Sue: When to Call a Lawyer

Americans are fond of saying—especially when something really wrong or unfair has happened—"I'll take it all the way to the Supreme Court." But, in fact, the period of transitioning from one job to another is probably the worst time to be involved in a lawsuit. It can be very expensive and time-consuming, and it will divert you from the very thing you should focus on the most, namely, your job search (a full-time job search requires 35 hours a week). Besides, the last thing you want prospective employers to find out is that you're suing your former company. The suspicion is that something went terribly wrong, and you are suspected of being a litigious person. So the impulse to sue should be treated like most other impulses: forget about it. Or at least wait until the impulse has cooled, and you've thought about it a lot before taking action.

That having been said, there may be reasons to consult with your attorney during the exit

process. If there is genuinely an issue relating to discrimination or criminal behavior that brought about your dismissal, you may be justified in seeking legal action. Consultation with your lawyer could reveal how strong a case you may have. Of course, the potential benefits of suing would have to far outweigh the aggravation you would have to endure. And what would be the purpose of suing? To get your job back? That would be a good idea only in very rare circumstances.

As you review all of the issues relating to your termination with your career coach, the latter will clearly point out when a matter requiring legal advice comes up. Career coaches are not lawyers and don't have the expertise you need for such issues.

One of the areas for consulting an attorney is non-compete agreements. Most of these are usually imbedded in the hiring agreements that may have been signed months or years ago, but, especially when you lose your job against your will, your employer might be at a disadvantage in trying to enforce a non-compete. You may be able to have a non-compete renegotiated—with the help of your lawyer—when you're settling all the matters relating to your departure.

Getting Your Next Job Soon: The Value of Outplacement

Career coaching that is provided by your employer when you're let go (that is, you don't pay for it) is known as outplacement. Some companies offer this service, others don't; it's a matter of finances and attitude. Once when we made a presentation to a human resource officer about Five O'Clock Club outplacement, we stressed that our program (a full year of coaching help) is a way of demonstrating that a company cares. We were shocked to be told bluntly, "But we don't care." This level of insensitivity is rare, and you should include outplacement on your list of requests as you negotiate an exit. Even if you work for a company known for its heartlessness, you should make the case for getting outplacement help.

The primary reason for doing this is that people who get job search coaching land better jobs faster. There's really no mystery about this: most people are not experts on how to find a job. Even people who have found themselves out of a job several times in their careers say, "Oh no, not again," because it is stressful and always presents new challenges. There's a lot of conventional job-hunting wisdom floating around—most of it wrong—and if you follow it, you're likely to get stalled or delayed on the way to your next job. Working with a coach means that you can avoid making costly mistakes; coaches have guided hundreds of people through the process and can offer invaluable guidance. Asking your employer for this kind of service is a way to give yourself a boost, which you will come to fully appreciate in the weeks and months ahead.

But what about money instead? Your employer may say, "Here's three months' severance and outplacement service *or* four months' severance. Which do you want?" Most employers are astute enough not to offer this option, because the impulse of most people is to say, "Show me the money!" But turning your back on job search help is simply not a smart move; it could very well translate into *several*

more months of unemployment, which means you've *lost* money.

A cushion of money is nice, of course, and who doesn't want the cushion of money to be as big as possible? Ironically, a large cushion of money can work against you: "Wow! I've got six months' severance. I can give myself a break and coast for a while." Many times people have arrived at the Five O'Clock Club in a panic: "I'm just about out of money. I've got to find a job fast." And it turns out that a big severance package is just about exhausted, and the person had been job-hunting half-heartedly; the extra cash had bred complacency and procrastination. It's very hard to get geared up for the hard work of job search if you've just been coasting for a while. Chances are, if you get signed up for outplacement, your coach will prod you out of the coasting mode as soon as possible (at least that's the way we do it at the Five O'Clock Club). Our research shows that people who don't get started on job search right away lose momentum and end up with much longer searches. Getting outplacement service as part of your exit package is one of the best ways to shorten your between-jobs status.

For full information about Five O'Clock Club outplacement services, visit our website www.fiveoclockclub.com or call the home office, 212-286-4500.

CHAPTER FIFTEEN

What Is
The Five O'Clock Club?

*America's Premier
Career-Coaching Network*

The
Five
O'Clock
Club

How to Join the Club

The Five O'Clock Club: America's Premier Career-Coaching and Outplacement Service

"One organization with a long record of success in helping people find jobs is The Five O'Clock Club."

Fortune

- Job Search Strategy Groups
- Private Coaching
- Books and Audio CDs
- Membership Information
- When Your Employer Pays

THERE *IS* A FIVE O'CLOCK CLUB NEAR YOU!

For more information on becoming a member, please fill out the Membership Application form in this book, sign up on the Web at: www.fiveoclockclub.com, or call: **1-800-575-3587** (or **212-286-4500** in New York)

The Five O'Clock Club Search Process

The Five O'Clock Club process, as outlined in *The Five O'Clock Club* books, is a targeted, strategic approach to career development and a job search. Five O'Clock Club members become proficient at skills that prove invaluable during their *entire working lives.*

Career Management

We train our members to *manage their careers* and always look ahead to their next job search. Research shows that an average worker spends only four years in a job and will have 12 jobs in as many as 5 career fields during his or her working life.

Getting Jobs . . . Faster

Five O'Clock Club members find *better jobs, faster.* The average professional, manager, or executive Five O'Clock Club member who regularly attends weekly sessions finds a job by his or her 10th session. Even the discouraged, long-term job searcher can find immediate help.

The keystone to The Five O'Clock Club process is teaching our members an understanding of the entire hiring process. A first interview is primarily a time for exchanging critical information. The real work starts *after* the interview. We teach our members *how to turn job interviews into offers* and to negotiate the best possible employment package.

Setting Targets

The Five O'Clock Club is action-oriented. *We'll help you decide what you should do this very next week to move your search along.* By their third session, our members have set definite job targets by industry or company size, position, and geographic area and are out in the field gathering information and making contacts that will lead to interviews with hiring managers.

Our approach evolves with the changing job market. We're able to synthesize information from hundreds of Five O'Clock Club members and come up with new approaches for our members. For example, we now discuss temporary placement for executives, how to use voice mail and the Internet, and how to network when doors are slamming shut all over town.

The Five O'Clock Club Strategy Program

The Five O'Clock Club meeting is a carefully planned *job-search strategy program*. We provide members with the tools and tricks necessary to get a good job fast—even in a tight market. Networking and emotional support are also included in the meeting.

Participate in 10 *consecutive* small-group strategy sessions to enable your group and career coach to get to know you and to develop momentum in your search.

Weekly Presentations via Audio CDs

Prior to each week's teleconference, listen to the assigned audio presentation covering part of the Five O'Clock Club methodology. These are scheduled on a rotating basis so you may join the Club at any time. (In selected cities, presentations are given in person rather than via audio CDs.)

Small-Group Strategy Sessions

During the first few minutes of the teleconference, your small group discusses the topic of the week and hears from people who have landed jobs. Then you have the chance to get feedback and advice on your own search strategy, listen to and learn from others, and build your network. All groups are led by trained career coaches with years of experience. The small group is generally no more than six to eight people, so everyone gets the chance to speak up.

Let us consider how we may spur one another on toward love and good deeds. Let us not give up meeting together, as some are in the habit of doing, but let us encourage one another.

Hebrews 10:24–25

Private Coaching

You may meet with your small-group coach—or another coach—for private coaching by phone or in person. A coach helps you develop a career path, solve current job problems, prepare your resume, or guide your search.

Many members develop long-term relationships with their coaches to get advice throughout their careers. If you are paying for the coaching yourself (as opposed to having your employer pay), please pay the coach directly (charges vary from $100 to $175 per hour) **Private coaching is *not* included in the Five O'Clock Club seminar or membership fee.** For coach matching, see our Web site or call **1-800-575-3587** (or **212-286-4500** in New York).

From the Club History, Written in the 1890s

At The Five O'Clock Club, [people] of all shades of political belief—as might be said of all trades and creeds—have met together. . . . The variety continues almost to a monotony. . . . [The Club's] good fellowship and geniality—not to say hospitality—has reached them all.

It has been remarked of clubs that they serve to level rank. If that were possible in this country, it would probably be true, if leveling rank means the appreciation of people of equal abilities as equals; but in the Five O'Clock Club it has been a most gratifying and noteworthy fact that no lines have ever been drawn save those which are essential to the honor and good name of any association. Strangers are invited by the club or by any members [as gentlepeople], irrespective of aristocracy, plutocracy, or occupation, and are so treated always. Nor does the thought of a [person's] social position ever enter into the meetings. People of wealth and people of moderate means sit side by side, finding in each other much to praise and admire and little to justify snarlishness or adverse criticism. People meet as people—not as the representatives of a set—and having so met, dwell not in worlds of envy or distrust, but in union and collegiality, forming kindly thoughts of each other in their heart of hearts.

In its methods, the Five O'Clock Club is plain, easy-going and unconventional. It has its "isms" and some peculiarities of procedure, but simplicity characterizes them all. The sense of propriety, rather than rules of order, governs its meetings, and that informality which carries with it sincerity of motive and spontaneity of effort, prevails within it. Its very name indicates informality, and, indeed, one of the reasons said to have induced its adoption was the fact that members or guests need not don their dress suits to attend the meetings, if they so desired. This informality, however, must be distinguished from the informality of Bohemianism. For The Five O'Clock Club, informality, above convenience, means sobriety, refinement of thought and speech, good breeding and good order. To this sort of informality much of its success is due.

Fortune, The New York Times, Black Enterprise, Business Week, NPR, CNBC, and ABC-TV are some of the places you've seen, heard, or read about us.

The Schedule

See our Web site for the specific dates for each topic. All groups use a similar schedule in each time zone.

Fee: $49 annual membership (includes Beginners Kit, subscription to *The Five O'Clock News,* and access to the Members Only section of our Web site), _plus_ session fees based on member's income (price for the Insider Program includes audio-CD lectures, which retails for $150).

Reservations required for first session. Unused sessions are transferable to anyone you choose or can be donated to members attending more than 16 sessions who are having financial difficulty.

The Five O'Clock Club's programs are geared to recent graduates, professionals, managers, and executives from a wide variety of industries and professions. Most earn from $30,000 to $400,000 per year. Half the members are employed; half are unemployed. ***You will be in a group of your peers.***

To register, please fill out the form on the Web (at www.fiveoclockclub.com) or call 1-800-575-3587 (or 212-286-4500 in New York).

Lecture Presentation Schedule

- History of the 5OCC
- The 5OCC Approach to Job Search
- Developing New Targets for Your Search
- Two-Minute Pitch: Keystone of Your Search

- Using Research and Internet for Your Search
- The Keys to Effective Networking
- Getting the Most Out of Your Contacts
- Getting Interviews: Direct/Targeted Mail
- Beat the Odds when Using Search Firms and Ads
- Developing New Momentum in Your Search
- The 5OCC Approach to Interviewing
- Advanced Interviewing Techniques
- How to Handle Difficult Interview Questions
- How to Turn Job Interviews into Offers
- Successful Job Hunter's Report

- Four-Step Salary-Negotiation Method

All groups run continuously. Dates are posted on our Web site. The textbooks used by all members of the Five O'Clock Club may be ordered on our Web site or purchased at major bookstores.

> The original Five O'Clock Club was formed in Philadelphia in 1883. It was made up of the leaders of the day who shared their experiences "in a spirit of fellowship and good humor."

The
Five
O'Clock
Club

Questions You May Have about the Weekly Job Search Strategy Group

Job hunters are not always the best judges of what they need during a search. For example, most are interested in lectures on answering ads on the Internet or working with search firms. We cover those topics, but strategically they are relatively unimportant in an effective job search.

At the Five O'Clock Club, you get the information you really need in your search, *such as how to target more effectively, how to get more interviews, and how to turn job interviews into offers.*

What's more, you will work in a small group with the best coaches in the business. In these strategy sessions, your group will help you decide what to do, this week and every week, to move your search along. You will learn by being coached and by coaching others in your group.

We find ourselves not independently of other people and institutions but through them. We never get to the bottom of our selves on our own. We discover who we are face to face and side by side with others in work, love, and learning.

Robert N. Bellah, et al., *Habits of the Heart*

Here are a few other points:

- For best results, attend on a regular basis. Your group gets to know you and will coach you to eliminate whatever you may be doing wrong or refine what you are doing right.

- The Five O'Clock Club is a members-only organization. To get started in the small-group teleconference sessions, you must purchase a minimum of 10 sessions.

- The teleconference sessions include the set of 16 audio-CD presentations on Five O'Clock Club methodology. In-person groups do not include CDs.

- After that, you may purchase blocks of 5 or 10 sessions.

- We sell multiple sessions to make administration easier.

- If you miss a session, you may make it up any time. You may even transfer unused time to a friend.

- Although many people find jobs quickly (even people who have been unemployed a long time), others have more difficult searches. Plan to be in it for the long haul and you'll do better.

Carefully read all of the material in this section. It will help you decide whether or not to attend.

- The first week, pay attention to the strategies used by the others in your group. Soak up all the information you can.

- Read the books before you come in the second week. They will help you move your search along.

To register:

1. Read this section and fill out the application.

2. After you become a member and get your Beginners Kit, call to reserve a space for the first time you attend.

To assign you to a career coach, we need to know

- your current (or last) field or industry
- the kind of job you would like next (if you know)
- your desired salary range in general terms

For private coaching, we suggest you attend the small group and ask to see your group leader, to give you continuity.

The Five O'Clock Club is plain, easy-going and unconventional. . . . Members or guests need not don their dress suits to attend the meetings.

(From the Club History, written in the 1890s)

What Happens at the Meetings?

Each week, job searchers from various industries and professions meet in small groups. The groups specialize in professionals, managers, executives, or recent college graduates. Usually, half are employed and half are unemployed.

The weekly program is in two parts. First, there is a lecture on some aspect of the Five O'Clock Club methodology. Then, job hunters meet in small groups headed by senior full-time professional career coaches.

The first week, get the textbooks, listen to the lecture, and get assigned to your small group. During your first session, *listen* to the others in your group. You learn a lot by listening to how your peers are strategizing *their* searches.

By the second week, you will have read the materials. Now we can start to work on *your* search strategy and help *you* decide what to do next to move your search along. For example, we'll help you figure out how to get more interviews in your target area or how to turn interviews into job offers.

In the third week, you will see major progress made by other members of your group, and you may notice major progress in your own search as well.

By the third or fourth week, most members are conducting full and effective searches. Over the remaining weeks, you will tend to keep up a full search rather than go after only one or two leads. You will regularly aim to have 6 to 10 things *in the works* at all times. These will generally be in specific target areas you have identified, will keep your search on target, and will increase your chances of getting multiple job offers from which to choose.

Those who stick with the process find it works.

Some people prefer to just listen for a few weeks before they start their job search and that's okay, too.

How Much Does It Cost?

It is against the policy of the Five O'Clock Club to charge individuals heavy up-front fees. Our competitors charge $4,000 to $6,000 or more, up front. Our average fee is $360 for 10 sessions (which includes audio CDs of 16 presentations for those in the teleconference program). Those in the $100,000+ range pay an average of $540 for 10 sessions. For administrative reasons, we charge for 5 or 10 additional sessions at a time.

You must have the books so you can begin studying them before the second session. (You can purchase them on our Web site or at major bookstores.) If you don't do the homework, you will tend to waste the time of others in the group by asking questions covered in the texts.

Is the Small Group Right for Me?

The Five O'Clock Club process is for you if:

- You are truly interested in job hunting.
- You have *some* idea of the kind of job you want.
- You are a professional, manager, or executive—or want to be.
- You want to participate in a group process on a regular basis.

- You realize that finding or changing jobs and careers is hard work, but you are absolutely willing and able to do it.

If you have no idea about the kind of job you want next, you may attend one or two group sessions to start. *Then* see a *coach privately* for one or two sessions, develop tentative job targets, and return to the group. You may work with your small-group coach or contact us through our Web site or by calling **1-800-575-3587** (or **212-286-4500** in New York) for referral to another coach.

How Long Will It Take Me to Get a Job?

Although our members tend to be from fields or industries where they expect to have difficult searches, *the average person who attends regularly finds a new position within 10 sessions.* Some take less time and others take more.

One thing we know for sure: **Research shows that those who get *regular* coaching during their searches get jobs faster and at higher rates of pay than those who search on their own or simply take a course.** This makes sense. If a person comes only when they think they have a problem, they are usually wrong. They probably had a problem a few weeks ago but didn't realize it. Or the problem may be different from the one they thought they had. Those who come regularly benefit from the observations others make about their searches. Problems are solved before they become severe or are prevented altogether.

Those who attend regularly also learn a lot by paying attention and helping others in the group. This *secondhand* learning can shorten your search by weeks. When you hear the problems of others who are ahead of you in the search, you can avoid them completely. People in your group will come to know you and will point out subtleties you may not have noticed that interviewers will never tell you.

Will I Be with Others from My Field/Industry?

Probably, but it's not that important. If you are a salesperson, for example, would you want to be with seven other salespeople? Probably not. You will learn a lot and have a much more creative search if you are in a group of people who are in your general salary range but not exactly like you. Our clients are from virtually every field and industry. The *process* is what will help you.

We've been doing this since 1978 and understand your needs. That's why the mix we provide is the best you can get.

Career Coaching Firms Charge $4,000–$6,000 Up Front. How Can You Charge Such a Small Fee?

1. We have no advertising costs, because 90 percent of those who attend have been referred by other members.

   A hefty up-front fee would bind you to us, but we have been more successful by treating people ethically and having them pretty much *pay as they go.*

   We need a certain number of people to cover expenses. When lots of people get jobs quickly and leave us, we could go into the red. But as long as members refer others, we will continue to provide this service at a fair price.

2. We focus strictly on *job search strategy,* and encourage our clients to attend free support groups if they need emotional support. We focus on getting *jobs,* which reduces the time clients spend with us and the amount they pay.

3. We attract the best coaches, and our clients make more progress per session than they would elsewhere, which also reduces their costs.

4. We have expert administrators and a sophisticated computer system that reduces our overhead and increases our ability to track your progress.

May I Change Coaches?

Yes. Great care is taken in assigning you to your initial coach. However, if you want to change once for any reason, you may do it. We don't encourage group hopping: It is better for you to stick with a group so that everyone gets to know you. On the other hand, we want you to feel comfortable. So if you tell us you prefer a different group, you will be transferred immediately.

What If I Have a Quick Question Outside of the Group Session?

Some people prefer to see their group coach privately. Others prefer to meet with a different coach to get another point of view. Whatever you decide, remember that the group fee does *not* cover coaching time outside the group session. Therefore, if you wanted to speak with a coach between sessions—even for *quick questions*—you would normally meet with the coach first for a private session so he or she can get to know you better. *Easy, quick questions* are usually more complicated than they appear. After your first private session, some coaches will allow you to pay in advance for one hour of coaching time, which you can then use for quick questions by phone (usually a 15-minute minimum is charged). Since each coach has an individual way of operating, find out how the coach arranges these things.

What If I Want to Start My Own Business?

The process of becoming a consultant is essentially the same as job hunting and lots of consultants attend Five O'Clock Club meetings. However, if you want to buy a franchise or existing business or start a growth business, you should see a private coach.

How Can I Be Sure That The Five O'Clock Club Small-Group Sessions Will Be Right for Me?

Before you actually participate in any of the small-group sessions, you can get an idea of the quality of our service by listening to all 16 audio CDs that you purchased. If you are dissatisfied with the CDs for any reason, return the package within 30 days for a full refund.

Whatever you decide, just remember: *It has been proven that those who receive regular help during their searches get jobs faster and at higher rates of pay than those who search on their own or simply attend a course.* If you get a job just one or two weeks faster because of this program, it will have more than paid for itself. And you may *transfer unused sessions to anyone you choose.* However, the person you choose must be or become a member.

The
Five
O'Clock
Club

When Your Employer Pays

*D*oes your employer care about you and others *whom they ask to leave the organization?* If so, ask them to consider the Five O'Clock Club for your outplacement help. The Five O'Clock Club puts you and your job search first, offering a career-coaching program of the highest quality at the lowest possible price to your employer.

Over 25 Years of Research

The Five O'Clock Club was started in 1978 as a research-based organization. Job hunters tried various techniques and reported their results back to the group. We developed a variety of guidelines so job hunters could choose the techniques best for them.

The methodology was tested and refined on professionals, managers, and executives (and those aspiring to be) from all occupations. Annual salaries ranged from $30,000 to $400,000; 50 percent were employed and 50 percent were unemployed.

Since its beginning, the Five O'Clock Club has tracked trends. Over time, our advice has changed as the job market has changed. What worked in the past is insufficient for today's job market. Today's Five O'Clock Club promotes all our relevant original strategies—and so much more.

As an employee-advocacy organization, the Five O'Clock Club focuses on providing the services and information that the job hunter needs most.

Get the Help You Need Most: 100 Percent Coaching

There's a myth in outplacement circles that a termi-nated employee just needs a desk, a phone, and minimal career coaching. **Our experience clearly shows that downsized workers need qualified, reliable coaching more than anything else.**

Most traditional outplacement packages last only three months. The average executive gets office space and only five hours of career coach-ing during this time. Yet the service job hunters need most is the career coaching itself—not a desk and a phone.

Most professionals, managers, and executives are right in the thick of negotiations with prospective employers at the three month mark. Yet that is precisely when traditional outplace-ment ends, leaving job hunters stranded and sometimes ruining deals.

It is astonishing how often job hunters and employers alike are impressed by the databases of *job postings* claimed by outplacement firms. Yet only 10 percent of all jobs are filled through ads and another 10 percent are filled through search firms. Instead, direct contact and networking—done the Five O'Clock Club way—are more effec-tive for most searches.

You Get a Safety Net

Imagine getting a package that protects you for a full year. Imagine knowing you can come back if your new job doesn't work out—even months later. Imagine trying consulting work if you like. If you later decide it's not for you, you can come back to the Five O'Clock Club.

We can offer you a safety net of one full year's career coaching because our method is so effective that few people actually need more than 10 weeks in our proven program. But you're protected for a year.

You'll Job Search with Those Who Are Employed—How Novel!

Let's face it. It can be depressing to spend your days at an outplacement firm where everyone is unemployed. At the Five O'Clock Club, half the attendees are working, and this makes the atmosphere cheerier and helps to move your search along.

What's more, you'll be in a small group of your peers, all of whom are using the Five O'Clock Club method. Our research proves that those who attend the small group regularly and use the Five O'Clock Club methods get jobs faster and at higher rates of pay than those who only work privately with a career coach throughout their searches.

So Many Poor Attempts

Nothing is sadder than meeting someone who has already been getting job-search *help,* but the wrong kind. They've learned the traditional techniques that are no longer effective. Most have poor résumés and inappropriate targets and don't know how to turn job interviews into offers.

You'll Get Quite a Package

You'll get up to 14 hours of private coaching—well in excess of what you would get at a traditional outplacement firm. You may even want to use a few hours after you start your new job.

And you get up to one full year of small-group career coaching. In addition, you get books, audio CDs, and other helpful materials.

To Get Started

The day your human resources manager calls us authorizing Five O'Clock Club outplacement, we will immediately ship you the books, CDs, and other materials and assign you to a private coach and a small group.

Then we'll monitor your search. Frankly, we care about you more than we care about your employer. And since your employer cares about you, they're glad we feel this way because they know we'll take care of you.

What They Say about Us

The Five O'Clock Club product is much better, far more useful than my outplacement package.

Senior executive and Five O'Clock Club member

The Club kept the juices flowing. You're told what to do, what not to do. There were fresh ideas. I went through an outplacement service that, frankly, did not help. If they had done as much as the Five O'Clock Club did, I would have landed sooner.

Another member

When Your *Employer* Pays for the Five O'Clock Club, *You* Get:

- **Up to 14 hours of guaranteed private career coaching** to determine a career direction, develop a résumé, plan salary negotiations, etc. In fact, if you need a second opinion during your search, we can arrange that too.

- Up to **ONE YEAR of small-group teleconference coaching** (average about five or six participants in a group) headed by a senior Five O'Clock Club career consultant. That way, if you lose your next job, you can come back. Or if you want to try consulting work and then decide you **don't like it, you can come back**.

- **Two-year membership** in The Five O'Clock Club: Beginners Kit and two-year subscription to *The Five O'Clock News*.

- **The complete set of our four books** for professionals, managers, and executives who are in job search.

- **A boxed set of 16 audio CDs** of Five O'Clock Club presentations.

COMPARISON OF EMPLOYER-PAID PACKAGES

Typical Package	Traditional Outplacement	The Five O'Clock Club
Who is the client?	The organization	Job hunters. We are employee advocates. We always do what is in the best interest of job hunters.
The clientele	All are unemployed	Half of our attendees are unemployed; half are employed. There is an upbeat atmosphere; networking is enhanced.
Length/type of service	Three months, primarily office space	One year, exclusively career coaching
Service ends	After three months—or *before* if the client lands a job or consulting assignment	After one full year, no matter what. You can return if you lose your next job, if your assignment ends, or if you need advice after starting your new job.
Small-group coaching	Sporadic for three months Coach varies	Every week for up to one year; same coach
Private coaching	Five hours on average	Up to 14 hours guaranteed (depending on level of service purchased)
Support materials	Generic manual	• Four textbooks based on over 25 years of job search research • 16 40-minute lectures on audio CDs • Beginners Kit of search information • Two-year subscription to the Five O'Clock Club magazine, devoted to career-management articles
Facilities	Cubicle, phone, computer access	None; use home phone and computer

The
Five
O'Clock
Club

The Way We Are

The Five O'Clock Club means sobriety, refinement of thought and speech, good breeding and good order. To this, much of its success is due. The Five O'Clock Club is easy-going and unconventional. A sense of propriety, rather than rules of order, governs its meetings.

J. Hampton Moore, *History of The Five O'Clock Club* (written in the 1890s)

Just like the members of the original Five O'Clock Club, today's members want an ongoing relationship. George Vaillant, in his seminal work on successful people, found that "what makes or breaks our luck seems to be . . . our sustained relationships with other people." (George E. Vaillant, *Adaptation to Life,* Harvard University Press, 1995)

Five O'Clock Club members know that much of the program's benefit comes from simply showing up. Showing up will encourage you to do what you need to do when you are not here. And over the course of several weeks, certain things will become evident that are not evident now.

Five O'Clock Club members learn from each other: The group leader is not the only one with answers. The leader brings factual information to the meetings and keeps the discussion in line. But the answers to some problems may lie within you or with others in the group.

Five O'Clock Club members encourage each other. They listen, see similarities with their own situations, and learn from that. And they listen to see how they may help others. You may come across information or a contact that could help someone else in the group. Passing on that information is what we're all about.

If you are a new member here, listen to others to learn the process. And read the books so you will know the basics that others already know. When everyone understands the basics, this keeps the meetings on a high level, interesting, and helpful to everyone.

Five O'Clock Club members are in this together, but they know that ultimately they are each responsible for solving their own problems with God's help. Take the time to learn the process, and you will become better at analyzing your own situation, as well as the situations of others. You will be learning a method that will serve you the rest of your life and in areas of your life apart from your career.

Five O'Clock Club members are kind to each other. They control their frustrations because venting helps no one. Because many may be stressed, be kind and go the extra length to keep this place calm and happy. It is your respite from the world outside and a place for you to find comfort and FUN. Relax and enjoy yourself, learn what you can, and help where you can. And have a ball doing it.

There arises from the hearts of busy [people] a love of variety, a yearning for relaxation of thought as well as of body, and a craving for a generous and spontaneous fraternity.

J. Hampton Moore, *History of The Five O'Clock Club*

The
Five
O'Clock
Club

Lexicon Used at
The Five O'Clock Club

Use The Five O'Clock Club lexicon as a shorthand to express where you are in your job search. It will focus you and those in your group.

I. Overview and Assessment

How many hours a week are you spending on your search?

Spend 35 hours on a full-time search, 15 hours on a part-time search.

What are your job targets?

Tell the group. A target includes industry or company size, position, and geographic area.

The group can help assess how good your targets are. Take a look at *Measuring Your Targets.*

How does your résumé position you?

The summary and body should make you look appropriate to your target.

What are your backup targets?

Decide at the beginning of the search before the first campaign. Then you won't get stuck.

Have you done the assessment?

If your targets are wrong, everything is wrong. (Do the assessment in *Targeting a Great Career.*) Or a counselor can help you privately to determine possible job targets.

II. Getting Interviews

How large is your target (e.g., 30 companies)?
How many of them have you contacted?
Contact them all.

How can you get (more) leads?

You will not get a job through search firms, ads, networking, or direct contact. Those are techniques for getting interviews—job leads. Use the right terminology, especially after a person gets a job. Do not say, "How did you get the job?" if you really want to know "Where did you get the lead for that job?"

Do you have 6 to 10 things in the works?

You may want the group to help you land one job. After they help you with your strategy, they should ask, "How many other things do you have in the works?" If *none,* the group can brainstorm how you can get more things going: through search firms, ads, networking, or direct contact. Then you are more likely to turn the job you want into an offer because you will seem more valuable. What's more, five will fall away through no fault of your own. Don't go after only one job.

How's your Two-Minute Pitch?

Practice a *tailored* Two-Minute Pitch. Tell the group the job title and industry of the hiring manager they should pretend they are for a role-playing exercise. You will be surprised how good the group is at critiquing pitches. (Practice a few weeks in a row.) Use your pitch to separate you from your competition.

You seem to be in Stage One (or Stage Two or Stage Three) of your search.

Know where you are. This is the key measure of your search.

Are you seen as an insider or an outsider?

See *How to Change Careers* for becoming an insider. If people are saying, "I wish I had an opening for someone like you," you are doing well in meetings. If the industry is strong, then it's only a matter of time before you get a job.

III. Turning Interviews into Offers

Do you want this job?

If you do not want the job, perhaps you want an offer, if only for practice. If you are not willing to go for it, the group's suggestions will not work.

Who are your likely competitors and how can you outshine and outlast them?

You will not get a job simply because "they liked me." The issues are deeper. Ask the interviewer: "Where are you in the hiring process? What kind of person would be your ideal candidate? How do I stack up?"

What are your next steps?

What are *you* planning to do if the hiring manager doesn't call by a certain date, or what are you planning to do to assure that the hiring manager *does* call you?

Can you prove you can do the job?

Don't just take the *trust me* approach. Consider your competition.

Which job positions you best for the long run? Which job is the best fit?

Don't decide only on the basis of salary. You will most likely have another job after this. See which job looks best on your résumé and will make you stronger for the next time. In addition, find a fit for your personality. If you don't *fit,* it is unlikely you will do well there. The group can help you turn interviews into offers and give you feedback on which job is best for you.

> *"Believe me, with self-examination and a lot of hard work with our coaches, you can find the job . . . you can have the career . . . you can live the life you've always wanted!"*
>
> Sincerely,
> Kate Wendleton

Membership

As a member of the Five O'Clock Club, you get:

- A year's subscription to *The Five O'Clock News*—10 issues filled with information on career development and job-search techniques, focusing on the experiences of real people.

- Access to *reasonably priced* weekly seminars featuring individualized attention to your specific needs in small groups supervised by our senior coaches.

- Access to one-on-one coaching to help you answer specific questions, solve current job problems, prepare your résumé, or take an in-depth look at your career path. You choose the coach and pay the coach directly.

- An attractive Beginners Kit containing information based on over 25 years of research on who gets jobs . . . and why . . . that will enable you to improve your job search techniques—immediately!

- The opportunity to exchange ideas and experiences with other job searchers and career changers.

All that access, all that information, all that expertise for the annual membership fee of only $49, plus seminar fees.

How to become a member—by mail or E-mail:

Send your name, address, phone number, how you heard about us, and your check for $49 (made payable to "The Five O'Clock Club") to The Five O'Clock Club, 300 East 40th Street - Suite 6L, New York, NY 10016, or sign up at www.fiveoclockclub.com.

We will immediately mail you a Five O'Clock Club Membership Card, the Beginners Kit, and information on our seminars followed by our magazine. Then, call **1-800-575-3587** (or **212-286-4500** in New York) or e-mail us (at info@fiveoclockclub.com) to:

- reserve a space for the first time you plan to attend, or
- be matched with a Five O'Clock Club coach.

Membership Application

The Five O'Clock Club

☐ **Yes! I want to become a member!**
I want access to the most effective methods for finding jobs, as well as for developing and managing my career.

I enclose my check for $49 for 1 year; $75 for 2 years, payable to *The Five O'Clock Club.* I will receive a Beginners Kit, a subscription to the *Five O'Clock News,* access to the Members Only area on our Web site, and a network of career coaches. Reasonably priced seminars are held across the country.

Name: _____

Street Address: _____

City: _____ State: _____ Zip Code: _____

Work phone: (_____) _____

Home phone: (_____) _____

E-mail: _____

Date: _____

How I heard about the Club: _____

Report From the Front Lines
The following *optional* information is for statistical purposes. Thanks for your help.

Salary range:

☐ under $30,000   ☐ $30,000–$49,999   ☐ $50,000–$74,999

☐ $75,000–$99,999   ☐ $100,000–$125,000   ☐ over $125,000

Age: ☐ 20–29   ☐ 30–39   ☐ 40–49   ☐ 50+

Gender: ☐ Male   ☐ Female

Current or most recent position/title: _____

Please send to:
Membership Director, The Five O'Clock Club,
300 East 40th St.-Suite 6L, New York, NY 10016

The original Five O'Clock Club® was formed in Philadelphia in 1893. It was made up of the leaders of the day who shared their experiences "in a setting of fellowship and good humor."

About the Five O'Clock Club and the "Fruytagie" Canvas

Five O'Clock Club members are special. We attract upbeat, ambitious, dynamic, intelligent people and that makes it fun for all of us. Most of our members are professionals, managers, executives, consultants, and freelancers. We also include recent college graduates and those aiming to get into the professional ranks, as well as people in their 40s, 50s, and even 60s. Most members' salaries range from $30,000 to $400,000 (one-third of our members earn in excess of $100,000 a year). For those who cannot attend a Club, *The Five O'Clock Club Book Series* contains all of our methodologies—and our spirit.

The Philosophy of The Five O'Clock Club

The "Fruytagie" Canvas by Patricia Kelly, depicted here, symbolizes our philosophy. The original, which is actually 52.5" by 69" inches, hangs in the offices of the Five O'Clock Club in Manhattan. It is reminiscent of popular 16th-century Dutch "fruytagie," or fruit tapestries, which depicted abundance and prosperity.

I was attracted to this piece because it seemed to fit the spirit of our people at the Five O'Clock Club. This was confirmed when the artist, who was not aware of what I did for a living, added these words to the canvas: "The garden is abundant, prosperous and magical." Later, it took me only 10 minutes to write the blank verse "The Garden of Life," because it came from my heart. The verse reflects our philosophy and describes the kind of people who are members of the Club.

I'm always inspired by Five O'Clock Clubbers. They show others the way through their quiet behavior . . . their kindness . . . their generosity . . . their hard work . . . under God's care.

We share what we have with others. We are in this lush, exciting place together—with our brothers and sisters—and reach out for harmony. The garden is abundant. The job market is exciting. And Five O'Clock Clubbers believe that there is enough for everyone.

About the Artist's Method

To create her tapestry-like art, Kelly developed a unique style of stenciling. She hand-draws and hand-cuts each stencil, both in the negative and positive for each image. Her elaborate technique also includes a lengthy multilayering process incorporating Dutch metal leaves and gilding, numerous transparent glazes, paints, and wax pencils.

Kelly also paints the back side of the canvas using multiple washes of reds, violets, and golds. She uses this technique to create a heavy vibration of color, which in turn reflects the color onto the surface of the wall against which the canvas hangs.

The canvas is suspended by a heavy braided silk cord threaded into large brass grommets inserted along the top. Like a tapestry, the hemmed canvas is attached to a gold-gilded dowel with finials. The entire work is hung from a sculpted wall ornament.

Our staff is inspired every day by the tapestry and by the members of the Five O'Clock Club. We all work hard—and have FUN! The garden *is* abundant—with enough for everyone.

We wish you lots of success in your career. We—and your fellow members of the Five O'Clock Club—will work with you on it.

—Kate Wendleton, President

The original Five O'Clock Club was formed in Philadelphia in 1883.
It was made up of the leaders of the day, who shared their experiences
"in a spirit of fellowship and good humor."

 **THE GARDEN OF LIFE IS** abundant, prosperous and magical. ❦ In this garden, there is enough for everyone. ❦ Share the fruit and the knowledge ❦ Our brothers and we are in this lush, exciting place together. ❦ Let's show others the way. ❦ Kindness. Generosity. ❦ Hard work. ❦ God's care.

Index